Message from General Eisenhower

Soldiers, Sailors and Airmen of the Allied Expeditionary Force!

You are about to embark upon the Great Crusade, toward which we have striven these many months. The eyes of the world are upon you. The hopes and prayers of liberty-loving people everywhere march with you. In company with our brave Allies and brothers-in-arms on other Fronts, you will bring about the destruction of the German war machine, the elimination of Nazi tyranny over the oppressed peoples of Europe, and security for ourselves in a free world.

Your task will not be an easy one. Your enemy is well trained, well equipped and battle hardened. He will fight savagely.

But this is the year 1944. Much has happened since the Nazi triumphs of 1940-41. The United Nations have inflicted upon the Germans great defeats, in open battle, man-to-man. Our air offensive has seriously reduced their strength in the air and their capacity to wage war on the ground.

Our Home Fronts have given us an overwhelming superiority in weapons and munitions of war, and placed at our disposal great reserves of trained fighting men. The tide has turned. The free men of the world are marching together to Victory!

I have full confidence in your courage, devotion to duty and skill in battle.

We will accept nothing less than full Victory!

Good luck! And let us all beseech the blessing of Almighty God upon this great and noble undertaking.

Dwight D Eisenhower
June 6, 1944

Contents

The day the Allies launched an all-out amphibious assault on the coast of German-occupied France was a pivotal moment in modern history. The vast armada that left the south coast of England and weighed anchor off the beaches of Normandy in the early hours of June 6, 1944, was there not only to liberate France from the tyranny of Adolf Hitler and his Nazis but to secure the freedom of Germany and the rest of Western Europe too.

'D-Day' was never meant to refer exclusively to this most momentous of occasions – rather it was a military term used to mean the day when a given attack or operation was to begin. H-Hour of D-Day was the precise time of that attack.

Now D-Day has come to refer solely to the day British, Canadian and American forces invaded Normandy.

Operation Overlord, beginning on D-Day, was the largest combined land, sea and air operation the world had ever seen and it went on until Allied forces crossed the River Seine in France on August 19. The initial assault phase of Overlord was Operation Neptune – which lasted until June 30.

Adolf Hitler's forces had dominated Europe since the 'blitzkrieg' days of 1940 but the American entry into the war in December 1941 and the defeat of Germany's armies on the Eastern Front against Soviet Russia in 1942 had put the dictator and his forces on the back foot.

The Allies were, however, keenly aware of Germany's efforts to create flying bombs, missiles, jet fighters and other advanced equipment – the so-called 'wunderwaffen' – and feared they might develop something truly war-winning, like the atomic bomb they were themselves developing.

Not only that, by early 1944 Joseph Stalin's seemingly unstoppable tank armies were inflicting defeat after bloody defeat on the Germans and pushing them inexorably backwards. Would Germany collapse and leave Stalin in control of the Continent?

There was a lot riding on the soldiers who stormed the beaches on D-Day – perhaps the hopes of the free world.

Seventy years on, their achievement remains undiminished. They had not, for the most part, been professional soldiers before the war. Rather, they were ordinary young people called upon and trained to do their duty at a time of unprecedented international crisis.

Historians have endlessly debated their equipment, their tactics and their leaders. Individual actions have been dissected, appraised and reappraised but throughout the courage of those involved has remained undeniable.

Omaha beach as it is today.
Anton Bielousov

Cover art by Neil Roberts

Author:
Dan Sharp

Design:
Leanne Lawrence

Reprographics:
Jonathan Schofield and Simon Duncan

Publisher:
Steve O'Hara

Group advertising manager:
Sue Keily,
skeily@mortons.co.uk

Marketing manager:
Charlotte Park

Commercial director:
Nigel Hole

Published by:
Mortons Media Group Ltd,
Media Centre,
Morton Way, Horncastle,
Lincolnshire LN9 6JR
Tel: 01507 529529

Printed by:
William Gibbons and Sons,
Wolverhampton

Many thanks to:
Neil Powell of
www.battlefieldhistorian.com
for most of the images used
in this publication. Clive
Rowley for help and advice.
Rosie Ward for map artwork.

ISBN: 978-1-911276-88-3

CHAPTER 1

This isn't goodbye – it's au revoir

Retreat from France and early invasion plans

The story of D-Day begins with Operation Dynamo – the retrieval of Britain's forces from France between May 27 and June 4, 1940. Even as the last evacuated soldiers were being brought ashore, the realisation was dawning on new Prime Minister Winston Churchill that Britain's armies had to somehow regain a foothold in France if Adolf Hitler was ever to be beaten.

The retreat from Dunkirk was both a catastrophe and a blessing for the British Army. The Second World War had begun in September 1939 when Adolf Hitler's forces invaded Poland, but for eight months Britain and France were largely unaffected. Then came the brief Battle of France.

The highly mobile German forces successfully overcame the combined might of the British Expeditionary Force (BEF) and the French Army in a matter of weeks.

The Panzer tanks of the Heer – the German army – were equipped with the latest technology. They had radios that enabled their commanders to communicate not just with each other but with air and other ground forces too. This sophisticated radio network enabled rapid decision making and manoeuvring that the Allies simply could not match.

Also, the bulk of the BEF's tanks were Vickers Light Tank Mk.VIs. These small vehicles could do 35mph but were armed only with machine guns.

Their armour was, at most, 14mm thick and this made them horribly vulnerable to the German Panzer II with its 20mm anti-tank gun which could punch through 20mm of armour at a range of 500m.

With the battle lost, the BEF left 331 Mk.VIs, 77 Matilda Is, 23 Matilda IIs and 184 Cruisers in France after Dunkirk – 47.2% of Britain's 1303 tanks. Even the Cruisers with their 40mm guns and slightly thicker armour had scarcely been able to hold their own against the equivalent German Panzer IIIs and IVs. A lot of old and outdated equipment had been abandoned or

Cruiser tanks of the 2nd Royal Tank Regiment of the 1st Armoured Division during the Battle of France in 1940. These vehicles, assuming they survived the fighting, would have been abandoned when their crews were evacuated at Dunkirk.

destroyed but, crucially, the men who had operated it and seen its shortcomings first hand had been saved.

The combat experience of these professional soldiers would prove invaluable during the four year run-up to D-Day and they would go on to form the nucleus of the invasion force at Normandy.

And with much of Britain's 1930s tank stockpile gone, renewed emphasis was placed on creating a tank that would be capable of defeating the Panzers seen in France. This resulted in significant revisions of the new A20 tank design that would become the A22 Churchill – a vital D-Day weapon.

All thoughts of re-engaging the ground war, either in France or elsewhere, had to

wait however since the next phase of the German blitzkrieg in the West was directed at an invasion of the British Isles. On July 16, 1940, when it became clear that Britain was determined to fight on and would under no circumstances consider terms for peace, Hitler issued Fuhrer Directive No. 16 which stated: "As England, in spite of her hopeless military situation, still shows no signs of willingness to come to terms, I have decided to prepare, and if necessary to carry out, a landing operation against her. The aim of this operation is to eliminate the English Motherland as a base from which the war against Germany can be continued, and, if necessary, to occupy the country completely."

WE SHALL FIGHT THEM ON THE BEACHES... WITH THE BUTTS OF BROKEN BOTTLES

In the immediate aftermath of the Dunkirk evacuation, on June 4 itself, Winston Churchill gave a lengthy speech to the House of Commons about the action, during which he said: "The whole question of home defence against invasion is, of course, powerfully affected by the fact that we have for the time being in this island incomparably more powerful military forces than we have ever had at any moment in this war or the last. But this will not continue.

"We shall not be content with a

defensive war. We have our duty to our ally. We have to reconstitute and build up the British Expeditionary Force again, under its gallant Commander-in-Chief, Lord Gort. All this is in train; but in the interval we must put our defences in this island into such a high state of organisation that the fewest possible numbers will be required to give effective security and that the largest possible potential of offensive effort may be realised. On this we are now engaged."

This was purely for the benefit of

public morale, and for the benefit of the Germans and the Americans, since Britain certainly did not have "incomparably more powerful military forces than we have ever had at any moment in this war or the last".

Just a moment later he gave a powerful indication of how he saw an invasion of Britain playing out and added a line at the end intended for American ears: "Even though large tracts of Europe and many old and famous states have fallen or may fall into the grip

A German 88mm flak gun in action against French light tanks during the Battle of France.

The invasion would be codenamed Operation Sea Lion and by now the Luftwaffe had already begun a sustained bombing campaign against first British ports and shipping, then RAF airfields and Britain's aircraft factories. The twin objectives were to achieve air superiority over Britain so that Sea Lion could proceed without fear of aerial attack – a concept that would return to haunt the Germans in 1944 – and to inflict serious damage on the Royal Navy.

The first objective could not be successfully completed since the RAF was able to successfully win the Battle of Britain, albeit at the cost of 544 aircrew and 1547 aircraft. The Germans lost 1887 aircraft and 3665 aircrew, of whom 2698 had been killed and the rest captured.

Defeating the Royal Navy was never likely to be a viable option since neither the Luftwaffe nor even the German Navy, the Kriegsmarine, had sufficient resources to deal with such a large and widely dispersed fighting force. Though plans were drawn up for Operation Sea Lion and preparations made, including the development of amphibious Panzers and the gathering of landing craft, it was formally abandoned on September 17, 1940.

Two months later, having won an unprecedented third term in office, US President Franklin D Roosevelt was given a memorandum on America's policy options in Europe penned by the Chief of Naval Operations, Admiral Harold R Stark. This suggested four different ways of following a plan originally drawn up the year before – Rainbow Five – which had posed a hypothetical situation where the US was allied with Britain and France fighting a war on two fronts against the Germans and Italians in Europe and the Japanese in the Pacific.

Stark's option A was to act defensively on both fronts. B was to attack the Japanese in

of the Gestapo and all the odious apparatus of Nazi rule, we shall not flag or fail. We shall go on to the end. We shall fight in France, we shall fight on the seas and oceans, we shall fight with growing confidence and growing strength in the air, we shall defend our island, whatever the cost may be. We shall fight on the beaches, we shall fight on the landing grounds, we shall fight in the fields and in the streets, we shall fight in the hills; we shall never surrender, and even if, which I do not for a moment believe, this island or a large part of it were subjugated and starving, then our empire beyond the seas, armed and guarded by the British fleet, would carry on the struggle, until, in God's good time, the new world, with all its power and might, steps forth to the rescue and the liberation of the old."

It was later reported that, after he'd sat down, Churchill turned to a colleague and muttered dryly: "And we'll fight them with the butt ends of broken beer bottles because that's bloody well all we've got."

British Prime Minister Winston Churchill in 1942, not long after America's entry into the war. Early preparations for a return to France were already being made.

Part of Hitler's blitzkrieg force – an armoured column of two Panzer IVs and two Panzer 38(t)s from Rommel's 7th Panzer Division somewhere in France in 1940. They worked in unison with air and other ground units in a way that the Allies were unable to match.

the Pacific but merely defend the British and French in Europe. C involved going on the offensive in both Europe and the Pacific, and D was to attack in Europe while defending against the Japanese.

The preferred choice, Stark said, was D or 'Dog' because: "I believe that the continued existence of the British Empire, combined with building up a strong protection in our home areas, will do most to ensure the status quo in the Western Hemisphere, and to promote our principal national interests. As I have previously stated, I also believe that Great Britain

requires from us very great help in the Atlantic and possibly even on the continents of Europe or Africa if she is to be enabled to survive.

"In my opinion, alternatives A, B and C will most probably not provide the necessary degree of assistance, and, therefore, if we undertake war, that alternative D is likely to be the most fruitful for the United States, particularly if we enter the war at an early date."

Until America declared war, Stark recommended that option A should be followed combined with a rapid build-up of

American military forces. Roosevelt accepted Stark's assessment of the situation and agreed that option D, 'Plan Dog' or 'Europe first' as it later became known, was the way to go.

Neither the American public nor Britain were initially made aware that this was the American government's intended course of action.

Meanwhile, having created a breathing space, and with British forces now engaged in battle against the Italians in Africa, Churchill made approaches to the Americans with the aim of involving them more directly in the war. The US had been supplying arms to the Western Allies since June 1, 1940, when President Franklin D Roosevelt declared tons of American small arms and ammunition to be surplus, thereby quietly allowing it to be sold to Britain.

Now Churchill argued that if Britain fell, its island colonies in the Caribbean and elsewhere could fall into German hands and result in a direct threat to the American mainland. This resulted in the US agreeing to lease a number of British island possessions in exchange for mothballed American naval destroyers.

Further talks with the US took place in January 1941 and on July 12, 1941, shortly after the beginning of Operation Barbarossa – the German invasion of the Soviet Union – the British and Russian governments signed the Anglo-Soviet Agreement by which they announced their intention to aid one another in the war against Germany.

While still technically neutral, the US openly declared its support for the British with the Atlantic Charter of August 14, 1941.

Royal Navy warships return to Britain with soldiers of the BEF after evacuating them from Dunkirk. Destroyer HMS Whitehall, D94, was damaged during the operation by German bombers.

Oil tanks burn in Dunkirk on June 5, 1940, just after the BEF's rescue during Operation Dynamo. The aircraft pictured in the foreground on the right is a patrolling RAF Coastal Command Lockheed Hudson.

Churchill desperately wanted Roosevelt to join the war and Roosevelt wanted to ensure that Britain had concrete goals for the way the world would look after the war if Germany was defeated. As a result, the charter both set out the goals of the Allied powers in the aftermath of the war and made it clear that America was supporting Britain in its war effort.

Among the charter's key points were: no territorial gains for either the US or Britain after the war; self-determination for all peoples; lowering of trade barriers; global

economic co-operation; freedom of the seas; efforts to be made towards a world free of want and fear and disarmament of aggressor nations plus global disarmament in the postwar period.

Germany and Japan, with whom animosity towards the Americans in the Pacific was already reaching boiling point, saw the charter as the beginning of an alliance against them. It was one of the factors that influenced Japan's decision to attack Pearl Harbor on December 7, 1941, finally bringing America into the war. Churchill's prayers had

been answered and he had already set other events in motion which would lead directly to the D-Day invasion.

ROUNDUP AND SLEDGEHAMMER

Just over a month earlier, on October 27, 1941, he had appointed Louis Mountbatten as Chief of Combined Operations. Mountbatten later recalled: "The very first day I reported to him, he said, 'You are to prepare for the invasion of Europe, for unless we can go and land and fight Hitler and beat his forces on land we shall never win this war.

You must devise and design the appliances, the landing craft and the techniques to enable us to effect a landing against opposition and to maintain ourselves there. You must take the most brilliant officers from the navy, army and air force to help plan this great operation. You must take bases to use as training establishments where you can train the navy, army and air force to work as a single entity. The whole of the south coast of England is a bastion of defence against the invasion of Hitler; you've got to turn it into the springboard for our attack'. This was October 1941, when the whole of our allies in Europe had been overrun and captured and conquered and the Russians looked like being defeated and the Americans weren't in the war.

"What a hell of a decision to make: to prepare for the invasion then. Then, when Churchill went over to meet President

German Waffen-SS tank men inspect an abandoned British Matilda II tank of the 7th Royal Tank Regiment in France in June 1940. The Infantry Tank Mk.II as it was officially known was Britain's most heavily armoured tank in 1940 and the loss of even 23 of them was a bitter blow.

Roosevelt a week after the Japanese attack on Pearl Harbor, they made their very brave decision: Europe first. We would beat the Nazis there before we crushed the Japanese, which, as the Japanese had just attacked them, was a courageous decision for the Americans."

With America now a willing participant in the war alongside the British, Plan Dog was brought into play. America would help beat the Germans first before turning its full attention on the Japanese. So from December 22 to January 14, 1942, Roosevelt, Churchill and their chiefs of staff discussed their objectives for the coming year. They decided that responsibility for manpower and war materials should be shared and combined and that the chiefs of staff of both nations should become the Combined Chiefs of Staff. They further confirmed that Germany, rather than Japan, was the 'prime enemy'.

Basic goals were established, such as maintaining the security of both Britain and the US, keeping lines of communication open, encircling Germany as far as possible and wearing down the German war machine. In practical terms, keeping Russia in the fight was vital to the encirclement goal and dropping an ever increasing number of bombs on Germany was deemed essential to depleting its ability to fight.

No plans for an invasion of France were discussed at this stage but the British were already working on two – Operation Roundup and Operation Sledgehammer. The first of these involved a full scale invasion in 1943 that would establish a base of operations in France, most likely through the capture of a major port, a build-up of troops, a breakout and then a race through the French countryside to attack the German industrial heartland of the Ruhr. The second, Sledgehammer, was only to be activated in an emergency such as the imminent collapse of Russia. All available forces would be sent to France as soon as possible and certainly before the autumn of 1942.

Meanwhile, Brigadier Dwight D Eisenhower, chief war planner to the US Army's Chief of Staff General George C Marshall, had been working on America's plans for how the war should unfold. Marshall and Roosevelt's representative Harry Hopkins brought Eisenhower's ideas to the British in April. This too involved a major operation in 1943 and in the meantime it called for the creation of "an active sector on this front by steadily increasing air operations and by raids and forays all along the coasts". It even called for something akin to Operation Sledgehammer if Russia got into dire difficulty.

The British were surprised and pleased that the Americans seemed to be thinking along the same lines. They were less pleased when Marshall came back in July and demanded that Sledgehammer be launched within three months as an opening phase for the commencement of Roundup.

Mountbatten said: "When General Marshall came over to see the British chiefs

Major-General Victor Fortune, centre, with German General Erwin Rommel, left, at St Valery on June 12, 1940. Fortune had led the 51st Highland Division, attached to the French 9th Army, which fought a rearguard action as the rest of the BEF was evacuated from Dunkirk from May 27 to June 4. A force of 209 'little ships' was assembled to evacuate the 51st from St Valery after it fought its way to the coast but fog and unsuitable beaches made this impossible. With the French breaking down around them, Fortune ordered his nearly 10,000 men to surrender and Rommel's 7th Panzer Division took them prisoner.

of staff he was enthusiastic about the idea of taking part in the invasion which I'd been ordered to plan. But he didn't seem to be able to appreciate that we couldn't stage it as quickly as he had hoped. We hadn't got the landing craft or the other things to go with it, hadn't got the men trained."

It was decided that a large scale landing had to be attempted, though, in the form of a raid rather than as an attempt to secure a

firm beachhead for further inland operations. It was further decided that the target should be a port. Dieppe was chosen by a process of elimination – Le Havre and Cherbourg were too big for a 'raid' to stand much chance of success, Boulogne was too heavily defended by coastal batteries and Caen and St Malo were beyond the range of effective RAF support. It was to prove a foolhardy decision. ■

Luftwaffe Heinkel He 111s during the Battle of Britain when Germany attempted to destroy the RAF.

Leading figures of the Atlantic Charter Conference pictured during a church service aboard *HMS Prince of Wales* in Placentia Bay, Newfoundland, in August 1941. Seated are US President Franklin D Roosevelt, left, and British Prime Minister Winston Churchill. Standing directly behind them are US Navy Admiral Ernest J King, US General George C Marshall, British General Sir John Dill, Admiral Harold R Stark and Royal Navy Admiral Sir Dudley Pound. To the far left is Harry Hopkins talking with W Averell Harriman.

A Royal Air Force Supermarine Spitfire Mk.IIA of 72 Squadron based at Acklington, Northumberland, flies over the coast in 1941. By now the threat of invasion had passed and even the Blitz was coming to an end as Germany concentrated its efforts on Operation Barbarossa – the invasion of the USSR.

EARLY RAIDS ON OCCUPIED FRANCE

The first 'foray' was Operation Biting on February 27-28, 1942. Aerial reconnaissance had by now identified a number of German radar stations in France and British scientists were keen to know how they worked. One particular station, Bruneval in northern France, was chosen and it was decided that an airborne assault had the best chance of successfully capturing the equipment intact, with the raiders being evacuated by boat afterwards.

C company of 1st Airborne Division's 2nd Parachute Battalion, led by Major John Frost, parachuted into France on February 27 and attacked the radar site. After a short battle they captured several important pieces of the Würzburg radar array and successfully withdrew by landing craft after another firefight on the beach. Three men were killed and seven wounded out of the 120 who took part.

Another mission on March 28 was also a success although the cost was considerably greater. Operation Chariot involved putting the dry dock at St Nazaire out of action. This important naval repair facility was the only one on the Atlantic coast capable of repairing the German battleship *Tirpitz*, and its loss would force the huge vessel to travel much further for repairs. The ambitious plan involved crashing an obsolete former US Navy destroyer packed with hidden time-delayed explosives right into the dock gates while commandos destroyed or disabled the rest of the facility. The soldiers would then escape on a flotilla of small vessels before the explosion.

After a diversionary bombing raid on the port, the *HMS Campbeltown* and 18 small boats approached St Nazaire. At 1.22am on March 28 the convoy was just eight minutes from the dock when it was lit up by searchlights.

The Germans flashed a signal demanding that the convoy identify itself and a Motor Gun Boat beside the *Campbeltown*, MGB-314, replied with a captured code. Both vessels were flying the German flag but there were short bursts of fire in response to which MGB-314 signalled: 'Ship being fired upon by friendly forces'. This bought a few minutes during which time the *Campbeltown* began accelerating towards the dock. Then every German gun along the seaward side of St Nazaire opened up. *Campbeltown* was hit numerous times but continued to accelerate even when gunfire raking the bridge killed the helmsman. The impact at 1.34am, later than scheduled, drove the *Campbeltown* 33ft into the gates and wedged it there.

The commandos went ashore and set about their task in the face of heavy enemy resistance. The small vessels they'd been banking on to get them home were all destroyed however and they had to try and escape St Nazaire on foot. Out of ammo and surrounded, they were forced to surrender. The *Campbeltown* exploded later that day as it was being inspected by German officers. They'd brought two British commandos with them who knew about the explosives. They remained silent and the blast, which killed them and every German in the area, caused such severe damage that the dock was put out of action for the rest of the war. A total of 622 men took part in the raid but only 228 made it home. A total of 169 were killed and 215 were captured. The Germans lost 360 men – most of them killed in the *Campbeltown* explosion.

Stuck fast on the southern caisson of the Normandie Dock, the heavily damaged *HMS Campbeltown* is examined by German soldiers. In the water in the foreground are the remains of the anti-torpedo nets *Campbeltown* tore through before hitting the dock.

CHAPTER 2

Slaughter at Dieppe

Learning how to invade – the hard way

Having prioritized Hitler's defeat in Europe over revenge for Pearl Harbor, US President Franklin D Roosevelt felt he needed quick results for the folks back home. The Americans therefore pressed Britain to 'get going' and invade France. The British already had plans to do so and were keen to try them out. The resulting mission was hastily planned, hastily executed and utterly disastrous.

Soldiers of the Queen's Own Cameron Highlanders of Canada transfer from a Landing Ship Infantry (LSI) to a Landing Craft Assault (LCA) ready for the attack on Green beach at Dieppe.

Outline plans for an attack on Dieppe were approved on May 13, 1942, under the codename Operation Rutter. The raid was to take place in late June or early July. On May 11, Mountbatten wrote: "Apart from the military objective given in the outline plan, this operation will be of great value as training for Operation Sledgehammer or any other major operation as far as the actual assault is concerned."

The Americans were equally enthusiastic about Rutter but could supply little in the form of direct logistical support given the tight timescale and the losses suffered at Pearl Harbor. The Royal Navy was stretched to breaking point by the necessity of guarding convoys of essential provisions against the U-boat threat in the Atlantic and was equally unable to provide substantial fire support for the raid. On the other hand, the RAF was hopeful that Rutter would serve to draw the Luftwaffe into a significant air battle which would deplete its stocks of aircraft in the West at a time when much of its strength was already being deployed to the East for the war against Russia.

The ground forces assigned to Rutter were originally to have been British but the Canadians pushed for an opportunity to test their mettle on the front line in a major operation and therefore the 2nd Canadian Infantry Division under Major General John Hamilton 'Ham' Roberts was given the job.

The aims established for the attack, now scheduled for July 4, were to destroy enemy defences, rail and dock facilities, a nearby airfield, radar and power stations and petrol dumps; to capture documents; to take prisoners and to remove German invasion barges that were being stored in the harbour.

Poor weather meant the raid had to be postponed and it was eventually cancelled on July 8, only to be reconstituted as Operation Jubilee shortly thereafter with a new target date of August 19. The raiding party would include around 5000 Canadians, 1000 British servicemen and 50 US Rangers.

The plan was simple. There would be a direct assault on four beaches in front of the town and one landing each on beaches down the coast on either side. From left to right these six beaches were code named Yellow, Blue, Red, White, Green and Orange.

Motor Launch ML 230 escorts four LCPs carrying soldiers of Les Fusiliers Mont-Royal, the Canadian 2nd Division's floating reserve, ahead of their run in to Red and White beaches. When they arrived they were met by a hail of machine gun fire.

On Yellow, eight miles to the left of Dieppe, No. 3 Commando would go ashore and knock out the coastal battery near Berneval-le-Grand.

The Royal Regiment of Canada and elements of the Black Watch of Canada would land on Blue at Puys while Red and White in the centre would be stormed by the Royal Hamilton Light Infantry, the Essex Scottish Regiment, Les Fusiliers Mont-Royal, 'A' Commando Royal Marines and the 14th Army Tank Regiment (the Calgary Regiment).

The Queen's Own Cameron Highlanders of Canada and the South Saskatchewan Regiment would land on Green, at Pourville, and on Orange, six miles to the right of Dieppe; No. 4 Commando including the US Rangers would eliminate the coastal battery near Varengeville-sur-Mer.

The Calgary Regiment, the operation's armoured support, was equipped with 58 new Churchill tanks. Three of them had flamethrowers and all would be modified to operate in shallow water. The Royal Navy was able to spare seven obsolete Hunt class destroyers and Polish destroyer *ORP Slazak* for artillery cover, plus more than 200 other vessels including landing craft, while the RAF would put up 74 squadrons, 66 of them flying fighters.

What little could be learned of Dieppe's terrain in advance of the operation depended on limited aerial reconnaissance and assessment of holiday photographs taken at the port. Precise details of the German forces at Dieppe and even the recently constructed coastal defences were unavailable but the beaches seemed suitable for both infantry and tanks.

THE ATTACK – YELLOW AND BLUE

The fleet set off for Dieppe late during the evening of August 18, 1942, with the first landings, on Yellow and Orange beaches, due to commence at 4.50am the following

An RAF Douglas Boston medium bomber during the Dieppe Raid. Bostons, escorted by Spitfires, attempted to provide close support to the troops on White beach but ended up being fired on by the Canadians on the ground who were unable to identify them. Six Spitfires were downed by 'friendly fire' during the attack.

day. Minesweepers moved ahead to clear a safe route across the Channel and the forces heading for Green and Orange beaches on the right successfully landed on time to begin the assault on Pourville and the gun battery at Varengeville-sur-Mer.

On the left, the convoy heading for Yellow and Blue, Berneval and Puys, hit trouble when it ran into German E-boats escorting an oil tanker at 3.48am. The E-boats managed to sink some of the landing craft with torpedoes before they were driven off and they were also able to warn the coastal defences of the Allies' approach. In addition, the raiding party's vessels had scattered during the attack and were still struggling to re-form by 4.50am.

One landing craft arrived in the right place at 4.45am, the other six arrived at 5.15am, most of them in the wrong place. At 5.30am, while the commandos from the six craft were still getting ashore, a German patrol turned up and opened fire. Many commandos were cut down as they tried to leave their vessels and the rest made a dash for the only exit off

the beach – a narrow gully.

This proved to be guarded however and it was impossible for the attack to proceed. At 7am the commandos, who had been pinned down for over an hour, decided to withdraw. When they got back to their boats they found they had been badly holed by gunfire and were no longer seaworthy. The Germans then launched an attack and the 82 surviving commandos were forced to surrender.

The 20 commandos who'd landed in the right place went undetected and managed to get clear of the beach. They advanced through woodland into Berneval itself where locals suggested that they could advance on the battery through an orchard. On the other side of this, they found themselves within 200m of the battery and opened fire. Although they were unable to defeat the numerically far superior force, they prevented the battery from firing on the main attack force at Dieppe for an hour and a half before their ammunition ran out and they were forced to withdraw to safety.

The Germans down the coast at Puys on Blue beach had also been alerted to the raid by the naval skirmish. The forces meant to destroy the machine gun and artillery positions covering the Red and White beaches at Dieppe were delayed by 20 minutes and during this time their protective smoke screen lifted. The 556 soldiers of the Royal Regiment of Canada and Black Watch ran for the sea wall but this offered no protection since the

Dead Royal Regiment of Canada soldiers lie where they fell on Blue beach. Trapped between the beach and fortified sea wall, they were gunned down by MG 34 machine guns in a German bunker. Its firing slit is visible in the distance, just above the German soldier's head to the left. Bundesarchiv, Bild 101I-291-1230-13 / Meyer; Wiltberger / CC-BY-SA

Within a short time of the initial assault, the beaches around Dieppe were littered with dead soldiers and wrecked British vehicles.

Germans had positioned a machine gun which overlooked it all the way down to the point where its base reached the sand. Two hundred Canadians were gunned down in minutes. Some managed to cut through the wire protecting the exit on to the sea wall and get off the beach but they were soon rounded up and a total of 264 men were captured.

ORANGE, GREEN AND SPOOK

At the other end of the attack front, No. 4 Commando landed on time at 4.30am. The unit split into two groups. The first, under Major Derek Mills-Roberts, was to move inland to cause a distraction while the second, under Lord Lovat, looped around to attack the battery at Varengeville from the rear. Lovat's group was spotted by the defenders as it neared the shore and a pair of pillboxes opened fire but the men managed to get to the beach, get off it and get behind the enemy emplacements to knock them out in short order. They then moved off in the direction of the battery.

Knocked out tanks at Dieppe.

Mills-Roberts and his group, including US Rangers, landed and got off the beach undetected. They cut off the communications between a nearby lighthouse, the battery's observation post and the battery itself before moving inland. Just an hour and 10 minutes after landing, Mills-Roberts and his men were positioned in a wood near the battery waiting for Lovat to attack. Then the big guns opened fire on the forces landing on Red and White beaches and Mills-Robert knew he had to act.

His men opened fire with rifles, Sten guns and mortars. One of them was US Ranger Corporal Franklin Coons – who then became the first American to kill a German during the Second World War. A British mortar bomb ignited German ammunition and there was an explosion that successfully silenced the battery.

Now Lovat's men moved in and their air support arrived. Captain Pat Porteous led the charge to capture the German position – an action for which he was later awarded the Victoria Cross. The guns were destroyed, a fact that the commandos signalled to the aircraft overhead using a large Union Flag. No. 4 Commando then withdrew and was safely evacuated.

The South Saskatchewan Regiment came ashore at 4.52am without being spotted but most of them had drifted away from the beach where they were supposed to be landing. As a result, they had to cross a heavily defended bridge in Pourville. With them was 22-year-old RAF Sergeant Jack Nissenthall, a radar specialist codenamed Spook, who was meant to steal the secrets of the German Freya radar system based near Dieppe just east of Pourville. He had been assigned an 11 man Canadian bodyguard with orders to shoot him if it looked like he was going to be captured.

The main thrust of the attack, made by the Saskatchewans and the Queen's Own Cameron Highlanders, failed when German reinforcements were rushed into the fray. Meanwhile, although Nissenthall and his men had been unable to enter the radar station, they did manage to cut its telephone wires. This forced the Germans to resort to radio communications and their messages were intercepted by Allied intelligence. Through this interception, the British learned valuable information about the location of German radar sites along the French coast.

Under heavy fire, 340 Canadians and Nissenthall managed to escape Green beach. One of the landing craft departing the coast sank just 650ft out and the Germans, who had orders to destroy the invaders rather than just repel them, shot the survivors dead as they swam back to shore.

Focke-Wulf Fw 190 A-2s of JG.2 based at Théville, France. This unit was already well accomplished at Spitfire killing before the Dieppe Raid.

Wrecked Churchills and bodies left on the beach after the raid.

German troops on the beach among the dead and wounded after the raid collapsed and the survivors either retreated or were captured.

Unlike many Churchills involved in the Dieppe Raid, 'Bert' managed to make it off the beach before being knocked out. It is pictured here being inspected by Germans.

THE MAIN ASSAULT – RED AND WHITE

Coastal defences on Red and White beaches, directly in front of Dieppe itself, were shelled by four of the task force's destroyers and bombed by five squadrons of Hawker Hurricanes as the Canadian assault force began to land. A smoke screen was also laid to cover the attack. The 58 Churchill tanks of the Calgary Regiment meant to be supporting the infantry were late and as a result the lead units, the Essex Scottish Regiment and the Royal Hamilton Light Infantry, had to carry out a frontal attack without armoured backup.

As the men charged towards the sea wall they were raked with machine gun fire from positions cut into the sides of the overlooking cliffs. At the wall itself, the Canadians found that it was too heavily defended with obstacles and were unable to get through. When they did arrive, only 29 tanks were even able to attempt the landing. Two of these ended up in deep water and sank. A further 12 got stuck on the beach itself as their tracks dug into the shingle without gripping.

The 15 tanks that did make it off the beach encountered an array of well-prepared tank traps and further obstacles that prevented them from entering the town. Those that survived were forced to turn around and go back to the beach where they provided covering fire for the infantry as they tried to get back to their landing craft alive. Every tank crewman who landed was killed or captured.

The reserve unit attempting to follow the Essex Scots and the Hamiltons on to the beach, Les Fusiliers Mont-Royal, sailed into a hail of machine gun fire from the shore. The Germans also started to use mortars and grenades and many of the landing craft were sunk before they even reached land. 'A' Commando Royal Marines was also sent in to support the lead units and suffered similarly high casualties on the way in. The marines' commanding officer Lieutenant Colonel Joseph Picton-Phillips, seeing what was happening, ordered his men to withdraw, only to be killed moments later.

The withdrawal from Red and White began at 11am, by which time the situation had become hopeless, and the battle was ended by 2pm with the Canadians and British having either withdrawn, been captured or been killed.

Dingo scout car 'Hunter' was disabled when a Churchill tank reversed into it. Throughout the battle, its crew were able to stay in contact with the headquarters ship HMS Calpe at sea. Canadian 6th Brigade commander Brigadier William Wallace Southam used the Dingo as his communications centre for a brief time. Bundesarchiv, Bild 101I-362-2211-04 / Jörgensen / CC-BY-SA

Weary survivors of Operation Jubilee arrive back in Newhaven, East Sussex, after the raid.

Some of the very few survivors of No. 3 Commando arrive back at Newhaven, East Sussex, after their hellish experience on Yellow beach, eight miles down the coast from Dieppe.

DEADLY BUTCHER BIRD

The Allies' 66 fighter squadrons at Dieppe were equipped primarily with Supermarine Spitfires. There were 48 Spitfire squadrons – 42 of them equipped with Mk. Vs, two with Mk. VIs and the remainder with Mk. IXs – plus units flying Hurricanes and Mustangs. They faced two German fighter groups, Jagdgeschwader 2 (JG2) and Jagdgeschwader 26 (JG26), with a total of about 200 aircraft between them. Both sides also fielded bomber squadrons, the Allies being equipped with Douglas Bostons, Handley Page Hampdens, Bristol Blenheims and B-17 Flying Fortresses while

the Germans operated Dornier Do 217 E-2s and E-4s.

The British, American and Canadian air forces had numerical superiority but they faced a formidable enemy. JG2 was led by 28-year-old Walter Oesau, an ace with 101 kills to his name. JG26's leader, Gerhard Schöpfel, 30, had 40 kills but when Oesau was grounded, Schöpfel flew with his men. Both fighter groups were equipped with the Focke-Wulf Fw 190, commonly known as the Würger or Shrike – the butcher bird, although JG26 also operated a small number of Messerschmitt Bf 109 G-1s. The Dieppe landings began at 4.50am and the

first German fighters were not scrambled until 6.20am. Even so, the first Spitfire was shot down just 23 minutes later.

A Hampden followed at 6.46am and then another Spitfire. The first Mustang went down in flames at 6.55am followed by a second at 7.02am. Just one Fw 190 was downed during this first phase of combat and the Luftwaffe withdrew for half an hour between about 7.30am and 8am. Then the onslaught was renewed.

A JG2 Fw 190 shot apart a Spitfire at 8.10am and another followed it down a minute later. A third was destroyed at 8.17am, this time by a JG26 Fw 190. The

Canadian prisoners are paraded through the streets of Dieppe after the raid.

Prisoners taken during the Dieppe Raid are watched over by German guards as they are taken into captivity.

The front and back of a German propaganda leaflet dropped over Britain following the Dieppe Raid. The Nazis had no qualms about photographing dead Canadian soldiers and using those photographs for propaganda.

German tally continued to rise throughout the morning with Spitfires and Mustangs falling like ninepins. There was another lull between 10.30am and 11.30am as the Luftwaffe pilots returned to their airfields to rearm and refuel.

Now it was the Allies' turn. At 10.32am, 22 B-17s escorted by Spitfires bombed Abbeville-Drucat airfield where part of JG26 was based. After the 10 minute raid, intended as a distraction, a Canadian flying one of the Spitfires said: "A quick glance showed that there was terrific activity on land, on the water and in the air. I saw an Fw 190 alone about 1500ft below me. I did a barrel roll to lose height, levelled out about 150 yards behind the Hun, opened fire and closed to a range of about 25 yards. Pieces of the Fw 190 about a foot square flew off from around the cowling. Just as both the enemy aircraft and I ran into a cloud, he blew up with a brilliant flash of flame and smoke.

"My windshield and hood were smothered in oil, and there was a terrific clatter as pieces of the Hun struck my plane. I broke away, hardly able to see over the hood. Afterwards my number two told me that one of the pieces he saw break off the enemy aircraft was about 10ft long.

"I did not realize at that stage that the debris of the exploded aircraft had done such serious damage to my Spitfire that I would have to bale out a few moments later."

At 11.30am, the full force of JG2 and JG26 was unleashed. Two Spitfires were shot down at 11.33am with more at 11.35am, 11.39am and 11.40am. This time some Fw 190s were blown out of the sky too and the ferocious clashes continued until 12.50pm when again the Germans withdrew.

At the climax of this battle, a Do 217 scored two direct hits on British destroyer *HMS Berkeley* forward of the bridge on the starboard side. This broke the ship's back, killed 15 of the ship's 146 strong crew and caused severe flooding of the forward compartments. The order was given to abandon ship and the survivors were picked up by *HMS Albrighton*, which then torpedoed the Berkeley to put it beyond the possibility of salvage by the enemy.

The two sides' air forces continued to fight throughout the afternoon with Gerhard Schöpfel shooting down his 41st kill, a Spitfire, at 4.30pm. He got his 42nd at 6.30pm. The last Spitfire to be shot down over Dieppe was destroyed at 7.43pm.

AFTERMATH

The Canadians and British sent 6000 men on the Dieppe Raid, 5000 of them Canadian. More than 900 Canadians were killed in the attack and 1874 were taken prisoner after it had failed. A further 600 were wounded. In addition, the British suffered 825 casualties during the sea and ground assault. Around two-thirds of them were Royal Navy personnel who had piloted the Canadians' landing craft and the remainder were commandos. The Germans suffered 311 dead and 280 wounded. In the air, the British lost 88 fighters to enemy action, 44 of them Spitfires, plus another 18 reconnaissance and bomber aircraft.

Fourteen more RAF machines were destroyed through accidents or mechanical failure. On the German side, JG2 lost 14 Fw 190s and JG26 lost just six. A further 28 aircraft, mostly bombers, were also destroyed. At sea, the British lost the Berkeley and 33 landing craft.

For the Allies, it had been a disaster which left many of those involved deeply embittered. The experience had taught a number of important lessons however and the invasion planners had been given a much clearer idea of areas where improvement was desperately needed. ∎

Commando officers Lieutenant Colonel the Lord Lovat, Captain Gordon Webb and Captain Boucher-Myers discuss the role of No. 4 Commando in the Dieppe Raid.

CHAPTER 3

Planning the invasion

Fighting for survival, landing craft and COSSAC innovations

The horror of Dieppe graphically demonstrated the importance of detailed reconnaissance and preparation in any future assault on Hitler's 'fortress Europe'. U-boats had to be overcome, supplies stockpiled and British and American forces melded together for a combined war of liberation. Planning on an epic scale was required.

In the wake of Dunkirk, when huge quantities of British weapons, equipment and vehicles were abandoned in France, factories across the nation worked around the clock to make up the shortfall.

British campaigns in Africa and elsewhere had to be supplied and as the war rolled on the factories grew dramatically in size and capacity. Raw materials and other essential supplies arrived in huge quantities by ship but the cost was high.

The Battle of the Atlantic saw hundreds of Allied warships and thousands of merchant vessels forcing their way through Germany's attempts to impose a naval blockade on the British Isles. Heavy cruisers such as the *Admiral Scheer* and powerful battleships such as the *Scharnhorst* and *Gneisenau* joined the German Navy's U-boat fleet in hunting down and picking off the supply convoys.

These raiders enjoyed significant early successes from June 1940 to February 1941, a period that the Germans called Die Glückliche Ziet – The Happy Time. Thousands of tons of vital supplies were being sent to the bottom of the sea and the nation was being slowly throttled. Overall nearly 3500 merchant ships and 175 warships were sunk, but by mid-1942 the threat was easing. The big capital ships had

been recalled to Germany and the effectiveness of convoy escorts began to improve, resulting in the number of U-boats destroyed beginning to rise significantly.

From January 1942 to June 1944, the US successfully shipped more than 17 million tons of supplies to Britain including everything from 800,000 pints of blood plasma to millions of cigarettes. Military materiel also made up a significant proportion of the total tonnage sent to

British ports including M4 Sherman tanks, artillery pieces and thousands of tons of bullets, shells and bombs.

In May 1942, Operation Bolero began – the movement of US troops and aircraft to Britain in advance of Operation Roundup, the first version of the invasion plan which foresaw the full scale attack being launched in 1943. The goal was to get a million Americans – 525,000 soldiers, 240,000 airmen and ground crews and 235,000

The Battle of the Atlantic was fought by U-boat submarines and surface raiders such as the powerful 'pocket battleship' *Admiral Scheer*, pictured here in the mid-1930s.

P-38 Lightning fighters make a refuelling stop in Iceland on their way to Britain in 1942 during Operation Bolero.

An LST in action on D-Day transferring tank and lorries on to a Rhino ferry bound for Gold beach. 'Virgin' is an Observation Post (OP) type Sherman tank belonging to the 8th Armoured Brigade.

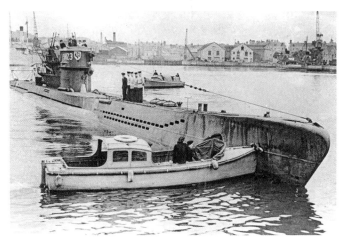

Germany primarily used U-boats such as this Type VII to prevent vital supplies reaching Britain from America and Commonwealth nations. U-1023 is pictured here in 1945, surrendering at Plymouth.

supply chain personnel – to Britain by March of that year.

While troop formations and tanks had to be moved by ship, it was decided that aircraft, specifically B-17 Flying Fortress bombers, P-38 Lightning fighters and C-47 Skytrain transports to begin with, would be flown over. Starting in Goose Bay, Canada, the pilots flew to airfields in Greenland for their first refuelling stop, to Iceland for their second, and then on to their final destinations in England or Scotland. Fighters were divided into groups, each led by a bomber which handled the navigation.

This wasn't quite as straightforward as it looked on paper however, since the pilots had to deal with unpredictable weather conditions, poor radio reception, rudimentary airstrips and compass problems caused by flying close to the North Pole.

The first flight took off on June 1, 1942, and arrived safely in England. Just over three weeks into the operation, on June 26, four B-17 bombers were lost out of a flight of 10 due to bad weather over Greenland. On July 15, six P-38s and two B-17s were forced to land on a glacier in Greenland due to bad weather over Iceland. While their pilots and crews were eventually recovered, the aircraft were left to sink into the ice. Despite these losses however, Bolero proved to be a success and continued on until January 1943 with a loss rate of 5.2%.

LANDING CRAFT SHORTAGE

Supplies were building up steadily but the failure of the raid on Dieppe in August 1942 put an end to Operation Roundup and its target invasion date of early 1943. It was realised that an assault on Hitler's Atlantic Wall required planning in far greater detail than the Roundup timescale had allowed.

Furthermore, Roundup was built on a foundation of British and Commonwealth forces going it alone. The entry of the Americans into the war meant there were now far more resources available and the experience of Dieppe had demonstrated that existing vehicles, weapons and equipment were inadequate.

American help was critical in one area in particular – landing craft. Without a huge number of vessels to ferry troops and equipment into an expanding beachhead, assuming one could be established in the first place any invasion, no matter how large its initial assault, was doomed.

With the tide turning in the Battle of the Atlantic, there was spare capacity in some of Britain's shipyards for work other than fitting out and repairing convoy vessels but it was the Americans who made all the difference. Chief of Combined Operations Louis Mountbatten said later: "The absolutely critical thing for an invasion is to get the troops across the water and for that you want landing ships and landing craft, and those we just didn't have.

"They had to be designed; they had to be built in large quantities at a time when all the shipbuilding facilities were required to fight the Battle of the Atlantic. But we got permission to get smaller yards to start building the landing craft and then we started converting merchant ships to landing ships. And above all, when the Americans came in, I persuaded General Marshall right away to double all the orders I'd placed in America. That's how we built up the landing craft at a time when nobody wanted them to be built up."

A bewildering variety of vessels were designed, mostly in Britain, for use during the invasion of France. There were, in the first instance, Landing Craft (LCs) and Landing Ships (LSs), the craft generally being smaller and the ships larger. Nearly all of the LSs, 1573, were made in the US, compared to just 24 in Britain. There were seven main types of LS ranging from the largest, the Landing Ship Tank (LST), to the Infantry (LSI but also in medium and large forms), Headquarters (LSH), Emergency Repair (LSE) and Dock (LSD).

Britain built many landing craft of its own – 1264 larger vessels and 2867 smaller ones. America made 2486 of the larger types and a staggering 45,524 small craft, though the majority of these were for use in the Pacific theatre. The most common types were the Higgins boat or Landing Craft, Vehicle, Personnel (LCVP), Landing Craft Infantry

A cavernous Landing Ship Tank (LST) prepares to disgorge its contents on to the shore.

Transferred to Britain during Operation Bolero, B-17E 'Yankee Doodle' was used to lead the first B-17 bomber raid against targets in Europe on August 17, 1942.

US Rangers on board a British Landing Craft Assault (LCA) off the coast of Weymouth.

(LCI), Tank (LCT), Support (LCS – in medium and large varieties) and Assault (LCA). During the D-Day assault itself, 236 LSTs and 837 LCTs were used plus thousands of their less substantial brethren. There were even LBBs, Landing Barge Bakeries, and LBKs, Landing Barge Kitchens, which amounted to seaborne catering vans for the troops who were taking part in the attack.

The most important landing craft for the Americans was the LCVP. This flat bottomed boat only needed 26in of water to operate in, had a tough pine log under the bow to absorb the shock of running into sandbars and a tunnel beneath the craft to protect its propeller from debris. It could hold 36 soldiers, 12 soldiers and a Jeep or up to 8000lb of any other cargo. For defence, it had a pair of .30 calibre machine guns. Top speed was 12 knots (13.8mph).

The LCA was the British equivalent of the LCVP. It was built in Hampshire by John I. Thornycroft & Company. Like the LCVP, it could hold up to 36 men and their gear or anything else that weighed up to 8000lb. Unlike the LCVP, its pair of Ford V8 engines could only power it up to seven knots (8mph), fully laden. Its four man crew had either two Bren or two Lewis guns to protect both themselves and the vessel. While the LCVP saw action all over the

world during the war, on D-Day it saw action primarily on the American beaches – Omaha and Utah. The LCA was used on Sword, Gold and Juno but also on Omaha and Utah. Men and equipment were being prepared but by the end of 1942 there was still no firm plan in place.

The Allied leaders, except Stalin whose forces were hard pressed by the Germans, gathered at Casablanca in Morocco from January 14-24, 1943. Aside from agreeing that they would only accept unconditional surrender from Germany, Churchill and Roosevelt, with Charles de Gaulle and Henri Giraud representing the Free French, decided that a cross-channel invasion of France was not, in fact, the best option.

The quintessential American landing craft – the Landing Craft, Vehicle, Personnel (LCVP), also known as the Higgins boat. It could operate in just 26in of water.

The Landing Craft Tank (LCT) had a similar name to the LST but was far smaller. This one is seen offloading an A15 Crusader tank in April 1942.

THE RISE OF COSSAC

It was agreed that a better plan for 1943 would be to attack Europe through what Churchill described as its "soft underbelly" – Italy. Still, it was also agreed that an organisation should be set up to plan Allied operations in Europe in 1944. No firm decision was taken on who should lead this organisation but a right hand man was chosen in advance for whoever would be picked. Lieutenant General Frederick Morgan was made Chief of Staff to the Supreme Allied Commander in March.

Morgan christened his organisation 'COSSAC' after his appointment's initials and the following month he was ordered to devise three plans. The first would be "an elaborate camouflage and deception scheme extending over the whole summer with a view to pinning the enemy in the west and keeping alive the expectation of large scale cross-Channel operations in 1943". This would encourage the Germans to waste resources and tie up forces along the French coast, making life easier for the Russians to the east.

The overall action was codenamed Cockade and it failed because the resources needed to make the operations look 'real'

Two of the big three at the Casablanca conference on January 22, 1943 – Franklin D Roosevelt and Winston Churchill.

were needed elsewhere for the real war effort and because there was a fear that resistance fighters in occupied countries might believe the invasion was real, rise up, and be brutally put down when the invasion failed to materialize. This resulted in too many people being told the truth and the Germans took no notice, moving ever more resources to the east to fight the Russians.

Organising the operation did, however, prove an invaluable experience for the COSSAC team in terms of deception tactics, disseminating false information, marshaling troops and managing the media.

COSSAC's second task was to plan "a return to the Continent in the event of German disintegration at any time from now onwards with whatever forces may be available at the time". This mission was codenamed Operation Rankin and its importance waned when it became clear that a German collapse was unlikely. However, its provisions and structures for dealing with German collapse when it did come became a part of Overlord.

OVERLORD (FIRST DRAFT)

COSSAC's third, and main, objective was to prepare plans for "a full scale assault against the Continent in 1944 as early as possible". A target date for this knock-out blow was established as May 1, 1944, and the Combined Chiefs of Staff required the plan by August 1, 1943, allowing nine months for

The central pier of the Mulberry established at Vierville. In the background are two Spud platforms arranged in T shape. Rumbling down the Whale pontoon roadway at vehicles of the 612th Tank Destroyer *HT Battalion* (Towed) assigned to the 2nd US Infantry Division. Pictured to the right are five Small Tugs (STs).

Lieutenant-General Frederick Morgan was COSSAC – the Chief of Staff to the Supreme Allied Commander – and the driving force behind much of the essential preparation work carried out before Operation Overlord could become a reality.

preparations. Morgan was told 29-30 divisions would be available for the attack by May 1 but that there would only be enough landing craft for five on the day.

Two landing zones were considered – the Caen area and Pas de Calais. Calais was close to England and its beaches were good but it was heavily defended. At Caen, the beaches were adequate, defences were less substantial and there was room for a significant beachhead. The port facilities of Cherbourg were also within easy reach so Caen was chosen.

For the attack to succeed, the German air force would need to be reduced, the number of landing craft increased and some form of artificial harbour devised. Diversionary operations would keep the enemy away from the Caen area and ahead of the attack, an air assault would hit German airfields. The landing beaches would be bombarded by naval vessels before three infantry and two armoured divisions were put ashore. Commando and airborne forces would take out coastal defences and cut lines of communication.

An area from coastal town Grandcamp-les-Bains in the west to Bayeux in the centre and Caen in the east would be taken on day one with Caen itself being captured by the first airborne wave. The assault force would then swing west to take the Cotentin Peninsula and Cherbourg within two weeks. By now 18 divisions would have been landed with 14 airfields created or captured to provide bases for 28-33 squadrons of fighters. What happened next would largely depend on what the enemy did.

The breakwater line of Phoenix caissons was supplemented by outdated merchant shipping vessels known collectively as Gooseberries. These were positioned behind the Phoenix and then sunk.

MULBERRIES AND PLUTO

The idea of creating an artificial harbour first emerged during a conference held at Largs in Scotland from June 29 to July 4, 1943, codenamed Rattle. Several different breakwater schemes were suggested and investigated including 'Lilo', which involved air-filled rubber chambers, a system which used bubbles to negate waves by forming a surface current, a steel and concrete floating construct known as Bombardon, a breakwater made of floating ships, a breakwater made of sunken ships and watertight concrete floats or caissons known as Phoenix.

The schemes chosen for further work were Bombardon, the sunken ships – to be known as Gooseberries – and Phoenix. The Gooseberries would be sunk during the assault itself to provide shelter while the Bombardon units would be positioned furthest out after the attack to form anchorages. The Phoenix units would then be filled with water and sunk to form the

The breakwater effect of the Phoenix caissons and sunken Gooseberry vessels – the 'outer wall' of a Mulberry harbour – is clearly visible in this image. A Spud pierhead and Whale pontoon roadway are visible in the background.

An essential part of the Mulberry harbour design was the use of hollow concrete boxes known as Phoenix. They were to be floated across the Channel and then sunk to form the Mulberry's outer sea wall. This one is being manoeuvred by Small Tugs (STs).

harbour itself – a Mulberry.

Further innovations were needed to get vehicles and supplies landed on the Mulberry to shore. Pontoon pierheads mounted on four legs, called Spuds, were designed to rest on the seabed at low tide and float when the tide came in. These would be connected to the shore by floating pontoon roadway piers called Whale. A non-floating roadway design known as the Hughes Pier was rejected as unsuitable. Excessively heavy equipment would be brought to shore on motorized pontoon ferries called Rhinos.

Getting all the necessary equipment and resources together to build the various Mulberry components took time and the project did not begin to come together until December 1943.

Another novel supply solution was Pluto – the Pipe Line Under The Ocean. This involved laying a reinforced tube all the way from Britain to the coast of France through which fuel could be pumped for Allied vehicles. Tests were begun to see whether this would be feasible.

RECONNAISSANCE AND ANVIL

Before the Mulberries or Pluto could be deployed, the invasion itself had to be a success. In October 1943, Morgan met General Dwight Eisenhower, then stationed in Algeria, to discuss plans for an attack in the south of France to divert attention away from the Overlord landings.

The chiefs of staff had ordered Eisenhower to draft the plans, codenamed Anvil, since he was commander-in-chief of

the Allies' Mediterranean forces at the time and it was they who would be required to carry it out.

When Eisenhower handed over his plans in November however, it was clear that he had drafted proposals for a full scale assault by two to three divisions, rather than a mere feint. He had also included the Free French in the plan which would strike into the heart of Vichy controlled France.

Morgan felt that this would divert too many resources away from the main thrust of Overlord further north but the French were keen and Stalin had been promised an attack in the south of France. A deadlock ensued that lasted into the following year but it also served to bring Morgan into direct contact with Eisenhower and the two men, despite their differences of opinion over Anvil, developed a mutual respect.

British General Bernard Law Montgomery arrived in London on January 2, 1944, to take up his appointment as commander of the 21st Army Group and the following day he had his first meeting with Morgan and his COSSAC staff at which he described their plan as "thoroughly bad".

Morgan's last weekly staff meeting was on January 14, 1944, when it was announced that Eisenhower would be in charge under the title Supreme Commander, Allied Expeditionary Force. Three days later he was in post and COSSAC was rolled into the command structure Eisenhower brought with him from North Africa, this being renamed Supreme Headquarters, Allied Expeditionary Force. Now work on detailed planning of Overlord could begin. ∎

FEARS OF A ROBOT BOMB ATTACK

While Morgan and COSSAC were in the early stages of preparing Overlord, in May 1943, they became aware that the Germans were rapidly building 11 large bases in northern France from which to launch long range rockets or missiles at Britain.

This threat was a wildcard in the Overlord scheme since it was uncertain how soon the German weapons would be ready for launch or how effective they would be. It was feared that the Allied invasion fleet might sail out into an aerial barrage against which there was no known defence.

Some of these sites, as it turned out, were for the unstoppable V-2 rocket while others were for the V-1 flying bomb or 'robot bomb' as it was referred to at the time. In November the first of 96 'ski slope' launchers for the V-1 was also discovered.

A bombing campaign, Operation Crossbow, was stepped up against the bases but even so plans to choose a different invasion zone that was out of flying bomb range were seriously considered. In the end it was decided to rely on bombing of the sites to reduce their effectiveness and keep the Caen area invasion on course.

CHAPTER 4

The final countdown

Deception and preparation for D-Day

With US General Dwight D Eisenhower now in overall command and British General Bernard Law Montgomery in charge of all ground forces for the first phase of Overlord, newly codenamed Operation Neptune, the five month run-up to D-Day began. While detailed planning was being completed and troops were being trained, an elaborate web of deception was being woven to keep German attention elsewhere...

Fresh from their successes in North Africa and Italy, Eisenhower and Montgomery took control of the organization and plans already painstakingly prepared by COSSAC and proceeded to apply their own combat experience to them.

Montgomery, in examining the COSSAC plan to land three divisions, quickly realized that this would be woefully insufficient for the establishment of a strong beachhead.

In a series of meetings with COSSAC in early January 1944, Montgomery dismissed suggestions that there would only be sufficient landing craft available for three infantry divisions and their armoured support and demanded that the plan be changed to allow for a stronger assault force.

The original three beaches chosen as landing areas, codenamed Juno, Gold and Omaha, did not create a wide enough front, he argued – a significant expansion on both sides was needed. He also wanted airborne landings to support both flanks.

COSSAC senior planning officer Brigadier Kenneth McLean said: "He took the line that

we must have more landing craft. He said it must be a five division front or no show, 'give me this or get someone else'."

A few days later, Eisenhower flew to London to take up command of the COSSAC organization and rapidly remould it into SHAEF – the Supreme Headquarters Allied Expeditionary Force. He also appointed General Omar Bradley as the commanding officer of all US ground troops following the invasion, which was to be Monty's show.

At Eisenhower's first meeting of all the senior Overlord commanders, representing army, navy and air forces, Montgomery outlined his proposal for a broader 50 mile invasion front. The navy baulked at the idea of having to provide hundreds of additional transports and the naval firepower necessary to support the extra landings. The air forces, for their part, considered that it would be a struggle to find the extra transports needed for the proposed airborne assault.

Therefore, to give them more time, the invasion date was pushed back from COSSAC's original May 1 deadline to May 31.

General Dwight D Eisenhower pictured wearing the symbol of SHAEF on his shoulder.

BODYGUARD, FORTITUDE, GARBO AND BRUTUS

During the conference held by Churchill, Roosevelt and Stalin at Tehran in Iran from November 28 to December 1, 1943, the British leader reportedly said to his Soviet counterpart: "In wartime, truth is so precious that she should always be attended by a bodyguard of lies."

This memorable nugget of Churchillian wisdom gave the grand scheme of deception concocted to cloak the Overlord build-up in secrecy its name – Operation Bodyguard. The COSSAC ruses of 1943, executed under the banner of Operation Cockade, had been failures, but those who devised them had learned their lesson and when the time came for Bodyguard they were ready to stage a spectacular hoax.

The operation's three objectives were to make it look as though the Calais area was the Allies' invasion target, to conceal any real details about Overlord and to keep German reinforcements away from the Caen area for at least two whole weeks after D-Day.

A scenario was invented where the Allies believed that bombardment of Germany from the air was the best way to win the war and that therefore building bombers was their top priority. This was not, in fact, too far from the truth – a key aspect of selling the lie.

In addition, rather than a single invasion, the Germans would be led to believe that there would be three simultaneous assaults, one in Norway, one in Calais and one in Italy.

Field Marshal Bernard Montgomery took the theoretical plans carefully devised by COSSAC and used his hard-won combat experience to remould them into a practical blueprint for the invasion of Normandy.

The iconic flaming sword logo of the Supreme Headquarters Allied Expeditionary Force.

GOING BEYOND TOP SECRET

During the planning of D-Day there were necessarily certain documents which made mention of the true time and place of the Normandy invasion.

When Neptune was adopted as the codename for the naval part of the operation, the planners realised that documents giving accurate information about its more sensitive aspects required the greatest protection from German intelligence.

For these documents they used the codeword BIGOT. This was a simple reversal of the code stamped on papers used by officers bound for Gibraltar ahead of the invasion of North Africa in November 1942 – To Gib. Anyone who would require direct access to BIGOT documents had to undergo strenuous background checks and if they passed they became 'Bigoted'.

Double agent extraordinaire Juan Pujol Garcia, codenamed Garbo because he played his role better than Greta Garbo, deceived German secret intelligence with an elaborate web of lies ahead of D-Day. They codenamed him Arabel.

Bodyguard was subdivided into several smaller operations, the largest being Fortitude – selling the idea to the Germans that invasions of Norway and the Calais coast were imminent. The tools for the 'sell' were dummy aircraft, airfields and landing craft, controlled 'leaks' of information, faked military radio traffic, high profile officers featuring in the media and German spies working for the Allies – double agents.

By this stage of the war, the Allies controlled the skies of Britain to such a degree that the dummies were practically useless. No German reconnaissance aircraft flew close enough to see them. The leaks too were distrusted by the Germans and therefore ditched as a deception method. That left the radio broadcasts, the high profile officers and the double agents.

After the war, MI5 agent Hugh Astor said: "By 1943 it was realised that all German agents operating in this country were under our control and this opened up the possibility of using deception. The agent fits into it by virtue of the fact that he's providing a channel of communications. He's been recruited by the Germans, he's been sent over here by the Germans, the Germans believe he's operating freely, and you've therefore got a direct line of communication with his German controllers.

"The deception plan for Overlord was brilliantly thought out. The cover plan created an imaginary army and we gave the Germans the impression that we had available almost twice the number of troops that were in fact in existence.

"It was quite interesting at the end of the war when we went through all their files and found they had recorded with details all these imaginary units, the names of their commanding officers, their divisional signs, call signs and all the rest of it; where they'd been stationed at different times, what training

they'd had, what equipment they'd had. All of this was imaginary and passed on by us.

"Only two agents were really used for the deception plan for Overlord. One was Garbo, the other was Brutus. The others played very small parts; they were sort of beating the triangle in the orchestra, just to fill in details from time to time."

Garbo was Spaniard Juan Pujol Garcia. He hated both fascists and communists but was able to create a right-wing persona for himself so convincing that the Germans recruited him, ordered him to London and told him to set up a sub-network of spies. Instead, he went to Lisbon and made up 'reports' from London composed of publicly available materials such as magazine articles and train timetables. He was again extremely convincing and began to make up additional agents on whom he could blame any mistakes he made.

The British, having previously rejected Garcia as an agent, now brought him on board and moved him to Britain. His fictional spy network was expanded to 27 agents – all funded by the Germans when in fact the money went straight into British coffers. The Germans codenamed him Arabel.

Brutus was similarly expert at fooling his German handlers. Roman Czerniawski was a Polish air force captain who had spent the early part of the war spying for the British in France. The Germans arrested him and

attempted to blackmail him into working for them in return for the safety of the spies he had recruited in France – 64 of whom had been arrested. He agreed, but as soon as he arrived in London he turned himself in to the British authorities. The Germans codenamed him Armand.

Both Brutus and Garbo now worked for the top secret MI5-backed Double Cross System organization, also known as XX (two crosses) or the Twenty Committee (two crosses being the Roman numerals for 20).

During Operation Fortitude, they each helped the Germans to build up a false picture of the forces supposedly massing in readiness for an attack on Calais. Their reports gave the genuine details of troops stationed in the central part of the English south coast, lending them credibility, but they reported few units in the south west, when hundreds were stationed there.

Reports of the southeast detailed both real and imaginary forces, particularly the entirely fictional 1st United States Army Group 'led' by US General George S Patton – who was at a loose end having been taken off the front line for slapping a shell-shocked soldier at a hospital in Sicily.

The double agents' reports were backed up with faked radio traffic between the 'units' in the south east. Rather than arousing suspicion by giving the Germans 'secret plans', the Twenty Committee

Royal Navy X-Craft submarine similar to the one used during survey missions to the Normandy coast.

allowed them to weave the tidbits of information they were given into their own tapestry of falsehood which strongly suggested that the greatest weight of troops was poised to strike at Calais.

It worked so well that the Germans not only spent a huge amount of time and resources fortifying Calais, but they also kept 15 divisions in reserve there even after the D-Day landings had begun, thinking that they were just a diversion.

Another branch of Fortitude, Fortitude North, kept 13 German divisions in Norway by similar means using a pair of 'turned' Norwegian spies, John 'Helge' Moe and Tor Glad, codenamed Mutt and Jeff.

LEARNING THE BEACHES

While the spies were telling tall tales to the Germans, engineers and scientists were using detailed information gathered during reconnaissance missions to build up a

picture of the real landing grounds.

The five French beaches selected and the surrounding area were subjected to intense scrutiny. Gradients were studied since this could mean the difference between troops arriving on relatively level terrain or having to slog up a steep natural incline towards the enemy defences.

Likewise, it was important to understand the tidal patterns at each potential site. Landing at high tide might carry a vessel over beach obstacles whereas landing just a little earlier could put the same vessel right on them.

Identifying natural barriers to inland progress such as cliffs, rocks and gullies as well as the layout of the German defences beyond the landing grounds themselves was vital. Even the consistency of the sand along different parts of the coast would need to be examined since tank tracks were better suited to compacted sand than loose shingle – as had been found to the Allies' cost at Dieppe.

Gathering the necessary samples, evidence and information to work this out was a formidable undertaking. A key element of this geological and geographical detective work was aerial photography.

Obtaining detailed photographs of the beaches to work out tide times was the task given to 140 Squadron, which operated an unarmed photoreconnaissance version of the Supermarine Spitfire and later, in 1944, the de Havilland Mosquito. Getting the images was no mean feat – pilots were

M10 tank destroyer 'Bessie' participates in the US Army training exercise on Slapton Sands. In the foreground are rolls of Sommerfeld Tracking mesh which was used to give tanks better traction on sand or weak soil. The mesh, nicknamed 'tin lino' was invented in Britain by German expatriate Kurt Joachim Sommerfeld.

Polish airman Roman Czerniawski, codenamed Brutus, was the other significant double agent of Operation Fortitude – convincing the Germans, who codenamed him Armand, that he was still working for them while feeding them a pack of falsehoods.

MONTY'S DOUBLE – OPERATION COPPERHEAD

Deceiving the Germans about Allied intentions was taken to extremes in the weeks before D-Day and one of the most unusual and elaborate operations involved training a man who closely resembled General Montgomery to ape his mannerisms before sending him to Gibraltar.

Brigadier Dudley Clarke, one of Britain's top counter-intelligence specialists, came up with the idea, later dubbed Operation Copperhead, after watching 1943 film Five Graves to Cairo in which British actor Miles Mander gave a convincing performance as Montgomery. Mander was eventually tracked down in Hollywood but Clarke had himself been fooled by the magic of the silver screen. In real life Mander was 6ft – far too tall to be mistaken for Monty who stood around 5ft 7in.

Another lookalike, Australian Meyrick Edward Clifton James, was spotted in a newspaper article and actor David Niven was called upon to recruit him, ostensibly for a screen test. When James turned up, he was told about the real role he was being asked to play.

Having agreed to impersonate Monty, James was fitted with a prosthetic finger to replace the one he'd lost during the First World War – Montgomery had a full set – and taken up for a test flight to make sure he didn't suffer from air sickness.

James was a habitual heavy smoker and drinker while the 'character' he was being asked to play neither smoked nor drank. He therefore had to give up both.

With Montgomery's consent, James shadowed him to learn his mannerisms. Through the Allies' network of double agents, the (true) fact was put about that Montgomery would command the ground forces on D-Day and then those same agents told their handlers that the general was flying to Gibraltar on May 26, 1944.

James made the flight and attended a breakfast with the British governor Sir Ralph Eastwood before leaving to catch a flight to Algiers. His takeoff was observed by Ignacio Molina Perez, a Spanish envoy and known German spy, who dutifully relayed his sighting of the 'general' to his handler.

After being paraded around in Algiers, where he met General Maitland Wilson, the supreme Allied commander for the Mediterranean, he was flown on to Cairo. Here he was kept hidden out of sight in a hotel room until well after D-Day.

There is no conclusive proof to suggest that the Germans either believed or disbelieved the ruse. James himself went back to being a jobbing actor and working in the Pay Corps. He was told not to talk about Copperhead and later felt that he had been treated "shabbily" by the intelligence services.

Aussie actor M E Clifton James played Montgomery for real to fool the Germans ahead of D-Day.

hampered by enemy patrols, cloud cover, bad weather and even high winds driving waves up beaches.

Each set of photographs, once it was complete, was analysed by the Royal Engineer surveyors of 1 Air Survey Liaison Section working with the Hydrographic Department's Tidal Branch to produce a gradient chart. Another of 140 Squadron's tasks was to produce detailed photographs from which 1:25,000 and 1:12,500 scale maps could be produced. After much painstaking work, the 'Benson' maps produced, named after 140 Squadron's Oxfordshire base, included everything from minor roads to the positions of bunkers and machine gun positions and even the lengths of bridges.

While 140 Squadron concentrated on high altitude photography for tides and mapping, the unarmed Lockheed F-5E Lightning aircraft of the USAAF's 10th Photo Reconnaissance Group flew extremely low level 'dicing' missions to photograph the German beach obstacles in close-up.

The group's pilots went 'dicing' 35 times, from May 6-20, 1944. The task involved switching on the aircraft's three sensitive cameras before speeding down the beach at 360mph at a height of just 25ft. The overlapping view from the cameras of one aircraft produced astounding images that gave Allied commanders a good idea of what they were likely to face on any given beach. On one occasion, pilot Lieutenant Allen Keith hit a seagull. It smashed through his outer windscreen but a layer of bulletproof glass stopped it from hitting him. Though he had to wipe blood and feathers from his goggles, he managed to continue with the mission.

Avoiding another Dieppe by assessing the consistency of the sand on particular landing grounds required a completely different approach. All existing data on the beaches concerned was compiled into 1:5000 scale maps but these were incomplete and even the data in hand had to be tested. As a result, on December 31, 1943, Royal Engineer Major Logan Scott-Bowden and Sergeant Bruce Ogden-Smith of the Special Boat Section were taken over to the French coast under cover of night. They donned rubber diving suits and backpacks containing measuring equipment and swam ashore on to what had already been designated Gold beach.

They took core samples and made measurements before returning to their support boat. Another mission, Operation Post Able, was carried out on January 16-21 to survey the American Omaha sector. This time an X-Craft midget submarine, X-20, was used to take measurements of the seabed near the shore using an echo sounder. Every night the same pair, Scott-Bowden and Ogden-Smith, swam ashore to collect samples which were later analysed to provide a more detailed picture of how troops and tanks would fare.

After the operation, Scott-Bowden was debriefed in London by General Omar Bradley – Commander in Chief of the American ground forces on D-Day. He gave an account of how well he thought the beach would bear the weight of tanks but

Exercise Tiger ended in disaster when German E-boats like this one attacked with torpedoes.

just before the end he said: "Sir, I hope you don't mind my saying but this beach is a very formidable proposition indeed and there are bound to be tremendous casualties." Bradley apparently replied: "I know, my boy, I know."

THE EXERCISE TIGER DISASTER

Numerous exercises and training sessions took place all over southern England during the run up to D-Day, but six weeks before the invasion, on April 22, 30,000 Americans gathered at Slapton Sands in Devon for a large-scale rehearsal. It was planned to last until April 30 and would involve nine tank landing ships loaded with men running up on to the beach. The 3000 inhabitants of the

nearby village of Slapton were evacuated to maintain the secrecy of the operation.

German E-boats, effectively fast patrol boats armed with torpedoes and 20mm cannon, were a constant danger to Allied vessels using the English Channel; and to ward off this threat the Royal Navy assigned a corvette equipped with a single 4in naval gun and four machine guns, *HMS Azalea*, and *HMS Scimitar*, a First World War destroyer with three 4in guns and four machine guns, to the exercise. These warships were backed up by three motor torpedo boats and a pair of motor gun boats.

The first four days of Exercise Tiger were taken up with beach organisational drills and exercises which passed without

incident. On the evening of the fifth day, April 26, the assault troops boarded their landing craft and set off out to sea so that they could then turn around and arrive on the beach at 7.30am on April 27.

In order to simulate the effects of a naval bombardment before they arrived, a heavy cruiser, the *HMS Hawkins*, was scheduled to fire live rounds from its 15 heavy calibre guns at a designated area of Slapton Sands between 6.30am and 7am. This would give the American instructors on the beach half an hour to inspect the cratered area for unexploded ammunition. On the day, several of the landing craft were late for the rendezvous and it was decided that the landing would be delayed until 8.30am.

HMS Hawkins received this information and altered the time of its bombardment accordingly – to between 7.30am and 8am. Several of the landing craft, however, did not get the message and landed at the previously appointed time. There is no official figure for the number of men killed by the bombardment but estimates range from 150 to more than 300.

While the main assault force had landed on April 27, a second wave was due to follow 24 hours later. This consisted of eight LSTs loaded with support troops, engineers and quartermasters, tanks, jeeps, trucks and other heavy equipment. Five landing craft from Portsmouth joined another three from Brixham and formed a line behind their escort *HMS Azalea* on the 27th.

The *Scimitar* had been due to join the formation but was unavailable so another destroyer, *HMS Saladin*, was brought up to fill the gap. Unfortunately, it didn't put to sea until early on April 28 and was a long way behind the convoy when, at 1.30am, seven E-boats attacked. The Germans had noticed unusual radio activity in the area and the surface raiders had been sent to investigate.

A German work crew, pictured middle left, flees in terror as the Lockheed Lightning F-5E camera plane that shot this photo begins its 360mph run across a Normandy beach at an altitude of around 25ft.

They launched a salvo of torpedoes at the landing craft, believing in the darkness that they were destroyers. When there were no hits, the E-boat crews reset the depth of their torpedoes for a shallower run and launched a second strike. Landing craft LST-507 was hit on the starboard side at 2.03am and caught fire. Fuel on board was ignited and the blaze spread rapidly.

A medical officer on board, Eugene Eckstam, said that the internal tank deck had become "a huge, roaring blast furnace" when seconds earlier it had been filled with men and vehicles. He wrote later: "Trucks were burning; gasoline was burning; and small arms ammunition was exploding. Worst of all were the agonising screams for help from the men trapped inside. But I knew there was no way I, or anyone else, could help them. I knew also that smoke inhalation would soon end their misery, so I closed the hatches into the tank deck and dogged them tightly shut."

LST-507 was abandoned by those who were able at 2.30am and the survivors of the 165 crew and 282 Army personnel on board were picked up by LST-515. Then a second vessel was hit, LST-531. It sank within six minutes and 424 of the 496 men who had been on board were killed. A third craft was hit in the stern but it managed to return to port.

While the E-boats circled the convoy like a pack of wolves, the men aboard the LSTs did their best to return fire and radioed for help but due to a clerical error the *Azalea* and the *Saladin* were using a different radio frequency and no help came. Radio stations along the coast did not answer the calls either due to the top secret nature of the exercise until it became apparent that they were indeed coming from the vessels

GIVING THE GAME AWAY (ALMOST)

Secrecy was paramount during the final stages of planning Overlord and anyone who threatened to give the game away was dealt with swiftly and harshly.

One US sergeant of German descent accidentally sent a package of top secret papers to his sister living in the German quarter of Chicago in March 1944. The packet broke open at the post office and the FBI was called. The man was arrested and, though cleared of espionage, was confined to quarters until after D-Day. In May, an American major was demoted and sent home after telling guests at a dinner party in London that D-Day would be before June 15. A navy captain who carelessly gave away details at another party was

likewise packed off home in disgrace.

On May 2, the Daily Telegraph printed a crossword with 'Utah' as one of its answers. Two weeks later, another answer was 'Omaha'. Then a third puzzle featured the answer 'Mulberry' and a fourth 'Neptune'. The teacher who compiled the puzzles, who'd been under surveillance since the second suspect answer, was then arrested.

It later transpired that the man had played an innocent game with his pupils, asking them to come up with answers which he would then work into the puzzle. One pupil had picked up the codewords while hanging around nearby military camps and listening to soldiers' talk before suggesting them in class without realising their significance.

involved in Tiger. Six small rescue launches put to sea but by the time they arrived it was too late for many of the men who spent hours struggling to stay afloat in the cold water. Estimates vary but the Exercise Tiger Trust places the figure at 637 dead.

Beyond the horrendous loss of life, the Exercise Tiger disaster was also a security problem. When Eisenhower heard what had happened, his first thought was of the 10 men lost who had been trusted with the highest level of security clearance – men who were 'Bigoted'. The word BIGOT, stamped in red, was first used on drafts of the Operation Neptune Initial Joint Plan in February 12, 1944, and thereafter appeared on all the most top secret D-Day documents.

If the Germans had managed to recover the bodies of the 10 officers with BIGOT

clearance or worse still had been able to pull any of them alive from the water and take them back to France for questioning the entire operation could have been placed in dire jeopardy. Fortunately all the missing Bigoted men were accounted for and Overlord's secrets remained secret.

By the end of May 1944, preparations were all but complete. Huge stockpiles of weapons, equipment, supplies and provisions had been amassed and hundreds of thousands of British and American servicemen were in a state of readiness, having spent months in training. Reconnaissance was complete and the Germans were still in the dark about what was to come. It only remained for the order to be given to commence the largest and most ambitious invasion the world had ever seen. ■

One of several photo reconnaissance versions of the Lockheed Lightning fighter – the F-5E. The camera apertures in its nose are clearly visible.

The Atlantic Wall

Rommel's formidable coastal defences

Adolf Hitler ordered the construction of defences stretching right the way along the Atlantic coastlines of the countries his forces had occupied – a total of 1670 miles – on March 23, 1942. By mid-1944, it comprised 16 'fortresses', two belts of mines each 1000 yards deep, thousands of heavy guns and tens of thousands of beach obstacles designed to rip open the hulls of landing craft. But it had been hastily built and some areas were better defended than others...

The directive ordering the construction of what became known as the Atlantic Wall demonstrated a remarkable foresight on the part of Hitler's military planners. Führer Directive 40 opened by stating that an assault involving British landing craft and large scale paratrooper and glider landings was likely.

It also accepted the possibility of the Allies achieving complete surprise through skillful deception and emphasised the need for the different branches of the German armed forces to work together in countering this threat.

Overall responsibility for organising the defences had, it stated, to be placed in the hands of one man and in the event of an invasion an immediate counterattack would be vital if the enemy was to be annihilated or thrown back into the sea.

That 'one man' was to be the Commander in Chief of German forces in the West. Hitler had appointed Field Marshal Gerd von Rundstedt to this position just eight days before Directive 40 was issued and therefore the defence of the coast fell to him.

However, in spite of the very stern language of Directive 40 heaping all responsibility for defence of the coast on his head and his head alone, von Rundstedt had little to do with it in practice. He was opposed to the creation of a 'wall' on principle. In October 1943, he sent Hitler a memo stating that the Atlantic Wall scarcely

Field Marshal Erwin Rommel inspects the Atlantic Wall. He was appalled at their poor condition when he was appointed to oversee the defences of Normandy in late 1943.

existed in reality and was little more than a propaganda tool. He told the dictator: "We Germans do not indulge in the tired Maginot spirit." He was referring to the vast

Maginot Line fortifications built by France along its borders with Germany after the First World War. When the Second World War broke out, the highly mobile German forces simply went around these defences.

In von Rundstedt's view, the best way to combat an invasion was by positioning armoured units well inland and moving them up rapidly by rail or road to meet any threat as it materialised – thereby concentrating the greatest force where it was needed rather than spreading it out thinly over 1670 miles.

With little support for the project forthcoming from von Rundstedt, the detailed work of preparing for the invasion Hitler had foreseen was carried out by Organisation Todt – Germany's civil and military engineering group – under the direction of Minister of Armaments and War Production Albert Speer.

Work on constructing, co-ordinating and improving the Atlantic coastal defences had

Rommel tours a Normandy beach to examine the defences.

One of the two gigantic concrete emplacements of the Marcouf battery on the north-eastern coast of the Cotentin Peninsula.

begun in earnest in mid-1942 but Speer, who was charged with the herculean task of coordinating all of Germany's resources to support the war effort, took a pragmatic approach. There was no imminent sign of invasion and no pressure from above to develop the defences so he diverted resources elsewhere. For example, repairing the damage inflicted by the RAF's Dambusters, 617 Squadron, during the Dams Raid saw 7000 Organisation Todt workers diverted from the Atlantic Wall for at least three months from May 1943.

When Hitler heard how little had been done he was concerned and brought in Field Marshal Erwin Rommel, the 'Desert Fox' of the North Africa campaign against General Montgomery in 1942, to take charge of the Normandy defences instead.

Rommel soon realised that a supreme effort would be needed to ready the defences against the invasion that was clearly being prepared across the English Channel. Organisation Todt's slave labour operations were dramatically increased on Rommel's orders and by June 1944 the Atlantic Wall, though by no means finished, was a significantly more daunting proposition for the invaders.

Concentrated on major ports and harbours but providing a degree of protection all along its length, the wall had consumed more than 17 million tons of concrete and some 1.2 million tons of steel.

A US soldier poses in one of four ferroconcrete coastal emplacements at Querqueville west of Cherbourg.

Wreckage of an American Waco CG-4A glider lies in a field of 'Rommel's asparagus' – tall wooden poles strung together with wires and topped with explosives.

NORMANDY BEACH OBSTACLES

Element C (also known as Belgian gates or Cointet-element)

Among the most difficult beach obstacles to overcome were these 3m wide, 2m high heavy steel fences. They could be mounted on concrete rollers, allowing them to be moved around, and were extremely difficult to get through once placed.

Designed by French Colonel Léon-Edmond de Cointet de Fillain, the obstacles were originally designed specifically to block tanks but vertical bars were later added to make them impassable to infantry too. The Belgian Ministry of Defence ordered 77,000 of them in July 1939 to form part of the Koningshooikt-Wavre Line – a Maginot Line-like defence against the threat of German armoured invasion. A total of 73,600 had been made by 28 Belgian companies before the surrender of the Belgian Army after just 18 days of fighting on May 28, 1940.

Unfortunately for the Belgians, the gates had not formed a continuous line and were therefore easily bypassed by the Germans. It is estimated that more than 20,000 'Belgian gates' were employed as part of the Atlantic Wall, with the rest being used for the defence of roads and bridges elsewhere.

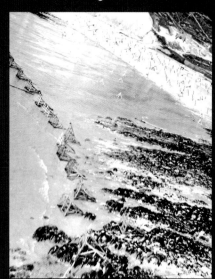

A line of Belgian gates photographed during an American photo reconnaissance mission.

Hedgehog (also known as Czech hedgehog)

This anti-tank defence consisted of iron rails welded or bolted together to form a spiky angular shape. In similar fashion to Element C, it was conceived as part of border defences by the Czech Republic but when Germany occupied the Sudetenland in 1938 it effectively acquired all of these defences including thousands of hedgehogs without firing a shot.

The basic hedgehog was relatively small at 4ft 7in high but the idea was that a tank attempting to shove it aside would end up running over it and getting stuck on top of it. Original hedgehogs manufactured by the Czechs consisted of three L-shaped metal brackets joined by rivets, bolts or welding. The 'arms' had square 'feet' to prevent them from sinking into the ground and a notch for attaching barbed wire.

A cluster of Czech hedgehogs near the Utah beach landing zone.

Wooden stakes (also known as Hochpfähle)

During an inspection of a beach at Neufchâtel-Hardelot, just south of Boulogne, on February 3, 1944, locally based soldiers demonstrated to Rommel a technique they had developed: using a high-pressure water jet to blast a hole in beach sand before inserting a tall wooden stake into it to create an effective obstacle.

The field marshal was so impressed he ordered that the technique be rolled out along the entire length of the Atlantic Wall where possible. Tests later revealed that the stakes were insufficiently strong to pose much of a threat to British landing craft so a larger design set at an angle was approved – the Hemmbalken or 'obstruction beam'. The Hochpfähle already put in were then topped with anti-tank Teller mines to increase their effectiveness.

The Germans made extensive use of wooden stakes topped with Teller mines as beach obstacles intended to damage or destroy landing craft.

In places, the Atlantic Wall employed complete turrets from outdated tanks as defensive positions.

Part of the Cherbourg defences. The coastal towns and villages of Normandy were often heavily fortified by the Germans in anticipation of the Allied invasion.

The greatest firepower was naturally concentrated in the areas where it was deemed that the level of threat was highest. The Calais region was defended by 93 heavy gun emplacements and 39 mobile heavy guns, compared to Normandy which had 27 emplacements and 20 mobile heavy guns.

All along the length of the wall were minefields, trenches, pillboxes, bomb shelters, command posts, tank traps and machine gun nests but, as an added defence, large areas behind the beaches were also flooded to make them impassable.

Coastal roads were blocked with solid concrete walls, huge tree trunks or dense coils of barbed wire, and seaside villages were turned into mini strong points with ordinary houses converted into bunkers and blockhouses. All beach exits were heavily mined and covered by overlapping fields of machine gun and anti-tank gun fire.

Numerous obstacles were positioned at the water's edge and within the tidal zone, designed to wreck landing vessels.

Obstacles were also placed in fields to wreck gliders as they attempted to land.

Rommel reasoned that a combination of defences and delaying tactics might just prevent the Allies from gaining a secure foothold long enough for reinforcements to arrive from their positions further inland. Another concern was the quality of the troops manning the defences.

There were a few experienced and highly capable units, such as the 352nd Infantry Division posted between Bayeux and Carentan, but many were 'static' units established for the express purpose of simply manning defensive positions. Some were those deemed unfit for any other service. Some were even former Soviet citizens brought over from the Eastern front and formed into 'Ost' units with German leaders. Their commitment was doubtful. Despite his misgivings, all Rommel could do was wait and hope to delay the Allies long enough for von Rundstedt's strategic forces to arrive on the scene. ■

CHAPTER 6

The right tools

Allied equipment and vehicles in Normandy

Getting past Hitler's vaunted Atlantic Wall and defeating some of the finest fighting units in Western Europe was going to take more than just modified tanks, powerful aircraft and well-equipped infantry – it was going to require all three working together.

While the British infantryman's burden had scarcely grown lighter in the generation that had passed since the First World War, he was better equipped.

Basic infantry weapons were the .303 calibre Lee-Enfield No. 4 Mk.1 rifle and Bren Mk.1 or Mk.2 light machine gun plus the pineapple-ridged No. 36 Mills bomb hand grenade. Some units were also equipped with Mk.2 Sten 9mm sub-machine guns, mortars, Vickers medium machine guns, 6-pounder anti-tank guns or PIAT hand-held anti-tank weapons.

The bolt-action Lee-Enfield rifle, which featured a 10 round box magazine, was little changed from the design that entered service with the British Army in 1895.

The Bren was first issued in 1938 and was an update of an earlier Czech design. Its name derived from the first two letters of the Czech city, Brno, where the earlier Zb vz 26 was made, and the first two letters of Enfield, the location of the Royal Small Arms Factory where it was made. It featured a distinctive curved magazine, could fire between 480 and 540 rounds per minute and could be shot from the hip if required. It was both reliable and effective.

The Sten was a recent invention in 1944, having been designed by Major Shepherd (the 'S' of Sten) and Harold Turnpin (the 't' of Sten) at Enfield (the 'en') just three years earlier based in part on a German design, the MP38. It was cheap to mass produce

British soldiers watch for signs of enemy counterattack while positioned in a house just south of the River Orne in Caen. The man on the left is carrying a Sten gun while the one on the right has positioned a Bren on the windowsill.

and could fire 500 rounds per minute. It was also inaccurate and jammed easily.

The tripod-mounted Vickers machine gun was the familiar and reliable design of 1912 which had featured so prominently during the trench warfare of the First World War but

the PIAT 'Projector, Infantry, Anti-Tank' was even newer than the Sten. It had been designed in 1942 and first used in combat just 11 months before D-Day. Firing a 2.5lb bomb, it operated on a spigot mortar principle where a pin ignited a propellant in the bomb itself, launching it towards its target.

In practice, the PIAT could be used to devastating effect. It was responsible for knocking out 7% of all German tanks destroyed in Normandy – a figure that would undoubtedly have been higher had the Germans not developed protective 'skirts' to detonate hollow charge rounds, such as the PIAT's mortar bombs, before they could penetrate the tank's own armoured skin.

Indirect fire mortars were particularly effective in Normandy and the British deployed three main types – the Ordnance SBML 2in mortar, the ML 3in and the ML 4.2in. Bangalore torpedoes, explosive charges inside a long pole that could be poked through barbed wire or onto minefields, were also used extensively.

American infantry attack over the body of a German soldier in France. The GI on the right is carrying an M1 Thompson submachine gun.

The US infantryman's anti-tank weapon of choice and still a household name, it's the bazooka. By 1944 German heavy tanks were all but immune to it.

An American infantryman fully kitted out.

AMERICAN EQUIPMENT

The US soldiers who took part in Operation Overlord used a whole arsenal of weapons which differed from those employed by their British counterparts.

The standard American rifle was the semi-automatic M1 Garand invented by French Canadian John Garand – pronounced to rhyme with 'errand' – in 1919. It was loaded using clips of eight .30-06 Springfield rounds slotted into its fixed magazine from above and in the hands of a trained soldier could be made to fire 40-50 accurate rounds per minute.

Troops were also issued with the M1 Thompson sub-machine gun, which had gained some notoriety during the 1920s Prohibition era as the Chicago gangsters' weapon of choice. Bank robbers Bonnie and Clyde used one too. Like the Garand it was invented in 1919 and named after its creator, US Army officer John T Thompson. It could fire more than 600 rounds of .45 calibre ammunition per minute – a rate which often resulted in a tendency for the barrel to rise off target during fully automatic firing.

The American equivalent of the Bren was the BAR 'Browning Automatic Rifle', invented in 1917 by John Browning. It saw

THE MIGHTY AMTRAC

The two main types of front line assault landing craft used on D-Day were the British Landing Craft Assault (LCA) and American LCVP (Landing Craft Vehicle, Personnel) or 'Higgins Boat'.

However, the Americans had another highly successful landing craft which saw action during the Pacific campaign but which simply wasn't used on D-Day.

The Landing Vehicle Tracked (LVT) or 'Amtrac' could only carry 18 fully equipped soldiers – half the number that the Higgins boat could manage – but it was amphibious. Using its tracks it could crawl right out of the water and deposit its load against a sea wall or other defensive position.

Following experiences during the Battle of Tarawa against the Japanese,

LVTs were also up-armoured to resist machine gun fire. There was even a variant equipped with a 75mm field gun, the 'Amtank', to provide better fire support.

US personnel brought to Europe from the Pacific were surprised to see that the landings would not involve Amtracs, even though 300 had been shipped to Britain, but it was explained that since there were no coral reefs to cross of the sort seen in the Pacific, the amtrac was unnecessary.

Had the European theatre commanders known what was in store for the US troops going in on Omaha they might have thought twice about employing Amtracs. As it was, the Amtracs were relegated to the reserves.

The LVT-3 Amphibious Tractor or Amtrac saw use primarily during the Pacific campaign against the Japanese. Some questioned why it was not used during the D-Day landings, despite being available.

A small fleet of Amtracs head for the shore during the Battle of Okinawa in 1945 – could similarly modified Amtracs have made a difference on Omaha beach?

A Projector, Infantry, Anti-Tank or PIAT crew prepare for action.

limited use with US forces towards the end of the First World War and underwent continuous development up until the M1918A2 variant appeared in 1938.

This could be toggled between a 300-450rpm rate of fire and 500-650rpm. It weighed 19lb compared to the Bren's 22lb. While the PIAT has hardly become a

household word, the fame of the American M1 anti-tank rocket launcher, commonly known as the Bazooka, is universal. While the concept of a tubular rocket launcher dates back to the First World War, the Bazooka as it is known today was the invention of US Army Lieutenant Edward Uhl in 1942. Weighing just 12.75lb itself, the

Bazooka fired 2.36in M10 self-propelled rockets. It got its name, initially just a nickname, from a novelty musical instrument played by American comedian Bob Burns.

The Bazooka earned a fearsome reputation almost immediately when it was deployed in Africa but it struggled to penetrate the armour of later German tanks and by 1944 it was largely obsolete as an anti-tank weapon. The Germans actually captured several examples and copied it as the Panzerschrek, making it larger to accommodate far more effective 88mm ammunition.

ARMOURED SUPPORT

Tanks played a critical role on D-Day and during the Normandy campaign that followed. Allied tanks have generally been regarded as inferior to their German counterparts and given the right conditions a tank such as the Panzer VI Tiger could and did annihilate whole formations of British or American tanks without loss.

The right conditions rarely prevailed however, and the deadliest German tanks were horrendously expensive and difficult to produce – resulting in relatively low numbers of designs such as the Panther, Tiger and Tiger II reaching the front line.

Against older and far more numerous German designs, such as the Panzer IV, III and earlier, Allied tanks such as the Sherman were evenly matched or superior.

In addition, the Dieppe raid had demonstrated how generally ill-suited unmodified tanks were to the task of amphibious assault so a multitude of add-ons were prepared to improve their usefulness and their chances of survival.

A DD or Duplex-Drive Sherman tank with its flotation screen lowered. In the water, this rose up to form a tall box-like structure around the tank, far taller than its turret. The commander could only see where he was going by standing up.

Armoured warfare specialist Major-General Percy Hobart, who was in charge of 79th Armoured Division Royal Engineers, was given the task of creating these 'funnies', mostly based on Churchill and Sherman tank chassis, in 1943.

By early 1944 he had come up with around 20 different designs. The most important of these for D-Day were the DD Sherman, AVRE, Crab, ARK, Fascine and Crocodile. Once the landing grounds were secure, Hobart's funnies quickly gave way to standard production models of the Sherman and Churchill plus Cromwells and M10 Wolverine tank destroyers.

M4 SHERMAN

Both British and American forces used Sherman tanks on D-Day and throughout the Normandy campaign. The M4A1 Sherman first saw service with the British 8th Army at the Second Battle of El Alamein in October 1942 where it overmatched German Panzer III and IV tanks. More than 50,000 Shermans were eventually built but even by June 6, 1944, it was outdated and had been surpassed by the German Panzer V Panther, Panzer VI Tiger.

The only Sherman that was truly effective against these monsters of the

ALLIED TANK SPECIFICATIONS

M4A4 Sherman Mk.V Firefly
Crew: Four (commander, gunner, loader/radio operator, driver)
Weight: 34.75 tons
Engine: 21 litre Chrysler A57 Multibank 30 cylinder (5 x inline-six) producing 425hp
Maximum speed: 25mph
Range: 120 miles
Armament: QF 17-pounder (7.62cm cannon, 1 x 7.62mm Browning M1919 machine gun in the turret, 1 x .12.7mm Browning M2 machine gun on a mounting on top of the turret. The latter was generally removed by crews however)
Armour: 89mm maximum (turret front)

A22 Churchill Mk.VII
Crew: Five (commander, gunner, loader/radio operator, driver, co-driver/hull gunner)
Weight: 37.9 tons
Engine: 21.3 litre Bedford horizontally opposed twin-six petrol engine producing 350hp
Maximum speed: 15mph
Range: 55 miles
Armament: QF 75mm cannon, 2 x 7.92mm Besa machine guns
Armour: 152mm maximum (front armour)

A27M Cromwell Mk.IV
Crew: Five (commander, gunner, loader/radio operator, driver, hull gunner)
Weight: 27.6 tons
Engine: 27 litre Rolls-Royce Meteor V12 petrol engine producing 600hp
Maximum speed: 40mph
Range: 170 miles on roads, 80 miles cross country
Armament: QF 75mm cannon, 2 x 7.92mm Besa machine guns
Armour: 76mm maximum (front armour)

battlefield was the British Sherman Firefly variant, which had the usual American 75mm gun removed and replaced with a high velocity British 17-pounder. Tests later showed that this actually had greater penetrating power even than the infamous 88mm KwK 36 fitted to the German Tiger.

The Sherman with the most prominent role on D-Day was the amphibious DD Sherman. The tank's lower hull was sealed and it was fitted with a tall all-round flotation screen, a bilge pump and 'Duplex Drive', hence DD, which amounted to a propeller at the rear linked to its engine. Its top speed in the water was about four knots, or 4.6mph.

Another variant of the Sherman to see extensive use on D-Day was the Crab, which was fitted with a spinning motorised cylinder at the front that pounded the ground with chains to detonate mines.

A22 CHURCHILL

Designed initially to cross trenches and fitted with a small turret ring that limited the calibre of its main gun, the Churchill nevertheless proved a valuable addition to the Allies' armoury. After the DD Sherman, perhaps the most important tank fielded by the Allies was a Churchill adaptation – the AVRE 'Armoured Vehicle Royal Engineers'. In place of a 6-pounder turret gun the AVRE was fitted with a huge 290mm 'Petard' mortar. This fired charges designed to blow holes in concrete emplacements and demolish walls. A sixth crewman, sitting beside and below the Petard's barrel, was added as a loader. AVREs could also carry a fascine. Among the many defences erected by the Germans along the Normandy coastline were deep ditches and dykes,

Renowned as the great tank killer of Normandy, in reality the Hawker Typhoon's greatest impact was psychological.

often deliberately filled with water. The fascine was a huge bundle of brushwood mounted on the AVRE's hull next to the turret. On approaching a ditch or deep shell hole it simply tipped the bundle in and then drove over it.

Other key modifications of the Churchill were the Crocodile flame-thrower and the Armoured Ramp Carrier or 'ARK', which had its turret removed and was fitted instead with a ramp at either end for filling in holes in defences or climbing walls.

A27M CROMWELL

After years of struggling to catch up with German tank developments – which favoured increasingly large main guns and heavy armour – the British finally hit upon a winner with the Cromwell. It was fitted with a powerful and reliable Rolls-Royce Meteor engine, had thickish 76mm armour and a largish QF 75mm main gun. While still outclassed by the likes of the Panther and Tiger, it was at least a match for the more numerous Panzer III and IV.

M10 WOLVERINE/ACHILLES

The M10 was created in 1942 using the mechanicals of the Sherman as a base but with lighter armour, an open-topped turret and a 3in M7 (76.2mm) anti-tank gun in place of the Sherman's smaller main weapon. On D-Day it was the standard Allied tank destroyer. The British had begun to receive M10s from the Americans the year before, in 1943, and nicknamed it 'Wolverine'. As with the Sherman, it was decided that it needed a bigger, British, gun.

Therefore work began on converting British M10s, of which there were 845 by the end of 1943, to take the same QF 17-pounder that was being fitted to M4 Shermans to create the Firefly.

While it was not present in huge numbers, the Wolverine/Achilles proved itself to be a valuable tool in taking on German armour in the close confines of Bocage country.

M10 Achilles
Crew: Five (commander, gunner, loader, loader's assistant, driver)
Weight: 29 tons
Engine: General Motors 6046 diesel engine producing 375hp
Maximum speed: 32mph
Range: 186 miles
Armament: QF 17-pounder cannon, 1 x .50 calibre Browning machine gun, 1 x Bren light machine gun
Armour: 57.2mm maximum

M7 Sexton
Crew: Six (commander, gunner, gun-layer, loader, wireless operator, driver)
Weight: 25 tons
Engine: 16 litre Continental R-975 nine-cylinder producing 400hp
Maximum speed: 25mph
Range: 125 miles
Armament: QF 25-pounder howitzer, 2 x Bren light machine gun
Armour: 32mm maximum

An American M10 tank destroyer lets loose on a target. The M10 was a highly successful weapon in Normandy and was responsible for knocking out a significant proportion of all German armour destroyed.

The Armoured Vehicle Royal Engineers or AVRE was a vital D-Day weapon. The huge 40lb bombs fired by its Petard mortar, nicknamed 'flying dustbins' because they were so large, were powerful enough to demolish sea walls and the sides of bunkers.

AIR SUPPORT

Huge numbers of fighter aircraft were flown in support of the Allied landings on D-Day – upwards of 170 squadrons – but they were scarcely needed. Very few German aircraft came near the invasion zone and Allied fighter pilots faced greater danger from friendly fire and from mechanical failure.

Heavy bombers were used to pound German rear positions and strategic assets such as rail yards too. Even after D-Day the Luftwaffe was in such a poor state, with much of its remaining strength deployed attempting to halt the Russian advance in the east, that the Normandy campaign was primarily a story of Allied air supremacy.

Hawker Typhoon

Designed as a direct replacement for the Hawker Hurricane, the Typhoon had never been intended to carry out attacks on ground targets but it was found that the type could carry a surprisingly large bomb load – up to two 1000lb bombs. It was first equipped with rockets in 1943 – four 60lb RP-3s under each wing. This weapon, already proven during use by Hurricanes, was devastatingly effective against tanks.

Throughout the Normandy campaign, the crews of German armoured fighting vehicles feared the arrival of Typhoon 'jabos' overhead. Analysis of destroyed tanks after the Normandy campaign showed a hit rate for air fired rockets of just 4% but the psychological effect of the attacks had been dramatic.

There were numerous instances where veteran tank crews, on spotting a Typhoon heading their way, immediately jumped out of their vehicle and ran for cover. This led to constant delay whenever armour was being moved around Normandy, particularly by road.

Republic P-47 Thunderbolt

The all-metal P-47 was huge and remains the largest, heaviest, most expensive piston engine fighter in history. It was used to great effect in Normandy as the USAAF's fighter bomber of choice. The most numerous variant in service was the P-47D.

Fighters and bombers

The British fighter of choice in mid-1944 was the Supermarine Spitfire Mk.IX, by far the most common of the later production Merlin-engined Spitfires and built in a bewildering variety of sub-types. While the bulk of the RAF's fighter strength was in Spitfires, a number of squadrons were operating the North American Mustang Mk.III, known to the Americans as the P-51B or C, on D-Day.

In addition to the Thunderbolt, the USAAF flew hundreds of twin-boomed Lockheed P-38F Lightnings on beach patrol and ground attack duties during the landings. Another American type used for ground attack was the Douglas A-20G Havoc. The British also used it during the Normandy campaign but renamed it the Douglas Boston IV. When night fell on D-Day, RAF de Havilland Mosquito NF Mk.XIX night fighters took to the air to

continue protecting ground forces from any potential Luftwaffe threat.

After fighter-bombers and fighters, the other key form of air support for the Allied forces was the heavy bomber might of the RAF's Bomber Command and the American Eighth Air Force.

More than 2300 sorties were flown by American heavy bombers on D-Day alone against German coastal defences and front line troops. Most commonly flown was the 'definitive' Boeing B-17 Flying Fortress – the B-17G. Also used were the Consolidated B-24 Liberator and B-25 Mitchell – the latter mostly by the RAF. Britain took delivery of around 900 examples in 1943. The Martin B-26 Marauder, primarily in B-26B form, was used by both the Americans and the British.

Britain also operated the Handley Page Halifax, most commonly the B Mk.III, and the Avro Lancaster B II for bombing. ∎

ALLIED FIGHTER-BOMBER SPECIFICATIONS

Republic P-47D Thunderbolt
Crew: One
Empty weight: 10,000lb
Loaded weight: 17,500lb
Engine: Pratt & Whitney R-2800-59 twin-row radial engine producing 2535hp
Maximum speed: 433mph at 30,000ft
Range: 800 miles
Maximum altitude: 43,000ft
Max rate of climb: 3120ft/min
Armament: 8 x .50 calibre M2 Browning machine gun, up to 2500lb of bombs or 10 5in unguided rockets

Hawker Typhoon Mk.Ib
Crew: One
Empty weight: 8840lb
Loaded weight: 11,400lb
Engine: Napier Sabre IIB piston engine producing 2200hp
Maximum speed: 412mph at 19,000ft
Range: 510 miles
Maximum altitude: 35,200ft
Max rate of climb: 2740ft/min
Armament: 4 x 20mm Hispano Mk.II cannon, 8 x RP-3 unguided air-to-ground rockets or 2 x 500lb or 2 x 1000lb bombs

THE GREAT PANJANDRUM

After Dieppe the Allies had a fair idea of the sort of defences they would be facing wherever they landed on the French coast.

As a result, the Directorate of Miscellaneous Weapons Development, part of the British Admiralty responsible for researching unconventional weapons, was given the somewhat open-ended task of coming up with something capable of demolishing 10ft high 7ft thick concrete walls or obstacles that could be launched from a landing craft.

The job was handed to Nevil Shute Norway, an engineer and novelist who had once served as deputy to bouncing bomb inventor Barnes Wallis on a Vickers airship project.

He calculated that making a tank sized hole in such a huge wedge of concrete would require more than a ton of explosives. The biggest problem was getting the explosives to the concrete. In the end, a device was constructed consisting of two wooden wheels, each 10ft in diameter, with the explosives positioned in a drum between them.

This outlandish rolling bomb was to be powered by cordite rockets attached to the outside edge of each wheel which would propel it up to a speed of 60mph before it hit the target, crashing through or over anything else in its path.

Norway rather poetically named it the 'Great Panjandrum' after a piece of nonsense prose written in 1755 by dramatist Samuel Foote as a means of testing orator Charles Macklin's claim that he could memorise any text at a single reading and repeat it verbatim.

This read: "So she went into the garden to cut a cabbage-leaf to make an apple-pie; and at the same time a great she-bear, coming up the street, pops its head into the shop. 'What! No soap?' So he died, and she very imprudently married the barber; and there were present the Picninnies, and the Joblillies, and the Garyulies, and the grand Panjandrum himself, with the little round button at top, and they all fell to playing the game of catch-as-catch-can till the gunpowder ran out at the heels of their boots."

Built at Leytonstone, the prototype Grand Panjandrum was tested on the beach at Westward Ho! in Devon on September 7, 1943. Only a small number of rockets were attached, far fewer than the operational version was expected to have, but even so, the device shot forward, span out of control and toppled over.

Three weeks later another test was conducted with more than 70 rockets and a third wheel for stability. Again, the vehicle went out of control. Some of the rockets flew off and shot over the heads of the observation team before crashing into the sea.

Efforts were made to control the device using steel cables but with its full complement of rockets it was too powerful and broke away from them.

A final test was conducted in January 1944 in front of Royal Navy officials. In the BBC documentary Secret War, eyewitness Brian Johnson described the scene: "At first all went well. Panjandrum rolled into the sea and began to head for the shore, the brass hats watching from the top of a pebble ridge. Then a clamp gave. First one, then two more rockets broke free. Panjandrum began to lurch ominously.

"It hit a line of small craters in the sand and began to turn to starboard, careering towards Klemantaski who, viewing events through a telescopic lens, misjudged the distance and continued filming.

"Hearing the approaching roar, he looked up from his viewfinder to see Panjandrum, shedding live rockets in all directions, heading straight for him. As he ran for his life, he glimpsed the assembled admirals and generals diving for cover behind the pebble ridge into barbed wire entanglements.

"Panjandrum was now heading back to the sea but crashed on to the sand where it disintegrated in violent explosions, rockets tearing across the beach at great speed."

The project was cancelled.

When the Great Panjandrum was being designed, this is how its creators envisioned it working against the Atlantic Wall – rolling out of landing craft, all rockets firing, and right into the Germans. In tests it fell far short of this ideal.

The Cromwell tank has been unfairly maligned as failing to measure up against the likes of the German Tiger or Panther but it was comparable or even superior to the far more numerous Panzer IV or StuG III.

The American Republic P-47D Thunderbolt. It was the heaviest and most expensive piston engine fighter of the Second World War.

CHAPTER 7

Crossing the Channel

The decision, final deceptions and crossing

Everything was ready. A tentative date of June 1 had been set for D-Day back in January 1944 but taking into account the tides needed to carry landing craft over beach obstacles and the benefits of a full moon for obstacle clearance teams working ahead of the landings, it was decided to push the date back to June 5...

The last day of May saw the first vehicles being loaded on to transport vessels in anticipation of the coming invasion of France. The paint had hardly dried on the white stars many bore on their roofs and sides – a last minute measure to prevent friendly fire.

Plans had been finalised for a frontal assault spread across five carefully surveyed landing zones, with paratroopers and glider-borne units dropping on either flank ahead of the main attack.

Stacks of orders and maps had been printed and were in the process of being sent out to senior officers ready for distribution to their subordinates once the order to begin the operation was given.

Bombing raids on targets across Germany and the occupied countries, and on infrastructure targets behind the invasion zone, particularly rail yards and radar sites, continued unabated – the RAF having already flown 11,000 sorties and dropped 37,590 tonnes of bombs during May alone. The bombers of the USAAF had not been idle either.

On June 1, Admiral Bertram Ramsay took operational command of the invasion fleet and his first act was to refuse both Churchill and King George VI permission to personally view the landings. The prime minister had been planning to embark aboard the cruiser *HMS Belfast* – which was

Rangers of E Company, 5th Ranger Battalion, at Weymouth as they load up in readiness for D-Day. E Company went ashore on Omaha beach.

to take part in the opening bombardment in support of Forces G and J – and the king, against Churchill's wishes, had insisted on accompanying him. Ramsay settled the matter.

That same day, Ramsay joined Eisenhower, Montgomery and Leigh-Mallory for the first of a series of twice-daily

weather forecasts from meteorologist Group Captain James Stagg. Stagg, a civilian given a military rank to lend him the appropriate authority among forces personnel, was the senior staff meteorologist given the task of collating and interpreting reports from three separate sets of forecasters – those of the Met Office,

A Sherman Firefly tank of C Squadron, 13th/18th Hussars at Portsmouth harbour prior to setting sail for Normandy. The 13th/18th landed on Sword beach.

Ships from Force O's bombardment fleet bound for Normandy on June 5. The front ship is the battleship *USS Texas*, followed by the British cruiser *HMS Glasgow*. Behind these are the battleship *USS Arkansas* and two French cruisers *Georges Leygues* and *Montcalm*.

Soldiers of the US 1st Infantry Division aboard an LCT ahead of the invasion crossing.

US Rangers waiting for the off at Weymouth in early June.

Royal Navy and USAAF. These reports frequently offered conflicting predictions and Stagg's job was complicated by the expectation that he should give the waiting military commanders just one report – the most accurate one. The USAAF forecasting team in particular consistently gave an over-optimistic interpretation of the data.

Earlier in the planning phase, dry-witted COSSAC leader Lieutenant-General Frederick Morgan had jokingly told him: "Good luck Stagg. May all your depressions be nice little ones, but remember we'll string you up from the nearest lamppost if you don't read the omens aright."

Stagg's June 1 report suggested calm weather ahead but the following day his forecasters had less positive news, predicting a deterioration to high winds, heavy seas and dense cloud cover by June 6. Eisenhower asked whether there was likely to be an improvement by June 7 and Stagg was forced to tell him that this, though not impossible, was unlikely.

While the weather outside Southwick House just north of Portsmouth, where the briefings were taking place, remained fine, the forecast given on the morning of June 3 was unchanged. By 9.30pm, Stagg was again forced to admit that conditions had taken a turn for the worse. It was now even raining at Southwick.

Eisenhower provisionally postponed the invasion for 24 hours, confirming the decision at the 4.15am briefing on Sunday, June 4 – and made the new D-Day Tuesday, June 6, but only if the weather began to show signs of significant improvement.

Most of the loading for D-Day had already been completed and thousands of men were on board their vessels, making final checks or simply waiting for the order to either begin the operation or stand down.

A convoy from Force U, one of the five naval assault forces of which there was one for each landing zone (Force U for Utah, Force S for Sword and so on), even set off

for France and had to be intercepted by a pair of destroyers which hurried out from Portsmouth to bring the landing ships back.

Eisenhower himself later recalled: "The final conference for determining the feasibility of attacking on June 5 was scheduled for 4am on June 4. However, some of the attacking contingents had already been ordered to sea, because if the entire force was to land on June 5, then some elements stationed in northern parts of the United Kingdom could not wait for a final decision on the morning of June 4."

Then, during the 9.30pm briefing that same day, Stagg announced: "Gentlemen, since I presented the forecast last evening some rapid and unexpected developments have occurred over the north Atlantic."

The weather forecast was showing, if not signs of improvement, then a greater delay

ahead of the coming bad weather than expected. A storm was still imminent but it was now moving more slowly. There was a window of opportunity.

Admiral Ramsay responded: "Let's be clear about one thing. If Overlord is to proceed on Tuesday I must issue provisional warning to my forces within the next half hour. But if they do restart and have to be recalled again, there can be no question of continuing on Wednesday."

Eisenhower asked Montgomery: "Do you see any reason why we should not go on Tuesday?" Monty's response was typically terse and to the point: "No. I would say 'go'."

The supreme commander paced silently up and down for a moment before saying: "Okay, let's go." The order was given and Overlord was under way.

The vast invasion fleet bound for Normandy as seen from the air.

SETTING SAIL AND SPOOFS

As bombing raids continued, targeting coastal defences, the invasion fleet set sail. It was to be a painfully slow overnight crossing in readiness for the early morning attack on June 6.

The invasion fleet was vast. Eight different navies supplied a total of 6939 vessels. Warships accounted for 1213 of these, 4126 were transports, including landing craft, there were 864 merchant craft and 736 ancillary vessels. The majority of vessels of all types were British since much of the US Navy was engaged in the Pacific.

Many of the soldiers and sailors of this unprecedented armada had already been on board their vessels for two days and while Forces S, J and G set off at 9am on June 5 from the congested Solent, Forces U and O carrying the American troops and equipment did not get going until 4pm. Coming from ports in Cornwall, Devon and Dorset, they had a less difficult and time consuming journey ahead of them.

The assault forces congregated at a pre-chosen rendezvous area 10 miles in diameter that was eight miles south east of the Isle of Wight. Known as Point Z, it quickly earned the nickname 'Piccadilly Circus'. Having formed up here, the convoys moved south towards the landing zones using narrow paths through the German coastal minefields already cleared by a small fleet of minesweepers.

British LCAs ferry US rangers out from Weymouth to their waiting troopship *HMS Prince Baudouin*.

ABOVE & BELOW Landing craft flying barrage balloons to defend against low level aerial attack. There was little danger of that on D-Day since the Luftwaffe stayed away.

The sea itself was choppy, with winds gusting up to force five and waves reaching 6ft in height. Many soldiers were soon suffering from sea sickness.

The Germans, meanwhile, had seen the same weather reports that had given Stagg so much trouble and believed that no attack could possibly take place. Rommel drove home to Germany for his wife's birthday.

To further mislead the Germans, the RAF conducted two operations on the evening of June 5, Taxable and Glimmer, using advanced technology to make it appear as though a separate large-scale naval attack was also under way elsewhere on the French coast.

Operation Taxable involved eight Lancaster bombers from 617 Squadron flying circuits over a group of 18 small vessels in the water below, 14 of them towing radar reflecting Filbert barrage balloons, and dropped thousands of strips of aluminium foil. This chaff, codenamed Window generally, and called 'Rope' when used in longer strips for Taxable, fluttered down from the sky and when picked up by German radar gave the impression of a much larger fleet approaching the French coast.

This was Special Task Force A.

Special Task Force B, set up for Operation Glimmer, involved a similar arrangement but with six Short Stirlings from 218 Squadron instead of eight Lancasters and just 12 boats to bob along with the Filberts.

Force A reached a point seven miles off the French coast north east of Le Havre by midnight and then made a 'run' at the coast to simulate a landing. The Germans opened fire on the 'fleet' and used searchlights to try and spot it but Force A then withdrew and the operation was concluded at 5am.

While this was going on, Force B had carried out a similar operation in an area further up the coast near Boulogne.

Ahead of D-Day, seven of the Germans'

long-range early warning radars had been destroyed by RAF Typhoons and Spitfires, leaving just enough to offer patchy coverage of the areas where Taxable and Glimmer were due to take place. On the night itself, further north than either of the two 'ghost fleets', four B-17 Flying Fortresses from the 803rd Bombardment Squadron and 16 Stirlings of 199 Squadron set up a screen of electronic jamming.

This was to mask the 'landings' but deliberately leaving a big enough gap for the remaining German radar stations to see something happening. One of the masterminds of Taxable and Glimmer, Dr Robert Cockburn, said: "Imagine the scene. A frightened under-trained young conscript radar operator sees the 'ghost' fleet on his screen and reports it to his headquarters as the long-expected enemy invasion force. So do his colleagues at other radar stations along the coast. Soon there appears a nice broad arrow on the situation map at the headquarters. The ghost fleet is now a military fact. If aircraft were then to fly into the area and report it clear of ships, would their reports be believed? Probably not.

"The operation was to take place at night and the aircraft might be far off their intended tracks. Once a broad arrow representing an enemy attack appears on the situation map at a military headquarters it is a military fact and it takes a lot to remove it."

ATTACK OF THE DUMMIES

There was one further trick that the Allies played on the defenders of the French coast on the evening of June 5. While the strange processions of circling aircraft, small vessels and bobbing balloons did their best to look like a second invasion force, the SAS and four further RAF squadrons staged a little invasion of their own – Operation Titanic.

This involved dropping 2ft 9in tall sack-cloth sand-filled dummy paratroopers known

LONG SOBS OF AUTUMN VIOLINS – THE FRENCH RESISTANCE ON D-DAY

From scattered and uncoordinated beginnings, the French Resistance had become a potent fighting force by June 6, 1944, working closely with British intelligence.

État-major des Forces Francaises de l'Intérieur (EMFFI) and the British Special Operations Executive devised four operations that members of the resistance would carry out during the D-Day landings or as soon afterwards as could be managed.

Plan Vert was a campaign of sabotage against what remained of France's already heavily bombed railway infrastructure, Plan Bleu involved the destruction of electrical plants, Plan Tortue was delaying tactics to slow the movement of German reinforcements and Plan Violet was the cutting of telephone and teleprinter cables.

The operations were coordinated via coded messages hidden within the content of the BBC's French radio service. These messages could take the form of apparently random sentences, snippets of poetry or quotations from books. Resistance cells were given lists of messages marked 'A' and 'B'. Hearing a message from 'A' meant preparations needed to be begun in readiness for the corresponding mission. The matching 'B' phrase was an order to carry out the mission immediately.

For example, shortly before D-Day, the first line of Chanson d'Automne 'Autumn Song' by French poet Paul Verlaine, "Les sanglots longs des violons de l'automne" or 'the long sobs of the violons of autumn' was on the 'A' list. It told resistance fighters in one network to prepare for an attack on rail targets. The second line of the poem, "Bercent mon Coeur d'une langueur monotone," was on the 'B' list and was transmitted on June 5.

A report compiled 23 years later found that on D-Day alone the French Resistance had been responsible for the destruction of 52 locomotives and railway lines had been severed in more than 500 locations. The telephone network in Normandy was also left barely functional due to huge numbers of lines being cut.

Canadian infantry aboard LCAs heading for their landing sites on Juno beach.

While the invasion fleet ploughed steadily through the choppy sea towards the coast of France, Short Stirling bombers like these were used to drop hundreds of dummy paratroops, Ruperts, to confuse the German defenders.

as 'Ruperts'. There were a variety of different types. Some were designed to land and then self-destruct, others had a bulky set of firecrackers attached to simulate rifle fire and still others had explosives fitted to simulate shellfire or grenades.

The first 200 dummies simulated an airborne assault in the Yvetot, Yerville and Doudeville area north east of Le Havre.

A further 50 were dropped in the Calvados region near to Maltot to the west of Caen and 200 more were deployed near Marigny west of Saint Lô.

A handful of SAS men also landed equipped with Very flare pistols, and battery powered gramophones. These were intended to play audio tracks including snatches of soldiers' conversations, shouted orders and gunfire with the aim of distracting and deceiving enemy troops.

The ruse worked in Le Havre, where the area commander sent a message to Berlin three hours after the SAS men and Ruperts had arrived to say that he had been cut off by enemy forces. A German officer of the 915th Grenadier Regiment in the Marigny area heard reports of the sounds generated by the SAS and sent his unit into a wooded area to 'flush out' the enemy. He was chasing shadows and continued to do so until well after the D-Day landings had begun.

Further reports of enemy activity were made at around 2am in the Saint Lô area but the level of alert was lowered when it was reported that the 'paratroopers' were actually dummies.

When SAS man Lieutenant Norman Harry Poole jumped from a Halifax and landed just ahead of his team to take part in Titanic at 12.11am on June 6, he became the first Allied soldier to land in Normandy. Four minutes later, British gliders began to land next to bridges spanning the Caen canal (later known as 'Pegasus Bridge') and the River Orne, heralding the beginning of Operation Deadstick.

Landing craft bound for Sword beach pass close by the headquarters ship of Force S, *HMS Largs*. In the foreground, an LCT has five DD Shermans on board with their swimming screens already raised.

Operation

The Allied landings on D-Day, June 6, 1944

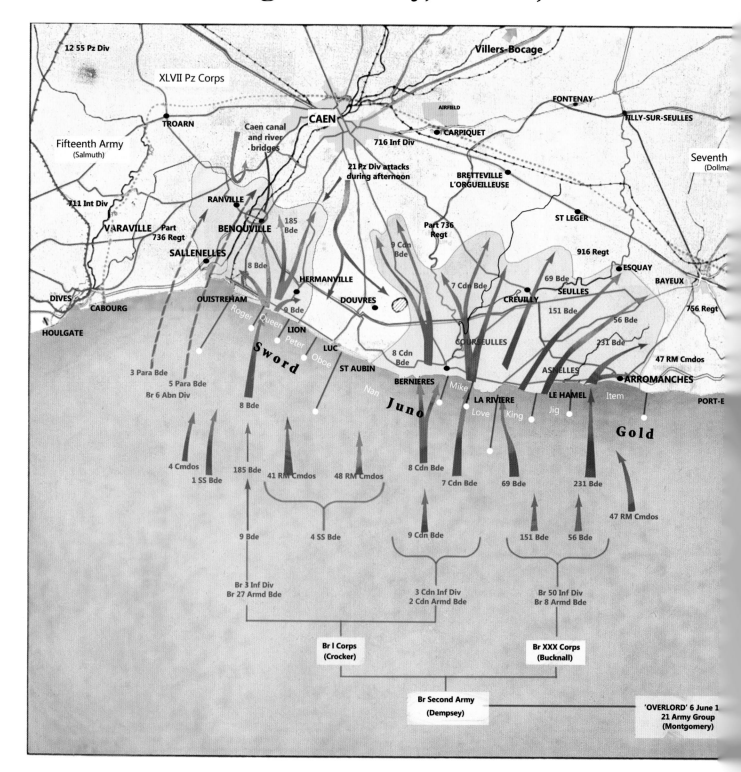

Overlord

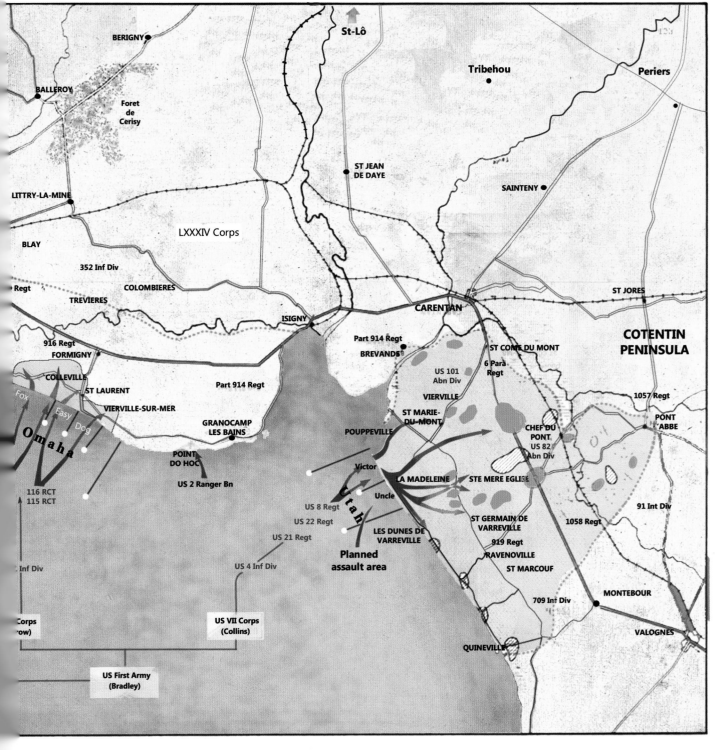

BERIGNY

BALLEROY

Foret
de
Cerisy

St-Lô

Tribehou

Periers

LITTRY-LA-MINE

BLAY

352 Inf Div

ST JEAN
DE DAYE

SAINTENY

LXXXIV Corps

COLOMBIERES

Regt

TREVIERES

ISIGNY

ST JORES

CARENTAN

COTENTIN
PENINSULA

916 Regt
FORMIGNY

COLLEVILLE

ST LAURENT

VIERVILLE-SUR-MER

Part 914 Regt
BREVANDS

Part 914 Regt

GRANOCAMP
LES BAINS

Fox

Easy

Dog

Omaha

POINT
DO HOC

US 2 Ranger Bn

116 RCT

115 RCT

Inf Div

Corps
ow)

US VII Corps
(Collins)

US 4 Inf Div

US First Army
(Bradley)

ST COME DU MONT

US 101
Abn Div

6 Para
Regt

VIERVILLE

ST MARIE-
DU-MONT

POUPPEVILLE

Victor

LA MADELEINE

Uncle

Utah

US 8 Regt

US 22 Regt

US 21 Regt

LES DUNES DE
VARREVILLE

Planned
assault area

STE MERE EGLISE

CHEF DU
PONT
US 82
Abn Div

1057 Regt

PONT
ABBE

91 Int Div

ST GERMAIN DE
VARREVILLE

919 Regt

RAVENOVILLE

ST MARCOUF

1058 Regt

709 Inf Div

MONTEBOUR

QUINEVILLE

VALOGNES

CHAPTER 8

'To hell with it, let's get cracking'
The airborne assault

While seemingly endless lines of Allied warships, troopships and landing craft steadily threaded their way through holes made in the offshore minefields meant to protect the French coast, hundreds of transport aircraft sped through the dark skies overhead. Before dawn broke on D-Day, Allied paratroopers were already causing chaos behind enemy lines...

Getting troops in behind the Atlantic Wall to prevent or delay German reinforcements from reaching the landing zone was deemed an essential part of the Overlord plan from its earliest days as a COSSAC project in 1943.

The original plan called for these airborne troops to also capture Caen and Cherbourg but by 1944 the emphasis had shifted firmly

The three Horsa gliders of D Company of the 2nd (Airborne) Battalion, Oxfordshire and Buckinghamshire Light Infantry at the eastern end of the Bénouville bridge, later known as Pegasus. The circular shape near the bridge is a gun pit.

towards protecting the seaborne invasion force from a counterattack.

On the right of the invasion front, two American airborne divisions would land behind Utah beach on the Cotentin Peninsula. On the left, three brigades of British airborne troops would land – one of which would capture strategic bridges across Caen Canal and the River Orne. Another would attempt to blow bridges across the River Dives, sealing off the only route into Caen from the east. It would also silence an artillery battery at Merville threatening Sword beach. The third would land later in the day to provide reinforcements.

THE 'COUP DE MAIN'

The British side of the operation was handed to the 6th Airborne Division commanded by Major-General Richard Nelson 'Windy' Gale and comprised the 3rd Parachute Brigade, the 5th Parachute Brigade and the 6th Airlanding Brigade.

Gale decided that the best way to take and hold the two vital crossing points, the Bénouville bridge over the canal and the Ranville bridge over the river, was a sudden

'coup de main' assault using gliders. Under cover of darkness, a crack unit would be towed across the Channel in gliders. They would silently descend, land as close to the targets as possible and seize them intact.

The glider troops would then have to hold them against any enemy units, no matter how strong, until a relief force arrived.

D Company of the 2nd (Airborne) Battalion, Oxfordshire and Buckinghamshire Light Infantry, led by Major John Howard was chosen for the mission and every night for several weeks beforehand they carried out exercises in darkness. During one practice run it became apparent that more men were needed so two platoons from B Company were drafted in plus 30 Royal Engineers of the 249th (Airborne) Field Company. They would remove any explosive demolition charges from the bridges.

This made a total of six platoons – three for each bridge – and exercises were carried out for six nights on two bridges over the River Exe near Exeter.

The six platoons, originally numbered 14, 17, 22, 23, 24 and 25, were renumbered 1 to 6 for the operation. They were led, in that

Troops of 6th Airborne Division are given a final briefing before a practice jump in spring 1944. This image is believed to have been taken at Netheravon in Wiltshire.

numerical order, by lieutenants Den Brotheridge, David Wood, Richard 'Sandy' Smith, Tony Hooper, Henry 'Todd' Sweeney and Dennis Fox.

The troops would be transported in six Airspeed AS.51 Horsa gliders. Each would carry two pilots from C Squadron of the Glider Pilot Regiment plus five Royal Engineers and 23 airborne infantrymen – 30 men per glider, though their usual maximum load was 28 – making a total of 180 men.

The relief force would be provided by the 7th Parachute Battalion, part of the 5th Parachute Brigade. If everything went according to plan, they in turn would be relieved at 11am on the day by commandos of the 1st Special Service Brigade who would make their way to the bridges after landing on Sword at 6am.

Less than a week before the mission, the teams were given a full briefing on the target by Howard. The bridges were separated by a 1650ft strip of marshy ground strewn with ditches and small streams.

The Bénouville bridge, defended by a trio of machine gun positions on the Caen side and one on the central strip, was the smaller of the two at just 190ft across, compared to the Ranville bridge's 350ft.

The Ranville bridge was more lightly defended with nothing on the central strip and a single pillbox with anti-tank and anti-aircraft guns on the eastern bank. To its north were two machine guns. Trench systems built up with sandbags had been dug in on both banks of both bridges.

Code words for the operation were also revealed. 'Ham' meant that the Caen Canal bridge had been taken intact while 'Jack' meant it had been destroyed. The code words for the river bridge were 'Jam' for captured and 'Lard' for destroyed.

The six teams' gliders took off from RAF Tarrant Rushton in Dorset at 10.56pm towed by Handley Page Halifax bombers, three each from 298 and 644 Squadrons. They crossed the Normandy coast at 12.07am flying at 6000ft. Encouraged by Major Howard, the men had loudly sung songs on the way over but they stopped when the tow cables were released.

The Horsa carrying 1 Platoon and Howard himself, touched down in a field at 90mph, crashed through several fences and ended up embedded in the canal bridge defences on the central strip at 12.16am – bang on target. The two pilots were knocked unconscious but everyone survived. The 2 Platoon Horsa came down at 12.17am and broke in half. Before anyone could save him, Bren gunner Lance Corporal Fred Greenhalgh fell from the wrecked aircraft into a large pond and drowned. Platoon leader Lt Wood was also thrown from the fuselage but landed uninjured on dry ground.

The 3 Platoon glider came down at 12.18am but it landed badly on swampy ground. The cockpit area was smashed up and Lt Smith was ejected through the wreckage. He landed in front of the still

Short Stirlings line up ready for the airborne invasion operations on June 5 at RAF Keevil, near Trowbridge in Wiltshire.

A ground view of the smashed up gliders of the 'coup de main' team, looking towards the Bénouville bridge. The canal is beyond the trees to the left.

Men of the 2/502nd Parachute Infantry Regiment, part of the 101st US Airborne Division, surround General Eisenhower on the evening of June 5.

A message for the Germans from the 6th Airlanding Brigades at RAF Harwell prior to take off on June 5. That night they landed in Dropzone W to the west of the Caen canal.

moving glider and it ran over his leg. Many of his men were badly injured in the crash and one later died. Only eight or nine men out of 30 were fit to continue.

Howard himself, Lt Brotheridge's 1 Platoon and Smith's 3 Platoon survivors moved to secure the bridge. Smith was limping badly but carried on nevertheless. Wood's 2 Platoon advanced towards the trenches on the bridge's north east side.

Just two German sentries were on duty on the bridge. The rest of the 50-strong detachment from the 736th Grenadier Regiment of the 716th Infantry Division was either at Ranville 1.2 miles away to the east with their commander Major Hans Schmidt, asleep or unaware of what was happening.

One shouted: "Fallschirmjäger!" (paratroopers) and ran to raise the alarm. The second fired a flare gun and Brotheridge shot him. Grenades dealt with the nearest machine gun positions while Brotheridge charged over the bridge with his men. The now-alerted guards managed to stage a brief defence from the western side of the bridge. Brotheridge was throwing a grenade when he was hit in the neck by machine gun fire. He died soon after, making him the first Allied soldier to die as a result of enemy action on D-Day.

Smith's men crossed the bridge next and cleared the western side, although Smith himself was wounded by a grenade blast. Wood, the third platoon leader, was shot in the leg while his men took the eastern side

but the bridge was now in British hands.

Lt Fox's 6 Platoon, heading for the river bridge, came down at 12.20am. 5 Platoon landed 2310ft off target a minute later but the last glider was missing. Realising he was the only one in a position to attack, Fox gave the order: "To hell with it, let's get cracking," and attacked. When the Germans responded with fire from a machine gun position, the platoon's Sergeant Charles 'Wagger' Thornton fired a 2in mortar bomb on to it and blew it up with a direct hit. The bridge was then taken. It was 12.26am and the codes Ham and Jam were broadcast.

THE LONGEST DAY

Catching up with Fox's men, 5 Platoon led by Lt Sweeney, nicknamed 'Todd' by his men after the infamous demon barber of Fleet Street Sweeney Todd, took up defensive positions on the eastern side of the river. The team's Royal Engineers found that the bridges had been wired for demolition but the explosives had not been fitted.

Now, surrounded by German forces on both sides of the bridge, it was a case of hanging on long enough for reinforcements to arrive from the 7th Parachute Battalion. Pathfinders for the follow-up drops by other 6th Airborne Division units began to arrive at 12.19am and at 12.52am the main parachute assault began.

Only a quarter of the 7th reached their rally point on time. About 100 men led by Lieutenant-Colonel Richard Pine-Coffin

gathered but without their radio equipment, Bren guns or mortars, all of which had been lost during the drop. By 1.10am, Pine-Coffin, apparently known to his men as 'Wooden Box', decided that he couldn't wait any longer and set off for the twin bridges.

The German response to all this was slow, uncoordinated and hampered by a complex chain of command. The man in charge of the bridge guards, Major Schmidt, having been in Ranville until now, boarded an armoured halftrack and set off with a motorcycle escort. At the bridge they were fired on and quickly captured.

At 1.20am, Generalleutnant Wilhelm Richter, the commander of the 716th Infantry Division, was informed that the bridges were still intact and in enemy hands. He contacted the 21st Panzer Division led by Generalleutnant Edgar Feuchtinger for help and he in turn ordered

German soldiers in the Orne area. It was soldiers such as these who fought the British 6th Airborne on D-Day.

A posed photograph showing an airborne infantry platoon about to take off in a Horsa glider (looking towards the rear of the aircraft). Note the cramped conditions, the flimsy infrastructure, chest harness and tiny porthole.

An Airspeed AS.51 Horsa glider is pulled off the runway by an Armstrong Whitworth AW.41 Albemarle.

the nearest unit, the 2nd Battalion of the 192nd Panzergrenadier Regiment, based at Cairon, west of the bridges, to attack.

Meanwhile, Colonel Hans von Luck of the 125th Panzergrenadier Regiment had also heard about the parachute and glider landings. He ordered his men to form up and move to the north and east of Caen.

A platoon of open-topped Marder I 75mm self-propelled guns from the 1st Company of the 716th's anti-tank section, which in the early hours looked and sounded like tanks, approached the Caen Canal bridge. Howard said: "We heard the ominous sound we most dreaded and that was the sound of tanks, and sure enough, round about half past one, two tanks were heard slowly coming down the road. The only anti-tank weapons we had were PIATs and we didn't have much faith in them."

In fact, only one PIAT anti-tank weapon was available to the defenders at that time and it was in the hands of Sgt Thornton since Fox's men had been moved from the Orne bridge to cover the canal.

Private Denis Edwards of D Company said: "Wagger Thornton let those tanks get really up close to him and then he let fly. We never thought those PIAT bombs would ever do much damage to a proper tank, but this flaming tank literally blew up, exploded. The whole thing went up. It was well-loaded with ammunition. I don't know what sort of ammunition it was, but within moments of

WHAT DID WAGGER BLOW UP?

Sergeant Charles 'Wagger' Thornton's spectacular destruction of a German armoured fighting vehicle in the darkness before dawn on D-Day at Pegasus Bridge has become the stuff of legend, but exactly what did he destroy?

American D-Day historian Stephen E Ambrose, who wrote Band of Brothers, believed it was a Panzer Mk.IV, as did Thornton himself. Private Eric Woods, who was beside Thornton at the time, believed it to have been a 'Renault'. Others have also described it as 'an old French tank'. Eyewitnesses in the area the following day however speak of seeing a wrecked 'half-track'.

Private Thomas Clare described seeing one of the crewmen blown clear of the machine wearing a black leather tank man's uniform.

The unit to which the vehicle belonged was almost certainly the 2nd Battalion of the 22nd Panzer Regiment, 21st Panzer Division. While the 1st

Battalion had 17 Mk.IVs per company for four companies, the 2nd had only, at most, half a dozen per company.

Its armour deficit was made up for with 39 captured French Somua S35 tanks and a selection of anti-tank guns that had been based on captured Lorraine and Hotchkiss chassis, the so-called Lorraine tractors.

Some revisionists have suggested that the vehicle was a half track such as a DEMAG D7 SdKfz 10, which had a gun mounted on the rear, but this didn't look much like a tank even in darkness and doesn't explain the crewman's leathers. Since there was no sign of a wrecked 'real' tank when daylight appeared, the most likely explanation would appear to be the Marder I, a smallish tank destroyer based on a Lorraine or Hotchkiss chassis.

The matter of Wagger's tank is perhaps a minor one, but has proven to be one of the most enduring D-Day mysteries over the last 70 years.

Wagger firing there were great spurts of green and orange and yellow as all the ammunition inside was exploding, making a hell of a din. And the other tank behind did a quick revving of engines and disappeared off up the road."

C-47 Skytrains towing gliders carrying American troops and equipment.

Men of 45 Commando Royal Marine, attached to 3rd Infantry Division for the assault on Sword Beach, march through Colleville-sur-Orne en route to relieve forces at the Bénouville bridge.

British paratroopers crouch beside the road north of Caen in this staged photo.

Three men from D Company's coup de main team photographed at Hérouvillette on June 15. From the left are Private Frank Gardener, Captain Brian Priday and Lance Corporal William Henry Lambley.

More of the 7th Parachute Battalion began to arrive, giving Pine-Coffin around 200 able-bodied men in three companies with whom to defend the position. The Germans tried again at 3am, using Marders, 20mm flak guns and mortars to attack the 7th's A and C Companies, positioned at Bénouville, from the south. The British were hard pressed and pushed back, but remained unbroken.

Securing new positions at Bénouville, the Germans dug in and waited for dawn while firing mortar and machine gun rounds at the defenders. When daylight finally appeared, it gave German snipers an opportunity to begin picking the British off.

At 9am, a pair of gunboats came motoring south towards the canal bridge. The first fired its 20mm gun at the defenders and 2 Platoon replied with a PIAT bomb which hit its wheelhouse, causing it to veer off into the bank. The second gunboat withdrew. An hour later a German aircraft appeared overhead and dropped a bomb on the bridge. This hit the bridge counterweight but failed to detonate. With more of the 7th having arrived, the British were able to

return to Bénouville and clear the Germans from their positions.

Shortly after noon, Col von Luck's advancing 125th Panzergrenadier Regiment was spotted by the British who were then able to call down an artillery barrage and air support which resulted in heavy losses for the 125th. Finally, at 1.30pm, leading elements of the 1st Special Service Brigade arrived. Private Stanley Wilfred Scott of 3 Troop, 3 Commando, was among the first to reach the beleaguered paras. He said: "At Le Port, opposite the church, we passed a para sitting with his leg up on a chair. He

had a shattered leg and he was guarding this little knot of prisoners and as we come along, like, he looks at us, didn't he? And what he said was unprintable. British Army language. Something like: 'Where the flaming hell have you been? About time.' There was none of the bagpipe playing and cheering and all that crap."

The sound of bagpipes was not far off however. The brigade's commander Brigadier Simon Fraser, better known by his title Lord Lovat, followed by his piper Bill Millin, soon arrived. It was in the nick of time, since the Germans were now in danger

Commandos from the 1st Special Service Brigade on the afternoon of D-Day having just crossed the bridges over the Caen Canal and the River Orne.

British vehicles cross the captured Caen Canal bridge with D Company's gliders still resting in the field beyond.

Aerial photograph taken on D-Day showing 10 British gliders landed in French fields.

An 8.4-ton Mk.VII Tetrarch light tank emerges from a Hamilcar glider. Carrying one of these made the Hamilcar very difficult to handle in the air.

of infiltrating and overrunning the position. The British survivors had pulled back to the western side of the Caen Canal and the eastern side of the Orne. The commandos swiftly moved to push the Germans back again, away from the bridges.

Millin got across to the central strip, as did Lovat, who then told the piper to play all the way over to the second bridge which he did. Millin said: "Lovat came over, and there's several casualties following him on the bridge, and from across the road appears this tall airborne officer, red beret on, marching along with his arm outstretched, and he said: 'Very pleased to see you old boy'. And Lovat said: 'And we're very pleased to see you old boy. Sorry we're two and a half minutes late'. We were more than two and a half minutes late."

At 9.15pm the 2nd Battalion of the Royal Warwickshire Regiment arrived from Sword to take over the bridge's defences. These were formally handed over by Howard at midnight. The Caen Canal bridge was later renamed Pegasus Bridge after the symbol of the 6th Airborne and the bridge over the Orne became known as Horsa Bridge.

BREACHING MERVILLE

While D Company was fighting to secure the bridges just after midnight, pathfinders were attempting to mark out the drop zones for the rest of the 3rd and 5th Parachute Brigades – the Operation Tonga landings.

The 5th's units were the 7th, 12th and 13th Parachute Battalions. The 7th's mission was to support D Company, and the others were to secure the area surrounding the bridges – Drop Zone N.

The 3rd's units were the 8th and 9th Parachute Battalions and the 1st Canadian Parachute Battalion. The 9th was tasked with attacking and securing the powerful artillery battery at Merville in Drop Zone V, while the 8th and 1st took care of the bridges across the River Dives in Drop Zone K to further secure the British landing zone's left flank. Heavy cloud cover, the huge number of

aircraft deployed for the operation, and the difficulties of navigating in darkness resulted in most of the teams being dropped in the wrong place.

Pathfinders aiming for N were dropped off-target and took 30 minutes to reach it, while a team heading for K hit N instead and set up radio beacons which caused some units of the 3rd to land in completely the wrong place. Another team, from the 9th, was virtually wiped out while attempting to mark the Merville Battery in Drop Zone V when an RAF Avro Lancaster bomber missed the battery and hit the pathfinders instead.

As a result, in contrast to the pinpoint accuracy of D Company's glider assault, both the 3rd and the 5th brigades were badly scattered by 1am. While the 7th headed for the twin bridges, the other components of the 5th, the 12th and 13th battalions, attempted to rally and secure Drop Zone N. The 12th had taken the village of Le Bas de Ranville on the eastern side of the bridges to the south by 4am.

The 13th took Ranville further to the east at around the same time. Both held their positions until they were relieved by forces moving up from Sword, having fought off

German assaults throughout D-Day and weathered heavy mortar and artillery fire.

In Drop Zone V, the 9th was particularly scattered. The battalion's leader Lieutenant-Colonel Terence Otway landed 1200ft outside V on a German command post. A fire fight resulted and Otway did not reach the rally point until 1.30am. An hour later, only 110 paratroopers out of about 550 had turned up with just one Vickers machine gun and a few Bangalore torpedoes.

The plan for taking the heavily defended Merville battery had relied on the whole battalion being present with breaching equipment. Knowing that the big guns had to be disabled before 5.30am to prevent them from wrecking havoc on the forces landing at Sword, Otway felt he had no choice but to begin the attack.

He set off at 2.50am with 150 men. Arriving within sight of the target at 4am he divided the men into four assault teams, one of each of the battery's bunkers. At the last minute, at 4.30am, two gliders appeared overhead carrying the Royal Engineers sappers who'd been assigned to handle the demolition side of the mission. The aircraft caught the Germans' attention and they opened up with everything they had.

Gliders of 6 Airlanding Brigade on the afternoon of June 6, a few hours before takeoff from RAF Harwell as part of the follow-up wave. The glider on the far left is marked 151, which shows it is one of the six Horsas of 195 Airlanding Field Ambulance destined for Dropzone W.

Slewing through this blizzard of gunfire, the first glider crash landed just 150ft from the battery, while the second caught fire and span into a field 1200ft away.

As the first glider went over, Otway ordered the assault. His men detonated their Bangalore torpedoes, clearing two routes through the battery's outer barbed wire defences, and charged. The defenders heard the explosion and turned to see the approaching paras. Caught on open ground, the British suffered heavy casualties. Just four of the men attacking the fourth bunker survived long enough to reach it and throw grenades through its air vents.

The other gun positions were also taken as the British discovered that in all the excitement the Germans had neglected to lock the battery's doors. The 150mm weapons expected by D-Day's planners turned out to be antiquated 100mm howitzers – still a threat to the beach, but far less so than had been feared. Most of the battalion's explosives had been used up in the attack and although the paras improvised with grenades they were unable to put all of them out of commission.

The back-up plan if the paras failed was for the *HMS Arethusa* to shell the battery during the landings and with the clock ticking the 9th withdrew together with the prisoners. Out of 150 men, 50 had been killed and another 25 wounded. After taking one of their secondary objectives, the village of Le Plein, the survivors withdrew to their rendezvous point at 5.30am.

MISSION ALBANY

The two American airborne formations involved in the first wave of D-Day landings were the 82nd Airborne Division, known as the All-American, and the 101st Airborne Division, the Screaming Eagles. Together they had around 13,000 men. Both were to land on the extreme right of the invasion force, on the Cotentin peninsula, behind Utah beach.

The 101st, led by Major-General Maxwell D Taylor, was given Mission Albany, which required it to land east and south of Sainte-Mère-Église in Drop Zones A, C, and D. It would then capture and secure four

causeway 'exits' behind Utah beach, destroy a battery at Saint-Martin-de-Varreville and capture or destroy a number of targets in the Douve River valley. The division would then clear its allocated zone of enemies, establish a defensive line and link up with the 82nd. The 101st comprised the 501st, 502nd and 506th PIRs plus support units, totalling some 6600 men, and Taylor jumped into Normandy with them.

The pathfinders due to land on A missed by about a mile and were unable to get their equipment to work. The C pathfinders had similar difficulties and the last group, heading for D, missed the drop zone and landed a mile off target, 10 minutes late.

The C-47s of the 101st were overloaded, only 40% had navigators on board, radio silence meant no-one could receive or give instructions and then they hit a bank of cloud. Some tried to climb over it, others tried to go under it, and some were forced to roll to avoid a mid-air collision. When the

Germans opened up with anti-aircraft guns, many pilots took evasion action and as a result their 'sticks' of paras were dropped haphazardly across a wide area.

The Screaming Eagles started jumping at 12.48am and the first down were the 502nd. The 2/502nd landed almost all together, but in the wrong zone. Their leader, Lieutenant Colonel Steve A Chappuis, landed with his own stick and almost no-one else in the right zone. The bulk of the 2/502nd therefore took no real part in the D-Day fighting.

Disorientated and without most of his own men, Lieutenant-Colonel Robert G Cole of the 3/502nd gathered together what men he could find – some from the 506th – and set off to secure the beach exits. By 7.30am, Exit 3 was secure and two hours later the Germans defending Utah, not realising the causeway was in American hands, tried to retreat across it. Cole's men gunned down 50-75 enemy soldiers.

US paratroopers with blackened faces inside a C-47 Skytrain. The shoulder patches indicate that they are from the 101st Airborne Division – the Screaming Eagles. These men are part of F Company of the 2/506th PIR. They are being transported to Normandy by the 439th Troop Carrier Group en route to Dropzone C. From left they are William G Olanie, Frank D Griffin, Robert J Noody and Lester T Hegland.

Paratroopers dropping from Douglas C-47 Skytrains.

Captain Kenneth L Johnson of the 508th PIR of the 82nd US Airborne smokes a cigarette in company with French civilians somewhere near Picauville in Dropzone N.

The 1/502nd's Lieutenant-Colonel Patrick J Cassidy also gathered together a small unit and found Exit 4 undefended. Exits 1 and 2 off Utah were to be taken and held by elements of the 506th under Colonel Robert L Sink. At the end of the day, only 2500 of the 101st's 6600 men were working together and a solid defensive perimeter had not been established.

MISSION BOSTON

Eleven minutes after the last Screaming Eagle jumped from a C-47, at 1.51am, the first All-American stepped out of another. The veteran 505th went first and carried out an almost uniquely accurate drop. The regiment's pathfinders, in Drop Zone O, successfully marked out the three battalion landing areas and as a result, 75% of the regiment landed within two miles of the designated drop zone.

In contrast, more than half of the 508th ended up more than 10 miles away from the correct drop zone. Private Thomas Porcella came down in the River Merderet. He was in over his head and had to jump up to take a breath. Rising to the surface, he saw the burning wreck of a C-47 in the sky just above him. He said: "I thought – oh my God! It's coming toward me!"

He tried to run, but in the end it landed right next to him. Crawling out onto the river bank, he heard a voice call out "Flash!" He recognised his friend Dale Cable and moved towards him. Cable shouted the warning again and was raising his rifle when Porcella remembered the correct response: "Thunder!" Disaster averted, the pair set off in search of other Americans.

The 507th was also way off target with several hundred men landing in swampland, where some drowned after being dragged under by the weight of their equipment. The headquarters' staff and company of 1/507th landed well within enemy territory and didn't manage to fight its way through to Allied lines until June 11.

The well-ordered 505th managed to complete two of its missions within hours of the drop. Capturing Sainte-Mère-Église was one of them. During the bombing raids which preceded the 82nd's drop, a house on

Soldiers of the 508th PIR of the 82nd US Airborne walk down a street along the wall of the cemetery around the church in Saint-Marcouf. The gun battery which sank the *USS Corry* off Utah beach was located next to the village. Technician Fifth Grade Donald J MacLeod covers the squad's rear in the foreground. The shoulder patch of the para on the right was censored.

one side of the town square had been set on fire by an incendiary.

The church bell was ringing as the All-Americans' landing started, calling the townspeople out to form bucket chains to put out the blaze. The German soldiers policing the town's curfew also came out to oversee the operation. Two sticks of paratroopers, one each from 1/505th and 2/505th, dropped directly over the town square – in full view of the Germans on the ground who opened fire.

Many were killed before they touched down, others were shot as they dangled helplessly from lamp posts or trees. One man, Private John Steele, was hit in the foot before his parachute snagged on a spire of the town's church.

Another man, Sergeant John Ray, landed in the square itself with Private Ken Russell. A German soldier came round the corner of the church and spotted them. Russell said: "I'll never forget him. He was red haired and as he came around he shot Sergeant

Ray in the stomach. And Sergeant Ray, while he was dying in agony, he got his .45 out and he shot the German soldier in the head and killed him."

Steele, deafened by the ringing church bell and in pain from his foot, pretended to be dead for more than two hours until the Germans realised that he was alive, got him down and took him prisoner. Russell, with bullets splashing off the cobbles around him, dashed out of the square and into the relative safety of nearby woodland.

The 3/505th captured the town at around 5am and freed Steele, killing 11 Germans and capturing another 30 in the process.

The American airborne had succeeded in completing many of its D-Day objectives, but by midnight there were still thousands of men scattered across the Cotentin peninsula, who were left fighting to survive. While thousands of British and Americans paratroopers stumbled around in the dark and fought to carry out their missions, the invasion fleet was finally nearing shore. ∎

An American Horsa glider in Normandy with its tail removed so that its cargo could be offloaded. The right wing has been damaged during landing.

This American Horsa has survived its landing in relatively good shape – just the front windows and tail have taken damage and its undercarriage is intact.

The race for Caen
Sword beach

Taking the city of Caen was regarded as critical to the early success of Operation Overlord. Positioned on the far left of the invasion front it could act as a lynchpin for the whole operation if captured quickly – or a thorn in the Allies' side if it was not. The British forces tasked with taking it landed on Sword beach...

British battleship *HMS Warspite* opens fire on the Normandy coastline in support of the landings on Sword.

The five mile wide stretch of coastline codenamed Sword was divided into four sectors from left to right: Roger, Queen, Peter and Oboe. Each of these was subdivided into three – Red, White and Green – but rocky offshore reefs meant only Queen White and Queen Red were viable landing grounds.

The attack on Sword was therefore to be concentrated in an area just 1.8 miles wide, allowing room for just two assault brigades and their supporting tanks. It also meant that the massed artillery of Force S could be largely focused on just one target zone around the seaside village of La Brèche with Queen Red to the left and Queen White to the right. Beyond the beach at La Brèche was a long line of seafront houses, many of which had been occupied by the Germans.

Particular targets for the assault were given their own codenames. Cod was a strongpoint on the beach in front of La Brèche housing an 88mm anti-tank gun; and Trout was another down the beach to the right at Lion-sur-Mer, defended by a pair of 50mm anti-tank guns. Still further along was a third at Riva Bella, codenamed Casino.

Inland were two large gun batteries – Morris with four 100mm guns and Daimler

ABOVE: Anti-tank gun emplacement at the top of the beach. This gun is probably the 50mm weapon located on the eastern edge of strongpoint Cod. The central defensive position of Cod housed an 88mm gun.

A Landing Craft Infantry approaches Queen Red Beach to the left of strongpoint Cod. Some of the tanks on the beach have been knocked out while others are trying to find a way off the sand.

The landings opposite strongpoint Cod. A Sherman Crab is burning on the beach and men are lying prone in the water. The two prominent villas on the right of the picture still exist and allow the scene to be pinpointed to the area to the east of the present day Rue de Rouen. The dark outline of the casemate housing the strongpoint's 50mm gun can be seen at the top of the beach, to the left of the house in the centre of the picture.

with four 155mm guns – and two further strongpoints, Hillman and Sole, housing headquarters bunkers of the local German garrison, the 736th Infantry Regiment.

Specific plans were drawn up for the capture or destruction of each of these targets.

The formation given the task of attacking Sword was the British 3rd Division, composed of the 8th, 9th and 185th Brigades and commanded by Major General Thomas Rennie. Two of the 8th's three battalions would lead the assault – the 2nd battalion of the East Yorkshire Regiment on Queen Red and the 1st battalion of the South Lancashire Regiment on Queen White. The third battalion of the three that made up the 8th, the 1st of the Suffolk Regiment, would provide the first follow-up wave.

Their armoured support would be DD Shermans from the 13th/18th Hussars (27th Armoured Brigade) plus a host of 'funnies' and other tanks operated by the 22nd Dragoons, Westminster Dragoons and 5th Assault Regiment Royal Engineers – all three part of the 79th Division.

Once Cod was overcome, the plan was for the 2nd East Yorks to eliminate Sole and Daimler near Ouistreham, the 1st South Lancs to press inland to the village of Hermanville and the 1st Suffolks to take Morris and Hillman.

While the 8th's three battalions were pacifying these strongpoints, the navy would keep Trout and Casino quiet by shelling them constantly until another unit, 4 Commando of the 1st Special Service Brigade, could land behind the 8th, advance along the shore and knock them out permanently. After 4 Commando would come 3 and 6 Commandos plus 45 Royal Marine Commando. They would rush inland to relieve D Company at the bridges over Caen Canal and the River Orne.

Two hours after the first landings, the next full brigade, the 185th, would start to land, followed by the 9th another two and a half hours after that. Both brigades would bypass the assault battalions of the 8th, no matter what their situation, and race for Caen.

Oblique aerial photograph taken before the invasion of the section of Sword beach to the right of Queen White sector. The villas along the seafront are between La Brèche d'Hermanville and Lion sur Mer. Hermanville is in the centre of the picture with Periers Ridge running across the middle distance.

THE D-DAY ALPHABET

The unusual code names given to the Normandy beaches by the Allies have a very simple origin – they were alphabetical.

The naming convention began with Omaha, which was originally on the westernmost end of the invasion front before Utah was added.

Omaha's beaches were named Able, Baker, Charlie, Dog, Easy and Fox, with George falling between Omaha and Gold. Then Gold itself had the next letters – How, Item, Jig and King, followed by Juno with Love, Mike and Nan and Sword with Oboe, Peter, Queen and Roger.

This loose invasion alphabet concluded when Utah was added to the plan to the right of Omaha with the out-of-sequence Tare, Uncle and Victor.

An AVRE team from 77th Assault Squadron has stopped on its exit from the beach at La Breche to allow some carriers from 3rd Infantry Division's machine gun battalion, 2nd Middlesex, to turn left from the lateral road towards Hermanville.

CAPTURING COD

Dozens of bombers took off from airfields all over the southern coast of England not long after midnight on June 6 and by 3am they were dropping thousands of tonnes of high explosives on the Atlantic Wall. It was the last aerial attack in a series that had gone on for weeks and seen the German defenders of Normandy routinely trooping down to their shelters in readiness for yet another sleepless night.

This time however, the follow-up was not still more bombs. Attached to Force S was the largest bombardment fleet of any D-Day landing zone. The big guns of the enormous

Troops of 101st Beach Group dig in at the top of the beach in front of the large casemate of German strongpoint WN18 near the junction of Queen and Roger sectors of Sword Beach.

battleships *HMS Warspite* and *HMS Ramillies* opened up on the coastal batteries behind Sword. Each warship boasted eight x 15in (381mm) guns plus a further 14 x 6in (152.4mm) guns. And they were joined by a further two 15 inchers mounted on the monitor *HMS Roberts*.

Sword itself was pounded by six cruisers – the *HMS Scylla*, *HMS Danae*, *ORP Dragon*, *HMS Frobisher*, *HMS Arethusa* and *HMS Mauritius*. These boasted a combined

total of 7 x 7.5in, 28 x 6in, 8 x 4.5in and 21 x 4in guns. And as daylight began to dawn, the bombardment force's 13 destroyers moved in close to shore and also opened up.

A small group of German E-boats tried to stop the bombardment but they could do little against such massed firepower. One of the 15 torpedoes they managed to fire before being driven off struck the Norwegian destroyer *Svenner* and broke it in two, but most of its crew were swiftly rescued.

At 4.45am a British midget submarine, *HMS X23*, which had been waiting submerged just off Sword since June 4, raised an 18ft mast and began flashing a green light seawards to guide in the first assault craft. This was invisible to anyone on shore but visible for up to five miles out to sea.

The 2nd East Yorks and 1st South Lancs clambered into their small wooden Landing Craft Assaults (LCAs) – 30 men to a boat – at 5.30am and began motoring slowly towards the beach. The 40 DD Shermans of the 13th/18th Hussars, still aboard their eight Landing Craft Tank (LCT) vessels, and the 'funnies' of the 79th Division aboard their 10 LCTs, did likewise.

LCT(R)s, LCTs modified to each carry 1064 x 5in rockets, accompanied the invasion fleet and opened fire when they were in range, rack after rack of munitions screaming into the air before slamming down into the bunkers, trenches and obstacles ranged along the shore.

At a distance of 15,000ft from the beach, 34 of the DD Shermans went into the water with their floatation skirts up. It was a long way from shore and the sea was choppy. Two sank before their tracks hit sand, their crewmen drowned. Another went down when it was accidentally rammed by an LCT taking evasive action to avoid some rockets that were falling short. When the naval artillery barrage subsided as the landing

A battery of self-propelled guns from one of the field regiments of British 3rd Infantry Division ready to fire in support of the infantry.

Traffic jams beginning to build up along the lateral road behind Sword beach. This view is looking westward towards the junction with the main road to Hermanville. Heavy traffic sapped the momentum of the British forces going ashore.

The main bunker of WN18. This concrete emplacement housed a 75mm gun used to fire in enfilade along the length of Sword Beach. The reinforced flanking wall on its seawards side made the position impervious to gunfire from warships. It was eventually knocked out by tank fire at close range.

craft neared the shore, the defenders opened fire. The surviving DD Shermans were on the beach at 7.24am, seconds before the infantry, but 10 were either knocked out in the surf or had their engines swamped as they struggled in the breakers.

The LCTs carrying Sherman Crabs, AVREs and other funnies also arrived on time, making it the best combined infantry and armour assault of the day.

Though it resulted in a lot of heavy hitting power concentrated in one place, the arrival of troops and tanks together on a strip of beach rapidly narrowing as the tide came in created a chaotic jumble of men and equipment. The 1st South Lancs' A Company suffered heavy casualties when it beached almost in front of Cod before any of the tanks had a chance to engage it.

Having lost their commanding officer, the South Lancs moved off down the beach to clear out houses along the sea front while C Company took on Cod itself, quickly joined by a company of the 2nd East Yorks. B Company of the 1st South Lancs, coming in behind A and C, found them still engaged in fighting the position and had to join in too. Tanks of the 13th/18th Hussars joined in but were sitting targets for Cod's massive 88mm gun.

It took nearly three hours to overcome the defenders of Cod and the 1st South Lancs suffered 107 casualties – about a quarter of the men they landed with. The 2nd East Yorks suffered a similar rate of attrition. In the end, the 2nd East Yorks took Cod after managing to get around behind the position.

Teams of combat engineers landed and began clearing away beach obstacles. They struggled to remove Teller mines from poles and dislodge hedgehogs from between beached landing craft and burning vehicles while under fire from snipers.

On the far left of Queen Red, 4 Commando led by Lord Lovat hit the beach in 24 landing craft and began disembarking ready for their trek to Casino. Before they had a chance to move however, they came under intense small arms fire from Cod.

Given little choice, the commandos advanced into the barrage and fought their way through the dunes to the left-hand side of Cod and on to the road which ran parallel to the beach in the direction of Ouistreham and strongpoints Sole and Daimler to the left of the main assault.

The task of capturing Casino was given to the two French troops of 10 Commando, which had been attached to 4 Commando for the landings. Casino had originally been exactly what its name suggested but the Germans had reduced it to rubble then dug into it to create an underground system of interlocking bunkers and tunnels surrounded by trenches, minefields and

Infantry from one of the beach groups by their shelters at the top of Queen White Beach the day after the landings. The location of this picture is around 200m to the east of the present day Place du Cuirasse Courbet.

British soldiers struggle ashore at 8.45am near the junction of Queen Red and White beaches opposite Cod. The men in the foreground with white bands on their helmets are Royal Engineers. In the immediate background are members of 41 Royal Marine Commando while further back are troops of the 2nd Middlesex Regiment.

Lord Lovat and his commandos go ashore on Queen Red Beach. He is the figure in the water to the left of the arm of the piper in the foreground, Bill Millin.

hidden machine gun posts. There was very little above ground.

The French leader, Captain Phillippe Kieffer, divided his men into two teams, both of which infiltrated the position through buildings to the rear before attacking with rifles, machine guns and grenades. Unfortunately, nothing the Frenchmen had made a dent in the nearest concrete bunker, which fired back at them with 50mm anti-tank guns and machine guns. A water tower was also used as a vantage point by German snipers to pick off the French commandos.

The attack faltered until a number of DD Shermans moved up from the beach, blew open the anti-tank gun position and dislodged the snipers from the tower with a few well-aimed shells. With these major impediments removed, the French advanced and cleared Casino.

The rest of 4 Commando made all haste to Ouistreham at the mouth of the River Orne to begin advancing inland towards the bridge downriver already being precariously held by the British airborne 'coup de main' team. They attacked a gun battery similar to Casino along the way but abandoned the assault when it became clear that the battery's guns had already been withdrawn by the Germans. Lovat sent 6 Commando on ahead to relieve the 6th Airborne at the River Orne

Commandos of Brigadier Lord Lovat's 1st Special Service Brigade moving inland. They have just left the beach and are heading for Colleville, making a detour right to avoid a minefield

Members of 4 Commando wait for orders to move further inland.

WO IST DIE LUFTWAFFE?

As the thousands of Allied ships taking part in Overlord appeared on the horizon and approached the shore, they seemed to the German infantry awaiting them in bunkers along the coast an ideal target for an aerial strike.

But the Luftwaffe was nowhere to be seen. It is reported again and again in accounts from German survivors of D-Day that they or their comrades' reaction to the fleet was to ask in exasperation: "Wo ist die Luftwaffe?" Allied air superiority was near total but it wasn't absolute. Sword saw the only German beach strafing run of the day.

A pair of Focke-Wulf Fw 190 A-8s flown by Wing Commander Josef 'Pips' Priller and Heinz Wodarczyk of I/Jagdgeschwader 26 took off from their airfield near Lille at 8am and managed a single run over the beach itself before beating a hasty retreat.

Earlier in the day, at just gone 5am, Helmut Eberspächer had led a sortie of four Fw 190 As from Schnellkampfgeschwader 10 against RAF Lancaster bombers from 97 Squadron, based at RAF Coningsby in Lincolnshire, that had been pounding the Pointe-du-Hoc battery just off to one side of Omaha beach.

In his log, Eberspächer recorded that three Lancs had been shot down but in fact the Germans managed to get four.

That evening, Junkers Ju 88 bombers of Kampfgeschwader 54 attempted to attack the British beaches but suffered heavy losses and were driven off.

Medics deal with the dead and wounded on Sword after the initial assault in the shelter of an abandoned AVRE tank from 79th Armoured Division. To the right is an M10 Wolverine from 20th Anti-tank Regiment.

bridge and they eventually arrived after fighting their way through four strongpoints and an artillery battery.

While 4 Commando went left on landing, 41 (Royal Marine) Commando landed at 8.45am and went right. The unit was aiming for the Trout strongpoint at Lion sur Mer, a nearby chateau and a radar station at Douvres. It was also meant to link up with other elements of its parent unit, 4th Special Service Bridge, due to land on Juno beach.

Clearing Trout proved to be simple, since it was undefended, but the chateau proved to be well garrisoned. Three AVREs joined the attack at 11am but when they were within 100 yards of the chateau a 50mm PAK hit them at close range and knocked them out. German mortars opened fire and the commandos sheltered in houses beside the road before withdrawing at 1.10pm.

Meanwhile, the 1st Suffolks had arrived along with self-propelled artillery and the 27th Armour Brigade, the Staffordshire Yeomanry. The beach had now been reduced to just 30 yards in width by the incoming tide, creating a huge traffic jam.

By 9am, the 1st South Lancs had already taken Hermanville but had dug in there instead of advancing. The 2nd East Yorks were moving to take Sole and the 1st Suffolks were headed for Colleville and strongpoints Morris and Hillman.

A jumble of men and machines, including beach group personnel, take shelter from German fire on Sword.

Wire defences at the top of the beach between strongpoints WN18 and WN20 were easily breached but were backed up on their landward side by minefields. In the background commandos from 1st Special Service Brigade are coming ashore from the infantry landing craft which brought them over the Channel.

DD Sherman tanks of B Squadron, 13th/18th Hussars and infantry of 2nd East Yorks moving along the lateral road towards Ouistreham.

M10 Wolverine from 20th Anti-tank Regiment gives supporting fire to men from 2nd East Yorks.

A disabled Sherman Crab from 79th Armoured Division on the beach near the western end of Queen White sector. Beside the tank steel matting has been laid on the sand to form a firm path towards the beach exit.

HOLDUPS AT BEUVILLE AND HILLMAN

Behind the 8th on to the same narrow landing zone of Queen White and Queen Red came the landing craft of the 185th Brigade, made up of the 2nd King's Shropshire Light Infantry, the 2nd Royal Warwickshire Regiment and the 1st Royal Norfolk Regiment.

The tanks meant to support these units, the Staffordshire Yeomanry, were mired in a traffic jam on the beach however so the 2nd KSLI went forward on foot with support only from 7th Field Regiment's M7 Priest self-propelled guns.

After initially encountering jubilant French civilians in Hermanville, they began to encounter stiff resistance at Periers Ridge. X Company came under sustained heavy mortar and artillery fire and discovered that the Germans had set up machine gun positions in the cornfields. Around 15-20 men were killed as platoons advanced into the corn to flush them out.

The Staffordshire Yeomanry, rushing to catch up with the infantry, ran headlong into the teeth of a German 88mm anti-tank gun. This knocked out five of B Squadron's Shermans before the remainder managed to target the weapon and blow it apart. Four Sherman Crabs from the Westminster Dragoons were also lost during the same action. Z Company of the 2nd KSLI engaged in a firefight with more German machine gunners on the ridge while W, X and Y companies continued the advance on Caen.

Mired by the traffic jams and waiting for orders, the 2nd Warwickshires and 1st Norfolks did not even begin their advance until well into the afternoon. At 3pm the Norfolks were ordered to advance to the left of the KSLI and the Warwickshires to the right but the Norfolks ended up passing through the 1st Suffolks at Colleville and out into cornfields too close to the as yet uncaptured Hillman strongpoint. The position's machine guns opened up and the battalion suffered 150 casualties in short order.

The lead companies of the Suffolks were actually in the process of taking Hillman,

Men of one of the beach groups wading ashore on Sword during the follow-up waves.

having already captured Colleville and Morris. Hillman, the headquarters of the German 736th Infantry Regiment, was huge – measuring 640m by 450m – and it took until well into the evening to finally winnow out its defenders using high explosives.

The 1st Suffolks were out of the race for Caen and dug in there as night fell.

D-DAY'S ONLY COUNTERATTACK

The third and final wave of the 3rd Division, the 9th Infantry Brigade, landed during the afternoon of D-Day and quickly found itself ordered into action against a coming German counterattack. Air reconnaissance reports made throughout the morning had tracked the progress of the 21st Panzer Division as it moved north and north west towards, and then into Caen. It had at least 90 tanks and two battalions of infantry and represented a major threat to the invasion.

The 2nd Lincolns, part of the 9th, took up positions to the right of Hermanville, their comrades in the 2nd Ulsters moved just beyond the town while the 1st King's Own Scottish Borderers were charged with defending St Aubin.

The panzers of the 21st assembled near Lebisey, north of Caen, directly in the path of the British advance and attacked at 4pm, immediately running into the 2nd KSLI.

The unit's Y Company had already entered Lébisey Wood, just three miles short of Caen, and reported seeing 40 or more enemy tanks, mostly Panzer IVs. A Squadron of the Staffordshire Yeomanry moved into the panzers' path on high ground near Biéville, along with every 6-pounder anti-tank gun the KSLI could muster. These were joined by a troop of

Men from 4 Commando moving along the narrow gauge railway behind the beach towards Ouistreham on their way to attack the battery there.

three M10 Wolverines from the 41st Anti-Tank Battery.

Y Company meanwhile engaged the German 192nd Panzergrenadiers supporting the tanks in a vicious firefight. Dozens of German soldiers were seen advancing to the right but the company held its ground. Sighting the approaching panzers, a Staffordshire Sherman commander shouted: "Nasties are coming!" from his open turret. Another British tank opened fire, making a kill. Now all the Shermans, Wolverines and 6-pounders were firing and the Germans slowed, two more Panzer IVs exploding as they suffered direct hits from the 2nd KSLI's guns.

The panzers now jinked around the defensive line and charged down the British right flank, pursued by the Staffordshires' Shermans. Three more panzers were hit and knocked out. B Squadron of the Staffordshires, equipped with Sherman Firefly tanks, was waiting for the Germans near Hermanville and succeeded in killing

another three before RAF Typhoons joined the fray and destroyed another four.

A total of 13 Panzer IVs had been destroyed and still more had suffered serious damage. The exhausted German tankmen had reached the coast but at 9pm, they saw 250 gliders carrying the next wave of British airborne troopers, the 6th Airlanding Brigade. This was too much.

Realising that they were hopelessly outnumbered and in danger of being cut off, the Germans tried to withdraw – only to encounter Canadians closing the gap between Sword and Juno.

Much confused fighting in the dark ensued and very few Germans escaped with their lives. The advance on Caen had stalled however. Y Company of the 1st KLSI and the Staffordshire Yeomanry supporting them were reluctantly withdrawn from their exposed position at Lébisey Wood.

By the end of D-Day, 28,845 men had been landed on Sword beach at a cost of 630 men killed, wounded or missing. ■

CHAPTER 10

'Don't take no prisoners'
Juno beach

Thirsty for revenge after the slaughter at Dieppe, the Canadians were out for blood at Juno. They suffered appalling casualties from beach obstacles and machine gun crossfire on the way in but once ashore they took the fight to the Germans in bloody and brutal combat...

Nan Red Beach just to the east of Bernières. B Company of the North Shore Regiment landed near the bottom of the picture, in front of the large house on the beach with a high sea wall. A Company landed to the right, opposite the seaside villas. The ground at the rear of the beach has been pockmarked by hundreds of 5in rockets fired from the LCT(R)s which accompanied the assault landing craft.

BELOW: Assault landing craft from *HMCS Prince David* and *SS Monowai* during their run in to Nan White beach on D-Day.

Observers on vessels out at sea late at night on June 5, 1944, saw the coast of Normandy lit orange, red and white by a massive aerial bombardment. The RAF alone kept up its attack for nearly six hours, dropping 5268 tons of bombs. Amid this ferocious onslaught came 230 Lancaster bombers of the Royal Canadian Air Force, dropping bombs on targets around Juno beach.

This was to be the Canadian point of invasion and at 5.30am the heavy guns of cruisers *HMS Belfast* and *HMS Diadem*, anchored off Juno, opened fire on its concrete bunkers, blockhouses and gun emplacements. Forty minutes later Force J's 11 destroyers joined in and yet more bombing runs were made along the five-and-a-half mile wide invasion front.

The Germans were not relying solely on the much vaunted Atlantic Wall at Juno however. Offshore was a reef that cleared the water's surface at low tide forming a natural barrier to any incoming vessels.

Landing craft moved forward under the naval barrage but rough seas led commanders to delay the troops' arrival for 10 minutes. They were already going in 10 minutes later than the troops on Gold beach so the tide could help them clear the hazardous reef.

Commandos landing on Nan Red beach.

Nan White Beach at Bernières in the late morning of D-Day. In the centre a bridge has been laid over the curved sea wall opening an exit for wheeled traffic.

The harbour entrance and estuary of the River Seulles at Courseulles. The picture was taken on the afternoon of D-Day with the tide half out. The earlier high tide has allowed two large LSTs to beach near the high water mark at the top of Mike Red beach.

As they neared the shore, eight landing craft carrying rocket launchers began to fire off salvos and M7 Priest howitzers still aboard their boats began to blaze away at targets on shore. Dense clusters of German obstacles lurked ahead though they were barely visible as the rising tide submerged them.

Juno's two primary invasion beaches were codenamed Nan and Mike. Nan, on the left, was the larger and was subdivided into three sectors with Nan Red covering St Aubin-sur-Mer at the furthest extreme, Nan White covering Bernières-sur-Mer in the centre and Nan Green covering the left side of Courseulles, a small port which sat astride the river Seulles. On the right of Juno were the two sectors of Mike. Mike Red covered the right of Courseulles and Mike Green covered the beach halfway from Courseulles to La Riviere on Gold.

Royal Marines from 4 Special Service Brigade headquarters arrive on Nan Red beach in the LCI(S) that has carried them over the channel. The steep ramps leading down from the light wooden craft made disembarkation difficult. Many men were tipped into the sea as the ends of the walkways bucked violently on the incoming waves.

THE JOHNS

Two companies of the Regina Rifle Regiment – the 'Johns' – two from the Royal Winnipeg Rifles and one from the Canadian Scottish Regiment led the attack at Courseulles backed up by Sherman tanks from the 1st Hussars and AVREs. The port had been fortified by the Germans and boasted three 75mm anti-tank guns, an 88mm, two 50mms, 12 machine gun positions and two mortars. All of these were reinforced with concrete and most with steel and earthworks, making them all but immune to the effects of naval artillery.

Before they could even reach this daunting arsenal however, the Allied landing craft had to run the gauntlet of beach obstacles. A Company of the Johns was first ashore at 8.05am and it came under heavy machine gun fire but 14 DD Shermans of the 1st Hussars had also landed and were able to bear the brunt of the defenders' firepower and return it in kind. The anti-tank gun emplacements were knocked out by direct hits from the tanks and the Johns were able to get inside the network of trenches and bunkers to put an end to German resistance on the beach before pushing into the port itself.

Accurate aerial photos taken in advance of the invasion and then enlarged had allowed the Canadians to carefully divide the port up into 12 'blocks' and each block was the responsibility of a particular unit. B Company, having landed 10 minutes after A, quickly overcame the surviving defenders on Courseulles' promenade with the aid of AVREs firing their heavy mortars into the defences before moving into the town. They cleared blocks two, three, four and 12 while A cleared one, five, six and seven. Block one, on the beach near the mouth of the Seulles river, had to be cleared twice because the Germans were able to retake it via an underground tunnel.

C Company landed at 8.35am and joined the fight, mopping up its designated blocks – eight, nine, 10 and 11 – in short order. Arriving at 8.55am, D Company suffered horrendous casualties when two of its landing craft struck mines. The resulting explosions tore the fragile vessels apart and pitched the surviving Canadians, many of them now injured, into the water 250 yards from the beach. Among the dead was D's commanding officer, Major Jack Love, and it took more than half an hour for the new acting CO to rally his men on the sand.

In spite of this setback and with fewer than 50 men left, D Company then set off in the direction of its D-Day target: a bridge over the Mue river more than two miles inland at a village called Reviers. C Company had by now finished up in Courseulles and it too pressed on, hot on D Company's heels. Shortly before noon, both companies were engaged in a firefight with a German headquarters position at Reviers and by 12.15pm they had been victorious – seizing the bridge and taking 20 prisoners into the bargain. By 3pm both A and B companies had also moved up and the battalion was able to gather all of its remaining strength at Reviers.

The Johns' two strongest formations, B and C companies, were ordered to continue the advance at 6pm, supported by B Squadron of the 1st Hussars. The Hussars'

Shermans took a beating at Fresne-Camilly when a German 88mm gun opened fire, knocking out six of the unit's 10 tanks in quick succession. A Company, now down to just 40 men, was left to guard Reviers while a similarly depleted D Company protected the battalion's left flank.

As the sun began to set, more than 100 men arrived fresh from the beachhead as reinforcements. Among them were survivors from D Company's landing craft disaster who had been picked up by the Navy. They carried German weapons to replace the ones they had lost and two even wore Navy uniforms, having been forced to wriggle out of their own during their swim to safety. The battalion dug in for the night at 10pm around Fresne-Camilly and Fontaine Henry, both about five miles inland from the coast.

THE LITTLE BLACK DEVILS

The Royal Winnipeg Rifles had taken severe casualties of their own during the battle for Courseulles. After landing on Mike Green at 7.49am, to the right of the assault, B Company had come under sustained machine gun fire from several directions at once. According to the Winnipegs' official history, The Little Black Devils: "Rushing the enemy, B Company encountered heavy enemy fire. Corporal Walter John 'Bull' Klos, badly shot in the stomach and legs while leaving the assault boat, made his way forward to an enemy machine gun nest. He managed to kill two Nazis before he was mortally felled. His hands were still gripped about the throat of his victim."

It took vital minutes for the Winnipegs' armoured support to arrive in the form of Sherman Crabs from B Squadron of the 22nd Dragoons. The other armoured

Troops of the North Nova Scotia Highlanders and Highland Light Infantry of Canada landing on Nan White. The picture was taken east of Bernières at high tide. The smoke in the background is from burning buildings in Courseulles, over a mile to the west.

element meant to be supporting them, AVREs of 26th Squadron, 5th Assault Regiment, Royal Engineers, were half an hour late. B Company had to fight its way up the beach through sheer tenacity and once it was clear it moved up into Courseulles via a small bridge. The other frontal assault unit, D Company, landed on the left. This was closer to the river and the entrance to the port but in front of a series of trenches and emplacements. D's armour backup, DD Shermans from A Squadron of the 1st Hussars, struggled badly with the rough seas and only seven made it ashore. Nevertheless, the company was able to overcome the defenders, cut a path through their barbed wire fences and move off the beach taking only light casualties. Before long they had moved on to Graye-sur-Mer, a small town set back from the coastline, and cleared it of German forces.

On the far right of Mike Red, the Canadian Scottish Regiment's C Company arrived all geared up to attack the 75mm emplacement that was its designated target, only to find that it had already been destroyed by high calibre naval shells. With this impediment taken care of, the Canadian Scots cleared paths through a minefield that was the Germans' only other defence before marching forwards and right, in the direction of St Croix-sur-Mer two miles directly inland from La Riviere on the left of neighbouring Gold beach.

An advance party from the 176th Workshop and Park Company, Royal Engineers, found its landing craft impaled on an obstacle on Mike Green, having been aiming to land on Nan Red. Lance Corporal Reg Clarke, who was part of the unit moving up in the wake of the Winnipegs' B Company, said: "An assault craft, broadside on to the beach, lay on its side next to us. It was shattered. Not a single Canadian soldier or crew member had made it. It was a bloody mess. Two bodies were actually hanging from the side where they had been blown by the force of the explosion.

"Obstacles were everywhere. One vicious looking pronged object with heavy explosive devices hung around the prongs was to our right. Quite a number of damaged assault craft, some on fire, were beached. There were armoured assault

The 9th Canadian Infantry Brigade lands over Nan White beach at Bernières during the late morning of D-Day. The width of the beach has been reduced to just a few metres by the incoming tide and the small stretch of dry sand at the top is becoming congested by troops and equipment, slowing the arrival of the follow up battalions.

DD Sherman of the Fort Garry Horse moving along the road from the centre of St-Aubin up to the seafront strongpoint. The tank is supporting B Company, North Shore Regiment, during its attack on WN27.

vehicles damaged and shattered by gunfire lying inert, not clear of the water as the tide was still coming in."

Private Ray Burge of the 2nd Devons, who should have landed on Gold beach, found his LCT had gone off course and he ended up on Juno's Mike sector instead. He said: "When we first landed, there was a Canadian officer there. We said, 'where do we go?' All he said was: 'Keep going down there and remember Dieppe and don't take no prisoners'. That was from a Canadian officer: 'Don't take no prisoners, just remember Dieppe'."

The Winnipegs' A and C companies landed at 8.05am and rapidly advanced off the beach and through open countryside. A Company went forwards and right, in the direction of St Croix-sur-Mer with the Canadian Scots following. The two units soon discovered, however, that the village was far from an easy target, coming under fire from eight separate machine gun positions.

C Company went straight on to another village, Banville. Here it encountered determined resistance from three machine gunners. Sherman tanks from the 1st Hussars were called up to help and along with D company, which had by now

Stranded Sherman DD tank of the 1st Hussars and a Bofors anti-aircraft gun beside a casemate at the top of Nan Green beach.

followed the line of advance, the Canadians managed to silence the German gunners.

Having overcome all opposition in both St Croix-sur-Mer and Banville by mid-afternoon, the whole battalion was able to

advance to Creully, about four miles inland, by 5pm. An hour later the exhausted Little Black Devils were digging in.

NAN WHITE

To the left of Courseulles lay Nan White sector, including Bernières-sur-Mer. The task of taking Bernières was given to the Queen's Own Rifles. When the ramp of the first landing craft dropped at 7.55am, 10 of the first 11 men to try and get out were shot dead. The sea front at Bernières had a wall up to 12ft high in places and the town, like the others along Juno beach, had been heavily fortified.

Among its defences were 12 machine gun positions and concrete bunkers for a 50mm KwK gun and an 88mm anti-tank gun. The first leading unit of the Queen's Own, B Company, suffered badly as the men ran into a hail of gunfire while trying to reach the sea wall. Four of the Fort Garry Horse DD Shermans meant to be supporting them suffered direct hits from the 88mm while swimming in and sank.

The sea wall on Nan Red beach after the assault. This picture was taken at high tide during the late morning when the width of the beach had been reduced to just a few metres.

A Canadian M10 Wolverine moves past a knocked out Centaur tank towards the strongpoint at Langrune. The house in the background formed part of the fortified position and was located alongside the high concrete wall which blocked entry into the compound.

Lieutenant-General Miles Dempsey (left) commander of British Second Army talking with Major-General Percy Hobart, commander of 79th Armoured Division. The 79th provided specialised armoured vehicles to tackle fortifications and obstacles whenever they were needed.

One member of B Company, Doug Hester, said: "We saw the five pillboxes on top of the sea wall. These were our first objective. About 500 yards out, they had us in their sights and began shooting. When the craft got into shallower water, the Royal Marines lowered the door.

"The three in front of me were hit and killed. By luck I jumped out between bursts into their rising blood. Cold and soaking wet, I caught up to Gibby. The first burst went through his backpack. He turned his head, grinning at me, and said: 'that was close Dougie'. The next burst killed him."

Despite the horrendous casualties, members of B Company managed to get close enough to the German pillboxes to knock them out with grenades and small arms fire. The unit had suffered 65 casualties but still advanced into the town.

Landing on the right the second leading unit, A Company, had a less difficult time getting from its landing craft to the sea wall but having climbed over it and cut through the barbed wire beyond it the unit was hit by heavy machine gun fire.

The assault's reserve unit, Le Regiment de la Chaudiere, landed at 8.30am but was pinned down on the beach while the Queen's Own attacked the town's defenders in house to house fighting. Advancing using covering fire, A and B companies quickly overcame the defenders and reach the town's central road. With the aid of the Fort Garry Horse's DD Shermans, the town was entirely in Canadian hands by 9am. By then both C and D companies had also landed. These suffered heavy casualties not from gunfire but from mines – half of their landing craft being blown up during the run in.

Landing behind the regiment, Private Frederick Perkins of the 5th Battalion, Royal Berkshire Regiment, said: "There were lots of dead Canadians about. As they'd hit the beach, beach obstacles were blowing up around them, landing craft were blowing up, hitting the mine obstructions on the beach, and the Queen's Own Rifles got caught with a crossfire by machine guns. They lost the majority of one of their companies and they were laying there. It was terrible to see."

An AVRE was used to lay a bridge up on to the sea wall, creating an exit from the beach suitable for vehicles and by 9.30am the Fort Garry Horse was in the town itself and forming up ready to advance.

German Prisoners under guard on Nan White beach at Bernières on D-Day. The troops with a white band around their helmets and a white circular patch on their sleeves are British beach group personnel, probably from the 5th Royal Berkshires.

Crew from 3rd Anti-tank Regiment RCA remove waterproofing from their M10 Wolverine after arriving on Mike Red beach

From here, the Queen's Own and their armoured support set off inland. By the early afternoon, C and B companies had got as far as Anguerny, six miles from the coast. D company had gone a mile further, reaching Anisy before night fell. Le Regiment de la Chaudiere, having left the beach at noon, advancing along the centre line between the Queen's Own on the left and the Regina Rifles on the right, got four miles inland – up to Colomby sur Thaon. The Queen's Own Rifles suffered the highest casualty rate of any Canadian regiment on D-Day – 143 killed, wounded or captured.

NAN RED

On the far left of Juno was St Aubin-sur-Mer, the primary stronghold of Nan Red sector. It had a central strongpoint housing a 50mm KwK gun with an excellent field of fire plus many smaller positions linked together by underground tunnels. The North Shore (New Brunswick) Regiment's B Company landed right in front of it at 8.10am in chest deep water. As with other sectors, the Germans opened up with machine guns as soon as the landing craft ramps fell.

The North Shores waded on to the sand dunes before sprinting forward but had to cover 300ft of beach before they could reach the village's sea wall. Once they were there, the survivors struggled to make any move forward and snipers began to pick them off one by one.

DD Shermans of the Fort Garry Horse's C Squadron landed shortly after the infantry but the first two ashore were hit by the 50mm gun and knocked out, followed soon after by the first pair of AVREs to land. The German strongpoint at St Aubin proved to be extremely difficult to overcome and nearly two hours later B Company was still at it. It wasn't until an AVRE managed to get ashore and hit the emplacement at close range with its heavy mortar that the North Shores were finally able to overcome it.

Meanwhile, the unit's A Company had landed to the right of B and without a major defensive position right in front of it the unit was able to go round the edge of St Aubin and enter it from the right-hand side, clearing it house by house. At 9.48am, while B Company was still on the beach and still battling the 50mm's defenders, A reached the coast road and joined up with the Queen's Own, who had taken Bernières.

Three minutes earlier, C and D companies had landed and moved into St Aubin. They bypassed the troublesome 50mm but were then being stopped in their tracks by a 75mm gun that had been brought up into the village during the assault. The Canadians fired several salvos of high explosive mortar bombs at it, putting it out of action, but were still held up by snipers shooting from the bell tower of the village church. An M7 Priest stopped them by blowing a hole in the tower.

As A and D companies were ending resistance within St Aubin itself, C Company gathered with two troops of Fort Garry Horse Shermans and advanced ahead of the others in the direction of Tailleville – which was directly inland over open countryside and occupied by a company of the German 736th Infantry Regiment. Even backed up by tanks and later A Company as it moved up from St Aubin, it still took six hours to dislodge the enemy. By the end of the day,

Tanks moving through the narrow streets of Thaon on the drive inland from the beaches. The Canadians pushed further inland from Juno than any other Allied forces managed on D-Day.

The beach at St Aubin-sur-Mer in the aftermath of D-Day. An American Republic Thunderbolt fighter-bomber has washed up beside the sea wall, along with a DD Sherman.

10pm, A, C and D companies were occupying Tailleville, while the exhausted B Company remained in St Aubin. The North Shores suffered a total of 125 casualties on June 6 – most of them from B Company.

JUNO'S COMMANDOS

Landing just 45 minutes behind the North Shores on Nan Red came the 420 men of 48 Royal Marine Commando. Their job was to move through the Canadians without engaging the enemy at St Aubin, who were supposed to have been well on their way to defeat by this point, and move along the coast to the left of the village in the direction of Langrune-sur-Mer – the very furthest left point of Juno.

The mission started to go wrong even before the men had set foot on land. Two of their six landing craft suffered severe damage from submerged beach obstacles and sank. Some commandos tried to wade ashore but the water was too deep and the tide too strong – many were drowned.

Marine Dennis Smith later recalled: "As we got close in, all hell broke loose. We were under fire not only from ahead but also from the left because we were on the extreme end of Juno beach and for five miles to our left there were no landings taking place. And because the tides were running high the underwater obstacles were still underwater and one or two of the boats were holed and stuck on these obstacles, way out."

Ashore, the commandos discovered the St Aubin strongpoint with its 50mm gun, machine guns and mortars waiting for them. Men tried to take cover on the beach and protect their injured comrades but DD Shermans from the Fort Garry Horse were still arriving at this point and, rolling up the beach, began to crush wounded commandos. One account tells of a commando officer, horrified to see this, furiously throwing a grenade at the Canadian tank responsible.

Sergeant Joe Stringer said: "We were exposed and as I came down the ramp two fellows immediately behind me were hit by machine gun fire. We lost a lot of men this way." He said it was chaotic on the beach with Canadians lying dead and wounded all around. "The Fort Garry Horse tanks were coming in at this time with their hatches down and a lot of wounded were being badly mauled by the tracks."

Marine Sam Earl said: "I kept running and then I saw a tracked vehicle coming from a ship and there were two of our chaps there. One of them, he'd got wounded and he lay there and this tracked vehicle came up, he couldn't move, and it ran him over and took his arm off. And the other chap, he bent down and tried to pull him and as he bent down a sniper got him in the head. When we went back two days after, to pick them up and bury them, we had a job to separate them two: the chap who was about to pick him up, his arms were round him and they were stiff."

After finally managing to leave the beach, the commandos dumped some of their heavier equipment in the garden of a house before fighting their way into the village alongside the North Shores.

It took three hours but the defenders of St Aubin were eventually subdued and the commandos were able to set off down the coast to the left in pursuit of their original objectives. The first of these was to take the German position at Langrune-sur-Mer and the second was to meet up with their colleagues from 41 Royal Marine Commando who had been due to land on Sword beach. This would effectively close the gap between Sword and Juno, forming a solid front line.

As they moved down the coast, the commandos came until fire from their own side – the naval vessels of Force J. Shells killed two men and wounded several more before the ships could be radioed and told to stop firing. When they got within sight of Langrune-sur-Mer the commandos realised that the mission would be more difficult than had been anticipated.

It was a row of seafront houses that had been reinforced and effectively turned into a small fortress. The road at either end had been blocked with 6ft concrete walls and there was a network of external trenches defended with machine gun posts. Facing the sea were a pair of bunkers, one housing a 75mm gun and the other a 50mm. On the inland side there was a field with signs declaring that it was a minefield.

The commandos' weapons – Sten guns, grenades, mortars and machine guns – were simply not enough to do the job. A team was sent ahead to try to fulfill the second of the unit's objectives but although they reached the agreed rendezvous point there was no sign of anyone from 41 Royal Marine Commando. At the end of D-Day the exhausted commandos had suffered more than 200 casualties and failed in both of their objectives. The next day however, the unit received support from a pair of Centaur

Late in the afternoon of D-Day followup troops land on Nan White beach at Bernières and trudge across the wide expanse of sand to the main beach exit near the Norman House.

Captured German 88mm gun casemate at the entrance of Courseulles harbour. The Canadians have used the concrete bunker to house a light anti-aircraft position on its roof.

IV tanks of the 1st Royal Marine Armoured Support Group that had been attempting to catch up with them following the landings on Juno. It was hoped that their 95mm howitzers would be able to blast a path into Langrune-sur-Mer and the first one rolled forward. It stayed on the road leading directly to the village to avoid the minefield on the inland side but the road itself had been mined and the tank was immobilized.

The second Centaur moved in, avoiding the mines, but it was found that even the high explosive shells of its large main weapon weren't powerful enough to put a hole in the German defences, although it was able to destroy a machine gun position. It turned around and returned to where the commandos were waiting.

The commandos' next gambit was to move forward and attempt to create a gap using Bangalore torpedoes but these were also found to be insufficiently powerful. At this point, two Canadian M10 Wolverine tank destroyers showed up and these were put to work firing armour piercing shells into the concrete wall covering the road. The Wolverines fired nonstop for over an hour and pincushioned the wall with holes until it began to crumble. Their ammunition now expended, they pulled back to allow a 1st Royal Marines Armoured Support Group Sherman and another Centaur forward. These tried again with high explosives and at last the concrete wall shattered and fell.

The marines were able to charge through the remains of the wall and spent the rest of the day mopping up the defenders until Langrune-sur-Mer was entirely in Allied hands.

KELLER AND THE 9TH

As the Canadian and British front line units advanced inland, Canadian Army commander Major General Rod Keller landed with his headquarters staff at Bernières-sur-Mer where he was irritated to find a jumble of tanks, self-propelled guns, carriers and trucks stuck in a traffic jam trying to exit the beach. While attempts were made to sort this out, Keller took stock of the situation. With Courseulles on the right and St Aubin on the left still partially in enemy hands, he realised that he would have to land the follow-up wave of troops, the 9th Canadian Infantry Brigade, at Bernières.

Unfortunately, by the time the 9th's landing craft began to arrive at 11.40am the traffic jams had grown worse and the infantry couldn't even get on to the sand.

With German artillery fire still landing sporadically on the beach, the Highland Light Infantry of Canada, The Stormont, Dundas and Glengarry Highlanders and The North Nova Scotia Highlanders were forced to sit and wait. Meanwhile, Keller set up his HQ in an orchard at 12.45pm and gave his brigade commanders their orders.

The North Nova Scotias, once they were ashore, formed up several miles inland from

German prisoners under guard by the sea wall between the Norman house and strongpoint WN28 at Bernières.

Bernières at Beny-sur-Mer, previously cleared by the Queen's Own Rifles, followed by the other two battalions. At 6.20pm the North Nova Scotias, most of them riding on the Sherman tanks of their armoured support, the Sherbrooke Fusiliers, moved forward past the Queen's Own and Le Regiment de la Chaudiere to continue the advance. They were delayed by German machine gun positions in the Colomby-sur-Thaon area but by 8pm they had reached Villons-les-Buissons – four miles from Carpiquet airfield on the outskirts of Caen.

The North Nova Scotias had advanced further from the beachhead than any other Allied unit on D-Day but now, with the bridge's other two battalions still back at Beny, the front line was overstretched. The men were ordered to dig in and prepare defensive positions against a counterattack which, it was feared, was imminent from the 21st Panzer Division. These panzers were already attacking the British 3rd Infantry

Major-General Rod Keller and some of his staff come ashore on Nan White at Bernières.

Division near Sword beach. The Allies landed 21,400 men on Juno beach during D-Day – the smallest number of the five landing zones – and suffered 1074 casualties, 961 of them Canadian. The total number of dead was 359 and another 47 men were taken prisoner. Juno was the second deadliest beach after Omaha. ■

CHAPTER 11

Blood on the sand
Gold beach

The idyllic, golden sandy beaches and pleasant little French seaside villages of Gold beach had become minefields littered with obstacles and bunker complexes sheltering heavy guns. The British forces going ashore found themselves under fire from positions inside chalets and hotels as they waded in...

Royal Marines of 47 RM Commando land on Gold beach at 9.30am on D-Day.

Soldiers of the 7th Green Howards cross King Green beach at about 8.30am. An 81st Assault Squadron AVRE, fitted with a Bobbin, is visible in the surf towards the right of the photograph, as are beach obstacles, Sherman tanks and other vehicles.

As four cruisers pounded the German coastal gun batteries, more than 140 assault landing craft, carrying 30 men each, motored through choppy seas towards Gold beach.

The cruisers – *HMS Ajax, HMS Argonaut, HMS Emerald*, and *HMS Orion* – had a total of 21 6in naval guns plus 8 x 5.25in guns and were firing off between four and six huge 112lb shells apiece every minute as the small troop craft moved in beneath the deafening barrage.

The men inside, their stomachs heaving as the boats lurched sickeningly on the swell, gripped their weapons and did their best to remained focused.

Accompanying these wooden troop vessels were larger tank carriers and still more craft converted to carry 1066 x 3in rockets which they began to launch in shrieking volleys at the beach defences as soon as the flotilla drew close enough to the shore.

Marines jump from their small LCA transports as larger LCT land behind carrying vehicles and heavy equipment on to Gold.

The plan had been to launch Force G's DD Sherman tanks into the water 5000 yards out and have them 'swim' in under their own power, but the tank units' commanders argued that the conditions were too rough. A decision was taken to drop the tanks right on to the beach instead, delaying their arrival.

The first landing craft hit the sand at 7.25am, their ramps dropping and men jumping into the surf. The vessels carrying the non-swimming tanks were arriving at the same time and there was confusion as boats jostled for space between wooden stakes, and steel 'hedgehogs'. Some boats were torn or blasted open by these defences, spilling men and equipment into the water, others spun around helplessly as the rough breakers caught them.

German machine guns, mortars and artillery pieces all along the five miles of beach opened up, cutting into the groups of British soldiers as they attempted to form up and advance. Tanks churning through the wet sand provided shelter as their crews opened fire on the fortified gun emplacements and bunkers ahead of them.

During the planning phase of D-Day, Gold beach had been divided into five codenamed sections. On the extreme left was a stretch known as King Red, encompassing the fortified seaside village of La Rivière.

To the right of that was open beach designated King Green and then came Jig Red in the centre. Jig Green was more open beach and Item was on the far right. These last two each partly covered another seaside village turned fortress, Le Hamel.

JIG SECTOR

Jig Green, just to the left of Le Hamel, also included a strongpoint known as Customs House and this was the landing zone of 231st Brigade – made up of the 1st Dorsets, the 1st Hampshires and the 2nd Devons.

These seasoned assault troops had fought in Sicily and Italy the year before and they'd been picked to lead the charge for that reason.

If everything went according to plan, the Dorsets would go straight forward and take Customs House while the Hampshires swung right and took Le Hamel. It was hoped that both strongpoints would have already been pounded into submission by American bombers of Eighth Air Force and a follow-up squadron of 12 RAF Typhoons, using 1000lb bombs.

In their wallowing landing craft approaching Jig Green, the Dorsets and Hampshires began to realise that this pre-emptive aerial assault had been less than effective as bullets began to splash into the water all around them. The DD Shermans

were meant to have gone ashore first, but due to the delay in their arrival, the troops wading from their landing craft after the ramps dropped were exposed and vulnerable. Heavy fire from at least five machine guns within Le Hamel's bunkers raked the beach ahead of them. Seeing what was happening, the steersmen of those landing craft yet to beach turned away to the left. Combined with ocean currents moving in the same direction, this meant that the Hampshires, now under a withering crossfire, were deposited in front of Customs House instead of the Dorsets. The Dorsets meanwhile were landed still further to the left on Jig Red, where they faced a relatively undefended section of open beach with marshes further inland.

The Hampshires' A and B companies were pinned down by machine-gun fire as soon as they reached the beach. The DD tanks were still at sea and although five other Sherman tanks rolled off landing craft 15 minutes after the Hampshires got there, all but one was knocked out within minutes

Vehicles coming ashore on Gold on D-Day.

by high-velocity armour-piercing rounds from a single 75mm Pak 40 anti-tank gun at Le Hamel. The last Sherman, a Crab minesweeper, evaded the gun and cut a safe path through the beach defences, reaching the coastal road that ran parallel above. It had turned in the direction of Le Hamel before the 75mm finally got it.

This heavy weapon, built into a fortified sanatorium and backed up by mortars and machine guns, was protected from naval shellfire by massive earthworks and concrete walls on the seaward side, the opening for its barrel facing sideways on to the beach.

Within minutes of landing, the Hampshires' commanding officer was seriously wounded and the battalion's headquarters' radios were put out of action, which meant there was no chance of calling in supporting fire from Force G's destroyers, which had sailed as close to the shore as they dared for just that purpose. By the time C and D companies had arrived 20 minutes later, casualties were mounting.

It was clear to the battalion's now acting second-in-command Major David Warren, leader of C Company, that advancing on Le Hamel directly was not going to succeed so instead he directed his men to flank it by pushing through Customs House and its surroundings defences to get behind the heavy defended village. This took several hours and in the meantime the Hampshires' follow-up battalion, the 2nd Devons, came ashore. One company of the Devons joined in the attack, while the rest moved down the coast to an artillery battery at Longues on the furthest side of Arromanches.

It had spent the morning blasting away at Force G's warships and had, in turn, been targeted first by the French cruisers *Georges Leygues* and *Montcalm* and the American battleship *USS Arkansas*, then by *HMS Ajax* and *HMS Argonaut*. Three of the battery's four guns were destroyed during

British Troops head inland from King Green towards Lavatory Pan Villa on the right. Note the Sherman Crab and AVRE on the left. Mont Fleury Battery was to the right of the house and 200m further inland.

Various vehicles on King Green including Sherman tanks, Universal carriers and an AVRE 'Bobbin'.

these exchanges, but one survived and it doggedly kept firing until 7pm. The battery's 184-strong garrison surrendered to the Devons the following day.

Once the Hampshires had succeeded in getting off the beach, bringing several newly arrived tanks with them, they were

able to get behind Le Hamel and take on its defenders, a company of highly trained and well-equipped soldiers of the German 352nd Division's 916th Grenadier Regiment, in fierce house-to-house fighting. The lethal 75mm gun was finally silenced when an AVRE nicknamed 'Loch Leven' fired its 290mm Petard mortar into the rear door of its bunker at close range. The tenacious German resistance at Le Hamel was finally ended by 4pm.

The battered Hampshires were then able to move beyond it towards Arromanches, further up the coast. Capturing this coastal town was a key goal of D-Day, since it was to be the site of a Mulberry artificial harbour.

LIBERATING 'PAREE'

As the 1st Hampshires advanced on Arromanches after defeating the defenders of Le Hamel, they encountered a radar station on a hill overlooking the town. It had suffered severe bomb damage during the early phases of D-Day and in the ruins they found two wounded German soldiers and a St Bernard cross dog. The Germans readily surrendered and the dog went with them as they were marched back to the beach by Sergeant James Bellows.

The prisoners told Bellows that the animal's name was Paree and they managed to smuggle it on to the landing craft that

'All looters will be shot – you have been warned'. LCT 886, heavily damaged while attempting to land its breaching team at Le Hamel, and which eventually drifted ashore near WN36. A hedgehog obstacle, with shell still attached, can be seen to the left.

Port en Bessin in British hands. The harbour entrance is to the left, anti-tank wall on the right. A sunken German anti-aircraft barge is in the foreground.

took them back to captivity in England. When the Hampshires later found out that the dog was still alive, they persuaded his new owner to give him up and adopted him as the regimental mascot under the new name Fritz. Bellows saw the dog again some years later. He said: "It just looked up at me and I said 'hallo Paree' and the dog went for me. I thought to myself 'I saved your life'." Fritz died in 1952.

The 1st Dorsets meanwhile, having landed further to the left of their intended destination, were able to get off the beach within 40 minutes of landing via the marshy land directly beyond the dunes. Their tank support was less fortunate and the heavyweight vehicles struggled with the uneven sand as they waded ashore from their landing craft.

Five Shermans got stuck in the water and their crews had to bail out when they became swamped. In addition, the two main road exits off the beach were soon blocked when, in each case, a Sherman and the AVRE following it were knocked out. Since the Jig Red area lacked natural obstacles and the boggy ground made it unsuitable for bunker building, the Germans relied heavily on minefields to defend it.

The Dorsets swept around the rear of Le Hamel, leaving it to the Hampshires, and faced a tough battle to clear the Germans out of Buhot and Puits d'Herode, a pair of tiny hamlets not far from the shore, en route to the area behind Arromanches. The Dorsets were still fighting at Buhot by the time reinforcements from 56th Infantry Brigade arrived at 2pm.

GOLD'S COMMANDOS

Hot on the heels of the Hampshires, Dorsets and Devons, into the chaos of Gold beach's Jig sector came 47 Royal Marine Commando. Comprised entirely of volunteers, this 420-man specialist unit made up of five troops – A, B, Q, X and Y – was not part of the main frontal assault.

Its mission was Operation Aubrey, the capture of Port en Bessin, a harbour town up the coast from Le Hamel and Arromanches – and a link up with the Americans as they moved inland from the Omaha beachhead. Port en Bessin was critical to the Allied invasion as it would be the focal point for the first phase of Operation Pluto, PLUTO being an acronym

for Pipe Line Under The Ocean. Pipelines would link berthed tanker ships to the shore and thousands of gallons of fuel would be pumped inland to keep the advancing Allied forces moving.

The commandos were told to avoid lengthy engagements with the Germans and move swiftly to meet their objectives. This meant getting ashore in the wake of the 231st Brigade battering ram, as it bludgeoned a path inland, and getting clear of the beaches as quickly as possible.

The commandos' landing craft approached a beach clogged with wrecked and burning landing craft, uncleared obstacles, sunken tanks and dead bodies. The tide had drawn in, and as the 14 vessels'

High tide on King Green at 9.45am. Just a sliver of beach is now available for disembarkation. Visible on the right through the haze is a Sexton self-propelled gun from 86th Field Regiment towing a 'porpoise' ammunition sled. The drowned vehicle is an M14 half-track.

Follow-up troops wade ashore from a landing craft on June 7. A bogged-down Sexton self-propelled gun can be seen on the left.

A Sherman tank of the Sherwood Rangers disembarks beside a bomb crater on Jig Red soon after 9am. Also visible are a 49th Flotilla LCT, an M14 half-track and an LCA.

marine crews tried to manoeuvre amid the debris they were sitting targets for the German gunners at Le Hamel, and while one was sunk by incoming fire another four hit mines or became impaled on beach defences.

Seven of the nine surviving landing craft were damaged, five of them so badly that they had to remain beached after dropping off the men they carried. The commandos landed along a 1500 yard stretch of beach between 9.45am and 10.15am, some having swum ashore from their wrecked landing craft, and began moving in small groups towards the planned rendezvous point at the church in Le Hamel. It quickly became clear that the village was still in enemy hands.

Forming up on the road at 11am, just three-and-a-half hours after the first British units landed on Gold, the commando unit's officers saw that 28 men had already been killed. A further 21 had been wounded, some of them seriously, and another 27 men were missing. To make matters worse, much of the unit's equipment had also been lost to the sea, including radios and ammunition.

Port-en-Bessin was nine miles away on foot through enemy-held territory and the remaining 344 men had to get moving. Giving Le Hamel a wide berth, the commandos took a cross-country route and reached a hill, known as Point 72, one mile south of Port en Bessin, by the evening. One man had been killed and a further 11 wounded, but the men had captured German equipment to replace what had been lost during their landing.

After digging in on the ridge and capturing two large underground positions and the German medics in them, the men got two hours' sleep. As first light broke on June 7, the commandos began patrols to assess Port en Bessin's defences and tried unsuccessfully to make contact with the Americans at Omaha.

During the day, two young Frenchmen turned up and gave the unit information about the German defences. One was then given a note for the German commander of the town's garrison demanding that he surrender. There was no response to this and it was decided that the attack would begin at 4pm with three of the five troops – A, B and X. Q would remain in reserve and Y would stay behind to guard Point 72.

Supporting fire from *HMS Emerald*, hit the port at 2pm and other vessels joined in. Shortly before 4pm two squadrons of Typhoons appeared overhead and launched a series of rocket and cannon attacks on German positions. Smoke shells were then fired to screen the commandos.

Port en Bessin had formidable defences. It was wedged between two 200ft cliffs – known as the Eastern and Western Features – which had been fortified with bunkers, trenches, minefields and barbed wire.

OUTGUNNED AND OUTFOUGHT
The German 352nd Infantry Division

The most formidable German force facing the Allies on D-Day was the 352nd Infantry Division, under Lieutenant General Dietrich Kraiss. It had 7400 men spread across nine battalions.

There were three front-line grenadier regiments, the 914th, 915th and 916th. In addition to the soldiers' usual personal equipment and weapons, these were each equipped with two 15cm sIG 33 heavy artillery pieces and three 7.5cm PaK 40 anti-tank guns. The first two also had six 7.5cm leIG infantry support guns, smaller artillery pieces, while the 916th had two of them.

The division's anti-tank battalion had a mix of 14 Marder II and Marder III armoured tank destroyers, 10 StuG III Ausf G armoured assault guns, and nine Flakpanzer 38(t) 20mm self-propelled flak guns.

Its artillery regiment had a range of 10.5cm leFH 16 and 15cm sFH 18 howitzers and its pioneer battalion had 20 man-portable flamethrowers and six mortars.

Panorama showing King Green and Jig Red sectors.

ATTACKING PORT EN BESSIN

A-Troop went in under mortar fire, reached the port's church and turned west before heading up a track on to the cliff slopes. As they moved up the cliff edge, two German ships in the harbour fired on them with flak guns, inflicting heavy casualties. Then Germans in the trenches above them opened up with withering machine-gun fire and threw down grenades. A gun battle ensued, but A-Troop was caught in the open and beaten back, suffering more casualties. The survivors retreated into the town, 12 men having been killed and 17 wounded in just a few minutes.

B-Troop had gone into the town right behind A-Troop, but had turned east instead of west at the church. As they approached the Eastern Feature, 12 Germans came forward to surrender. While these were being taken in, a pair of machine guns opened up on the commandos and they scattered, taking shelter in houses.

Q-Troop, which had been held in reserve, moved forward from Point 72 to support B-Troop with the unit's commanding officer, leaving just Y-Troop and the unit's headquarters staff in the area around Point 72. As night fell, German reinforcements overran the hill, forcing the British to retreat down towards Port en Bessin. Bottled up in the port the surviving 280 commandos, many of them having been wounded, were in a desperate situation.

They did what they could however, clearing the town and making preparations to continue the mission. It was getting dark by the time the commandos were able to mount an attack on the Eastern Feature, but even so, a small team of 30 men got into the defences and attacked a bunker. The team's commander, Captain Cousins, was killed in the attempt, but his men broke into the bunker and killed the Germans inside, giving the commandos a foothold.

The same team then fought their way through a series of concrete defensive positions, trenches, gun emplacements and barbed-wire fences. The feature's 120 defenders clung on, but by the early hours of June 8 the Eastern Feature was in British hands. The next day the commandos repeated the feat with the Western Feature and reoccupied their position outside the town too.

KING SECTOR – FIRST WAVE

The first British soldiers ashore on King Red, the furthest point to the left of Gold, were DD Sherman tank crews of the 4th/7th Dragoon Guards, rather than infantrymen. Even though they were dropped right on to the beach at 7.20am the three squadrons of tanks still struggled to get ashore. Under the breakers the sand was uneven and in places sandbars, which grounded landing craft, gave way to channels capable of swallowing a Sherman.

Just like Jig sector, there were numerous obstacles built into the beach to tear open landing craft and these also hampered the

tank crews as they coaxed their vehicles on to dry land. As the first troops from 69th Brigade – the 5th East Yorkshires and the 6th Green Howards – began to join them, an 88mm Pak 43/41 gun on the left at La Riviere, positioned sideways-on like the 75mm at Jig's Le Hamel, opened fire. The Pak 43/41 was the most powerful anti-tank gun used by the German army during the war – able to penetrate the thickest armour of any Allied tank at long range – and it began destroying tanks one by one.

Unlike the situation at Jig though, tanks had poured on to King Red beach in force. In addition to the 4th/7th Dragoons, there were AVREs and Sherman Crabs from the 6th Assault Regiment and the Westminster Dragoons. As the 88mm swung around,

trying to pick out a new target from the huge selection on offer, a Crab got close enough to put a shell right thought the narrow slot of its emplacement – destroying it and killing its crew.

Despite the loss of their main anti-tank weapon and the sheer number of tanks still coming ashore, the German defenders of La Riviere were determined to make a fight of it. The 5th East Yorks, on the left of the attack front and therefore tasked with taking on La Riviere, were pinned down behind the sea wall at the top of the beach by concentrated machine-gun fire.

Having arrived with their radio equipment intact though, the battalion was able to call down naval heavy artillery on to the rear of the fortified village, while men

Soldiers from the 2nd Essex disembark on Gold beach from their Canadian LCI (Large) about 12.30pm.

Armoured bulldozers clear the beach as more Shermans land.

DD tanks from the 4th/7th Royal Dragoon Guards, supporting 69th Brigade, advance near Rucqueville on the morning of June 7.

The 88mm casemate at La Riviere (WN-33), showing the massive walls on either side of the embrasure, which protected it against observation and fire from sea or inland. The sign at left reads 'wheels exit', indicating that non-tracked vehicles were to head inland from the beach at this point.

Gold beach from the air.

A Sherman with its wading gear still fitted motors down Gold beach.

climbed over the sea wall and advanced first on to the coastal road dividing it from the beach and then into the village itself.

An AVRE and a group of DD Shermans rolled up off the beach and into La Riviere, blasting German positions to rubble as they went. A company of infantry managed to get behind the village and attack enemy positions from the rear. It was all over for the defenders by 10am, the East Yorks having suffered 90 casualties.

To the East Yorks' right, the 6th Green Howards made short work of the positions facing them, thanks to a trio of AVREs. Their Petard mortars – cracked open one bunker before the Green Howards moved in and finished the job. A Sherman Crab made a path through the minefields at the top of the beach near La Riviere and a safe road inland was established.

Beyond the road that ran parallel to the beach, the Crab's crew discovered that the Germans had failed to destroy their own crossing point over an anti-tank ditch so they drove across it. A final obstacle, a shell crater blocking the road inland, was covered using a bridge-laying AVRE and suddenly the way into France was open. The trickle of vehicles using this route soon became a flood as the Green Howards, East Yorks and 4th/7th Dragoon Guards formed up and raced towards their objectives. The Green Howards' D Company broke off to attack the heavy artillery positions at Mont Fleury – a hill overlooking King sector.

B and C companies swung right towards Crepon, a village en route to their primary target – Villiers-le-Sec. Here the Green Howards, East Yorks and 4th/7th Dragoon Guards ran into a German counterattack.

Lieutenant Colonel Ernst Meyer, commander of the 915th Grenadier Regiment, part of the 352nd, had been told to stop the British. He was given 10 mobile assault guns – Marders and StuG IIIs – and a mixed bag of shaken survivors from other units to add to a single battalion of his own men and the 352nd's fusilier battalion, totalling more than 1000 soldiers. The battle began at 4pm and the German assault guns managed to destroy four of the Dragoons' Sherman tanks, but 'Battlegroup Meyer' was no match for the Green Howards and East Yorks.

Meyer was killed and fewer than 100 of his men escaped death or capture. The British made a lucky discovery too – a map found on Meyer's body revealed the locations of all German units along the coast. The Germans mounted a desperate attempt to recover his body, but failed.

KING SECTOR – SECOND WAVE

Behind the leading trio of the 6th Green Howards, 5th East Yorks and 4th/7th Dragoons came the 7th Green Howards who, despite initially struggling to make their way through the crowded beach area, pushed on past the German artillery positions at Mont Fleury and attacked a second battery behind it at Ver-sur-Mer. This was equipped with four smaller 100mm guns, but rather than firing them or even trying to defend them, its 50-strong garrison had retired to their concrete shelters and the Green Howards quickly took them prisoner.

Next in line after the 7th Green Howards, at 11am, were the three battalions of 151st Infantry Brigade – the 6th, 8th and 9th Durham Light Infantry. The final brigade of 50th Division to come ashore, at around midday, was the 56th which was comprised of the 2nd South Wales Borderers, the 2nd Gloucestershire and the 2nd Essex. They had been meant to come in behind the Hampshires, Dorsets and Devons on Jig, but fire from Le Hamel made this too risky so they arrived not far from where the 151st Brigade had gone in.

All the while, support units were driving ashore still more tanks including Centaurs, jeeps, Bren carriers, mortars, machine guns, field artillery pieces and dozens of trucks laden with supplies of every sort.

While the first attacking waves dealt with German resistance around the beachhead, the fresh troops of 56th Infantry Brigade had orders to leapfrog these skirmishes, seize the region's capital city, Bayeux, and establish a front line a mile and a half beyond it.

In the lead were the 2nd South Wales Borderers and 2nd Essex, followed by the 2nd Glosters. They advanced very slowly and by midnight Bayeux, though undefended and within reach, had not been taken. Meanwhile, the three Durham battalions of the 151st Brigade advanced up behind the Green Howards and East Yorks on their left and Borderers, Essex and Glosters on their right. They had reached the main road that ran from Bayeux to Caen by 8.30pm and had continued on well beyond Villiers-le-Sec, before being halted by darkness not far from the eastern outskirts of Bayeux.

A total of 24,970 men had landed on Gold by midnight at a cost of 413 casualties – 182 of whom were from the 1st Hampshires and 90 were from the 5th East Yorkshires. ∎

THE MAN THEY COULDN'T KILL
Stanley Hollis – D-Day's only VC

The house with the circular drive on King Green beach nicknamed 'Lavatory Pan Villa'. This photo was handed to tank crews of the 4th/7th Royal Dragoon Guards shortly before H-Hour on D-Day.

The first viable route inland from King Green was up a track which ran past a large farmhouse nicknamed 'Lavatory Pan Villa' because of its broad circular driveway. A bunker complex had been built around it.

Earlier in the day, D Company of the 6th Green Howards had been preparing to go ashore from *SS Empire Lance*. The unit's commanding officer Major Ronnie Lofthouse handed a box of condoms, for waterproofing the ends of rifles, to Sergeant Major Stanley Hollis to pass around.

Hollis, a gruff 6ft 2in 31-year-old veteran from Middlesbrough, replied: "What are we going to do? Are we going to fight the Germans or f**k them?"

D Company went ashore with only light casualties, although Hollis saw a man jump off a landing craft into a submerged shell hole and get cut to pieces by the vessel's propeller as it passed over him. They managed to get past the minefields at the top of the beach and on to the track which led to Lavatory Pan Villa before they came under machine-gun fire and were forced to take cover.

At first the men couldn't tell which direction the bullets were coming from but then Lofthouse spotted a well-camouflaged bunker near the farmhouse. He pointed it out to Hollis, who then got up and ran at it, firing his Sten 9mm submachine gun.

The Germans fired back but missed and Hollis was able to jump on top of the bunker and toss a grenade through the firing slit. After it went off, he climbed down and opened the bunker's back door. Two of the Germans inside were dead and the rest were in no condition to continue the fight. He then marched down a connecting trench to another bunker, changing the magazine of his Sten as he went, and took all 20 of the Germans inside prisoner.

Advancing further inland with his men, Hollis was shot in the face by a German sniper. The bullet only grazed him but caused him to bleed freely.

Three hours after landing, D Company reached Crepon on the main road to Bayeux and was again held up by the enemy. Hollis and his platoon had been ordered to clear a farmhouse, which they found to be empty. The Sergeant Major then decided to have a look round the back and was immediately fired upon. He saw two dogs jumping up at someone through a gap in a hedge and what looked like a German field gun in the orchard beyond.

Hollis ordered eight men to shoot up the hedge with Bren guns. They got up, ran to carry out his orders and were shot dead. Hollis, armed with a PIAT launcher and two other men carrying Bren guns then crawled forward towards the field gun through a dense patch of rhubarb.

At the edge of the rhubarb, Hollis fired his PIAT and missed. The Germans then fired their field gun and also missed, blowing the chimney off the farmhouse behind him. Realising he was overmatched, Hollis retreated, only to discover that the two men he'd taken with him had remained behind and were now pinned down. He told Lofthouse: "Well, I took them in, I will try and get them out." Taking a Bren gun, he went back to the men's position alone. The field gun's crew opened fire on him with Spandau machine guns but missed and Hollis returned fire from the hip to keep their heads down until his two soldiers could escape.

For these two actions, Stan Hollis was awarded D-Day's only Victoria Cross. His citation read: "Wherever fighting was heaviest, Sergeant Major Hollis appeared, and in the course of a magnificent day's work he displayed the utmost gallantry, and on two separate occasions his courage and initiative prevented the enemy from holding up the advance at critical stages. It was largely through his heroism and resource that the company's objectives were gained and casualties were not heavier and, by his own bravery, he saved the lives of many of his men."

He died in 1972 aged 59.

Sergeant Major Stanley Hollis of the 6th Green Howards.

CHAPTER 12

From the jaws of defeat
Omaha beach

It was understood from the outset that Omaha beach would be difficult to assault without the units involved suffering at least moderate casualties. As it was, the Americans barely managed to avoid catastrophe.

The *USS Texas* fires on Omaha while LCT 763 makes its way into shore.

The American approach to assaulting Normandy was somewhat different to that of the British and Canadians by necessity. Rather than utilising a host of specialist weaponry such as Sherman Crab mine flails, demolition charge-firing AVREs or ARC bridge carriers, the US forces were forced to rely on the carefully coordinated application of overwhelming firepower.

During the planning stages of Overlord, having seen and been impressed by Hobart's funnies, the US Army assumed it would be using AVREs and even put in orders for 25 Crabs and 100 Sherman Crocodile flamethrowers. These plans had to be cancelled however and the orders went unfulfilled because British industry could barely keep up with demand from the British Army for these specialist vehicles, let alone the US.

Troops of E Company, 16th Infantry Regiment, 1st Infantry Division wade on to Fox Green from their LCVP at H-Hour on D-Day.

LCVPs carrying American soldiers on the final run in to Omaha beach.

White clouds billow from a smoke grenade set off by enemy fire on board LCVP PA26-15 at 7am on its way in to Fox Green.

Prior to the expansion of the invasion front to include what became Utah beach, Omaha was the furthest point to the right and as such was the beginning of the Normandy beach 'alphabet'. It was divided up, from right to left, into Able, Baker, Charlie, Dog Green, Dog White, Dog Red, Fox Green, Fox Red, Easy Green and Easy Red sectors.

As with the other beaches, Omaha was defended in the first instance by numerous obstacles including Belgian gates, stakes topped with Tellermines and hedgehogs. There were 3700 of these and others on Omaha, more per square foot of beach than anywhere else on D-Day. In addition, there was a bank of slippery shingle positioned at the high water mark and beyond that a sea wall in several places. Rows of barbed wire came next along with minefields.

At the top of the beach rose a steep 150ft grassy slope or bluff – a feature not seen on other invasion beaches – bookended by vertical cliffs. The only way off Omaha short of climbing the bluff, which was just about possible for troops but impossible for vehicles, was via five gullies. Only two of these were suitable for motorised vehicles.

The Germans had naturally fortified each gully to the greatest possible degree with wire, obstacles, trenches and tank traps. They also built bunkers housing machine guns and anti-tank weapons into the sides of the bluff. There were 14 'Widerstandsnester' concrete strongpoints numbered WN60 to WN73 and they were made up of 85 machine gun nests, 35 Nebelwerfer rocket launcher positions, 35 pillboxes, 18 anti-tank guns, eight concrete bunkers housing guns that were 75mm or larger, six mortar pits and six tank turrets.

The forces assigned to tackle this formidable landing ground were known as regimental combat teams. On the left, going in on Fox Red and Green and Easy Red and Green, would be the 16th RCT, which was the 16th Infantry Regiment of the 1st Division 'The Big Red One' with various support units.

On the right, tackling Dog Red, White and Green and Charlie, was the 116th RCT. This was the 116th Infantry Regiment of the

Landing craft drop their troops off on Easy Red near WN62 and WN64 at H-Hour. The soldiers advance with water up to the waist in front of LCVPs PA 26-18 and PA 26-19.

29th Division and its support including combat engineers whose job it would be to remove beach obstacles. Once the first two RCTs had gone in, followup waves would see another two landed by noon. Armoured support for the 16th was to be provided by the 741st Tank Battalion while the 116th was supported by the 743rd Tank Battalion.

Right of Charlie, 2nd Ranger Battalion of the Provisional Ranger Group was to take the fortified clifftop artillery battery at Pointe du Hoc with its six 155mm guns.

THE OPENING BARRAGE

Force O gathered off Omaha beach at 3am on June 6. The infantry who would form the first wave began clambering into their assault craft at 4am and by 6am they were almost in position to begin their final run. Many were suffering from seasickness as a result of the choppy waters they had been motoring through for nearly two hours.

Covering the assault were the battleships *USS Texas* and *USS Arkansas,* four light

cruisers – *HMS Glasgow* and *HMS Bellona* and the French *Montcalm* and *Georges Leygues* – and 12 destroyers.

German onshore batteries began to fire at the destroyers *USS Emmons* and *USS Doyle* at 5.30am but the first vessel to begin fighting back was the *Montcalm*. Then the destroyers *USS Baldwin*, the *Doyle*, the *Emmons* and *USS Harding* started shelling the batteries too, silencing them by 5.51am.

A minute later *USS Arkansas's* 12in guns opened up and *HMS Glasgow* pounded the bluff above Dog Red and Easy Green. *Georges Leygues* and *HMS Tanatside* used their 4in and 6in guns to blow chunks out of the bluff above Easy Green and Easy Red.

By now nearly all the vessels were firing at onshore targets. It was an impressive display of raw firepower and 10 minutes after it began, 446 B-24 Liberators from the US Army Air Force flew over the coastline and dropped some 13,000 bombs – but none hit their targets. The night before the assault, orders had been changed and the drop was delayed by 30 seconds because it was feared that US units might be hit. This was enough time for the bombers to fly far inland and completely miss Omaha's defences. Shortly before the first landing craft were due to touch down, nine LCT(R)s opened up with a deafening barrage of rockets intended to detonate minefields, carve out craters in the beach for the attackers to shelter in and blast away some of the defensive obstacles.

Some troops reported seeing the rockets miss the beach and splash down in the water instead but many did hit home.

It had been planned that the DD Shermans of the 743rd Tank Battalion, going in with the 116th Infantry on the right, would launch at 5.30am and swim in under their own steam. The officers of the LCTs carrying the 743rd had so little faith in the unit's 'swimming' tanks they insisted on dropping them right on the beach.

One LCT sank on the way in but the remainder made it on to Dog Green and Dog Red between 6.30am and 7am. Four tanks were knocked out before they got to the beach leaving 40 out of 48 Shermans to provide fire support as the 116th went ashore.

On the left-hand side of the assault, Companies B and C of the 741st Tank Battalion (B/741st and C/741st) had driven their amphibious Shermans into the sea as ordered at 5.40am some 15,000ft from the shore. Many sank before travelling more than a few feet. Just two managed to swim all the way in and a further three were taken in by the skipper of their landing craft who'd watched the first of the four tanks he was carrying sink like a stone when it rolled off the ramp. This left the soldiers of the 16th on Easy Red beach supported by just five out of 32 DD Sherman tanks.

A/741st was equipped with regular Shermans and Sherman dozers and three of these were sent to the bottom when a mine blew a hole in their landing craft.

A view of WN64 up on the bluff at the back of the picture as seen from Easy Red.

THE INFANTRY

While the tanks were struggling, the infantry were arriving. Their landings commenced at 6.31am though most of their craft ground to a halt on a series of sandbars between 50ft and 300ft from dry land.

Lieutenant Jimmy Green, commanding a landing craft in the first wave carrying members of the A/116th, said: "We went flat out and crunched to a halt some 20 or 30 yards from the shore line. The beach was flat so that we couldn't go any further so the troops had to go in single file up to their waists in water and wade to the shore through tide runnels.

"They all made the beach safely and formed a firing line at a slight rise. At this time there was a lull in the German firing. They had been plopping mortar shells around us and firing an anti-tank gun but suddenly they ceased firing."

The infantry, now on Dog Green, were advancing on the gully which led up the bluff to Vierville when abruptly the German positions opened up, cutting down almost every man in the line. Around 100 members of A/116th were killed or seriously wounded within a few seconds. Troops who'd landed at the same time on Dog Red and Easy Green further to the left suffered the same fate. The Gap Assault Team demolition crews following the first wave were hit as well.

Team 11 was hauling its rubber boat filled with explosives ashore in front of the St Laurent gully when an 88mm round hit it and detonated the cargo, killing all the engineers in a massive explosion. Team 7 had set charges on obstacles and was about to blow them up when a landing craft collided with a post and detonated the Tellermine on it plus six others and all the team's explosives in one prodigious blast.

Team 15 were killed when another shell hit the landing craft of the neighbouring Team 14 and detonated their explosives. Having planted their explosives on obstacles on part of Easy Red, Team 12 hesitated, fearing the blast would kill wounded soldiers nearby. Then a mortar round ignited them anyway, obliterating the team and the wounded men.

By 7am many of the first wave had become casualties. Some units had lost all of their officers and every radio set was either wrecked by seawater, destroyed or attached to the body of a dead man and out of reach to the survivors.

Photographer Robert Capa, working for LIFE magazine, went in with the 16th. He said: "The flat bottom of our barge hit the earth of France. The boatswain lowered the steel covered large front, and there, between the grotesque designs of steel obstacles sticking out of the water, was Easy Red beach. My beautiful France looked sordid and uninviting, and a German machine gun, spitting bullets around the barge, fully spoiled my return.

"Then men from my barge waded in the water. Waist-deep, with rifles ready to shoot, with the invasion obstacles and the smoking beach in the background – this was good enough for the photographer. I paused for a moment on the gangplank to take my first

Soldiers of the 18th Infantry Regiment watch the shore as they head for Easy Red at around 10.30am. They landed just west of WN65, which was still held by the Germans at that time.

Sailors aboard their vessel watch helplessly as a large explosion, possibly that of a mine, goes off on Easy Red sector. The man to the right wears a US Navy talker's helmet.

American follow-up assault troops, carrying full equipment, move on to Omaha.

Two regiments of US reinforcements begin to arrive at noon. This vessel was headed for the beach between WN64 and WN65 which was already in American hands.

real picture of the invasion. The boatswain who was in an understandable hurry to get the hell out of there, mistook my picture taking for explicable hesitation, and helped me make up my mind with a well-aimed kick in the rear.

"The water was cold, and the beach still more than 100 yards away. The bullets tore holes in the water around me, and I made for the nearest steel obstacle. A soldier got there at the same time, and for a few minutes we shared its cover. He took the waterproofing off his rifle and began to shoot without much aiming. The sound of his rifle gave him enough courage to move forward, and he left the obstacle to me. It

was a foot larger now, and I felt safe enough to take pictures of the other guys hiding just like I was."

He said that he had tried to move away from the beach obstacle but the machine gun fire was too intense.

"Fifty yards ahead of me, one of our half-burnt amphibious tanks stuck out of the water and offered me my next cover. I sized up the situation. There was little future for the elegant raincoat heavy on my arm. I dropped it and made for the tank. Between floating bodies I reached it, paused for a few more pictures, and gathered my guts for the last jump to the beach. Now the Germans played on all their instruments, and I could

not find any hole between the shells and bullets that blocked the last 25 yards to the beach. I just stayed behind my tank.

"I didn't dare to take my eyes off the finder of my Contax and frantically shot frame after frame. Half a minute later, my camera jammed – my roll was finished. I reached in my bag for a new roll, and my wet shaking hands ruined the roll before I could insert it in my camera.

"I paused for a moment… and then I had it bad. The empty camera trembled in my hands. It was a new kind of fear shaking my body from toe to hair and twisting my face. An LCI braved the fire and medics with red crosses painted on their helmets poured

THE BEAST OF OMAHA

Overlooking the left-hand side of Easy Red beach, where photographer Robert Capa landed with the 16th, was strongpoint WN62.

At a machine gun position encased in thick concrete was 21-year-old German Corporal Heinrich 'Hein' Severloh of the 352nd Infantry Division.

He had watched in disbelief as the invasion fleet appeared. Beside him a comrade, Sergeant Krone, said: "They must be crazy. Are they going to swim ashore? Right under our muzzles?"

WN62 had precise ranges to beach obstacles painted on the inside of its forward viewing aperture so Severloh, manning the MG42 machine gun, knew precisely where to fire to hit any given target on the beach below. The men of the 16th leapt from their landing craft and began wading ashore at around 6.30am.

Severloh said later: "My order was to get them when they were still in one line, one after the other, before they started spreading. So I did not have to swing my gun sideways. I saw how the water sprayed up where my machine gun bursts landed, and when the small fountains came closer to the GIs, they threw themselves down. Very soon the first bodies were drifting in the waves of the rising ride. In a short time, all GIs down there were shot."

He estimated that over the next seven hours or so he fired 12,000 rounds from his machine gun plus another 400 from a pair of rifles and believed he had personally killed more than 1000 American infantrymen.

In fact, Severloh kept firing even when the positions on either side, WN61 and WN63, were overrun and only deserted his position in the afternoon when it was clear that the defences around him had fallen. He fled to Colleville and surrendered on June 7. He survived the war and died in 2006.

US Rangers at the foot of Pointe du Hoc prepar climb on to the top of the promontory.

from it. I did not think and I didn't decide it. I just stood up and ran toward the boat. I stepped into the sea between two bodies and the water reached to my neck. The rip tide hit my body and every wave slapped my face under my helmet.

"I held my camera high above my head, and I suddenly knew that I was running away. I reached the boat. The skipper was crying. His assistant had been blown up all over him and he was a mess."

SLAUGHTER ON THE BEACH

On the right-hand side of the attack, Dog Green, Richard Merrill, a captain in the 2nd Ranger Battalion, quickly realised that his mission to meet up with the other rangers at Pointe du Hoc was already over before it had begun. He said: "We thought getting across the beach would be no problem – but it didn't turn out that way.

"The tide was lower than we thought. There was a longer area to cross, and it was cross-stitched with fire. Small arms fire, machine gun fire, mortar fire, artillery fire. I was the first one off the craft. Captain Frank Corder, from Texas, was the next man off. And I remember Frank's exact words: 'This is no place for Mrs Corder's little boy Frank.'

"You knew the shortest path was a straight one right across the beach. You'd hear 'zip zip', just strings of machine gun bullets and automatic weapons criss-crossing paths. You're soaking wet and everything is heavy. You'd try to time it to run and you'd fall. You'd run on a dry piece of sand and then hit water and immediately

tumble, get up and keep going. I don't remember anyone right with me. I was just hoping the others were coming behind me.

"There were bodies around in the water, and there were others once you got across. One of the men from my boat, we saw him get hit and tumble and get up, and we were hollering 'Keep going Rusty!' I saw Frank Corder too, but he was tough to recognise because he'd lost an eye and teeth."

Nine companies landed in the first wave but only A/116th and the Rangers, landing on the right, were where they were supposed to be. E/116th ended up on Easy Red in the 16th's area where its survivors, having lost most of their equipment swimming ashore, mixed with those of E/16th and F/16th. The latter had landed near the Colleville gully and when the ramps of its landing craft dropped the Germans were able to fire right into them. Half the company was killed within two minutes. G/116th was 3000ft off to the left of its intended destination and landed relatively unscathed thanks to smoke blowing across the beach.

F/116th landed where G/116th should have been and was hit by the defences of the Les Moulins gully. It suffered heavy casualties. I/16th drifted off Omaha entirely and landed an hour and a half after H-Hour at 8am having had two of its six boats sink. Another one got stuck on an obstacle and the remaining three were damaged by artillery or mines.

L/16th landed half an hour late, also way off to the left, but managed to cross 600ft of beach relatively intact. A/116th took the heaviest casualties on Dog Green to the right – every soldier who had been in the company commander's landing craft was killed – and the rangers who landed with them lost 35 men out of 64 before they had

More reinforcements wade ashore on Omaha.

A soldier stoops to readjust his heavy load as more troops head for the shore.

reached the cliff on the far right of the beach.

All companies with the exception of L/16th were scattered and pinned down. Most were leaderless. Surviving combat engineers had managed to blast six gaps through barbed wire and mines to the top of the beach – one on Dog White, one on Easy Green and four on Easy Red.

A small group of men from E/16th managed to get through one of the Easy Red gaps and made its way up the bluff to attack one of the strongpoints, WN62, from behind. Meanwhile, F/16th knocked out one of position's pillboxes with a bazooka.

Small groups of soldiers also managed to begin attacking WN61, the main strongpoint on Fox Green before a tank of the 741st knocked out the position's 88mm gun with a direct hit. Another bunker of WN62 was blasted by a Sherman at 7.45am.

BACK FROM THE BRINK

Out at sea, Rear Admiral Bryant and his fellow naval officers could only look on and await requests for fire support. He wrote: "After our allotted time, our fire ceased, and we awaited calls from our fire control officers sent ashore in the landing parties, but none came. Later we learned that nearly all had been killed." Having arrived at 7am amid the bodies and horribly wounded

American assault troops of the 3rd Battalion, 16th Infantry Regiment, 1st Infantry Division move along the base of a cliff at Colleville-sur-Mer past piles of equipment.

A large group of American assault troops having gained the comparative safety offered by the chalk cliff at their backs take a breather before moving on.

SAVING PRIVATE RYAN

The dramatic and horrifying opening sequence of 1998 American war film Saving Private Ryan depicts Company A of the 116th and a company of the 2nd Rangers landing in the teeth of German machine gun fire on Omaha's Dog Green and Charlie beaches.

Empire magazine has called it the "best battle scene of all time" and it regularly appears in 'best of' lists whenever war films are mentioned.

Shot in Ireland at a cost of $12 million, the sequence involved 1500 extras including more than 20 amputees who portrayed seriously wounded GIs.

Twelve real Second World War landing craft were used during filming – 10 LCVP 'Higgins' boats and two LCMs which took the place of the British LCAs that carried the rangers in. Forty barrels of fake blood were used to turn the seawater red.

A young GI is treated for concussion and an injury to his right cheek at the foot of the cliff of Colleville sur Mer under WN60 on Fox Red among others exhausted and wounded belonging to the 3rd Battalion of the 16th RCT.

survivors of the first wave, the second wave found itself pinned down at the water's edge by machine gun and mortar fire.

On the far right, B/116th, C/116th and D/116th were meant to follow the now broken A/116th in on Dog Green but they were scattered by the strong offshore tide much as the first wave had been and some landed right off Omaha under the cliffs to the side. Those members of B/116 that landed in the right place then joined the survivors of A/116th in their struggle to stay alive at the water's edge.

H/116th landed on the border of Dog Red and Easy Green and was badly mauled by the defences there – at Les Moulins.

C/116th was drawn to the left and landed on Dog White, away from the deadly machine guns of Dog Green. Here, smoke from grass fires covered their advance and

they managed to jog up to the sea wall with few casualties. The similarly intact 5th Rangers then joined them and the entire Dog Green assault was diverted to the left to land on Dog White instead.

An hour later the beaches were heavily congested with burning vehicles, wrecked landing craft and scattered debris. Many of the most badly injured GIs drowned as the tide rose over them.

DUKWs bringing in artillery and supplies were picked off one after another as they tried to land. Brigadier General Norman Cota and Colonel Charles D W Canham of the 116th landed at 7.30am – Cota on Dog White and Canham on Dog Red. They found their men huddled behind obstacles, unwilling or unable to move. Canham, who had been shot through the wrist shortly after landing, screamed at his men to get up and start killing Germans. He roared at one lieutenant huddled in the remains of a pillbox: "Get your ass out of there and show some leadership!"

Finally galvanising the men, from F and G/116th, into action he led them up and over the bluff. Cota led his own party of men from C/116th up to a point at the base of the bluff where the undulating terrain sheltered them from the German crossfire.

Knocked out US vehicles covering Dog beach west of Les Moulins, after the assault on the beach. The tank, Ceaseless, is from C Company of the 743rd Tank Battalion.

LCT 207 was meant to land on Dog White at 8am carrying SPGs of the 58th Armoured Field Artillery Battalion but found it was unable to do so. It finally landed on Dog Red at 4pm instead. The smoke is from landing craft destroyed earlier in the day.

84 D-DAY – OVERLORD

They began to climb. Simultaneously, the 5th Rangers on Dog White blew four of their own gaps in the wire and also started up the bluff. The three different parties met up at the top and began to fan out.

At 9am, the *USS Frankford*, nicknamed 'the Hot Dog' arrived off Easy Red sector with the commander of Omaha's destroyer fleet, Commodore Harry Sanders, on board. He saw what was happening, realised fire control teams on the beaches had been killed, and ordered his vessels to get in close to the beach and fire at anything which looked like a target.

At 10am, Cota's small group had grown sufficiently in size for him to send a force of C/116th and 5th Rangers into Vierville beyond Dog White and Dog Red while still more rangers moved to cut off the village's access roads.

THE WOODEN BATTERY

Off to the far right of the Omaha battlefront was the battery at Point-du-Hoc which had been mercilessly pummeled by US Navy shellfire first thing in the morning on D-Day. The 2nd Rangers assigned to put the big guns out of commission, 200 men in 10 British LCA landing craft with DUKWs carrying ladders, arrived 40 minutes late due to a navigation error.

The boat carrying the unit's commanding officer had sunk way out at sea, reducing the small flotilla to nine, but when they arrived they set off their rocket-powered grappling hooks as planned. The DUKWs could not reach the base of the cliff for their ladders to be of any practical use because shellfire from the *USS Texas* had caused part of the stone cliff face to collapse into a slope of rubble.

The German garrison had exited their bunkers by now and, spotting the rangers immediately below them, opened fire causing 15 casualties. At this point the *USS Satterlee* provided close fire support from its four big 5in guns and drove the Germans back. Minutes later the first rangers were at

US reinforcements arrive on Omaha. Vehicles are stranded on the shingle bank and cannot cross. To the far left, the valley of Colleville is still in German hands.

the top of the shattered cliffs and after reaching the battery itself they discovered that the huge artillery pieces Allied intelligence had thought would be there had been replaced with wooden decoys.

When the rangers eventually found the real guns inland, they spiked two of them with grenades and broke their delicate sighting instruments. The Germans swiftly fought back and the rangers were soon besieged on the clifftop and fighting for their lives. A relief force fronted by Sherman tanks eventually arrived on the morning of June 8.

Back on the main invasion beach on D-Day, as further waves landed on Easy Red and Easy Green, and the German defenders were gradually worn down, more and more men made it up over the bluff.

The tide had turned and the Americans gradually overwhelmed each of the 13 defensive positions before moving inland about a mile by the end of the day.

The total number of men landed on Omaha by midnight was by far the highest of any D-Day beach, in spite of everything, at 34,250. According to the official record, by the end of the day the Americans had suffered 2374 casualties – comprising 694 dead, 1349 wounded and 331 missing.

In later years there was a substantial amount of recrimination over these dramatic early losses. The USAAF's failed bombing raid at the outset was blamed, as were the Allied planners who failed to take note of how heavily defended Omaha was. Those who decided to follow orders and put their DD Sherman tanks into the sea 5000 yards out were criticized as were those who fired the opening salvos of rockets.

The American achievement in securing a victory on Omaha, albeit a narrow one, has since become a legend which has outshone many others' achievements on D-Day and become the popular modern image of the invasion as a whole. ∎

Troops of the 2nd Infantry Division scale the bluffs of Omaha before moving inland on June 7. The photo was taken from the top of WN65.

Nicholas Fina from I Company of the 3/16th stares at the photographer after being wounded during the assault on Fox Green.

CHAPTER 13

'We'll start the war from right here!'
Utah beach

The landings on Utah were in sharp contrast to those on Omaha – orderly, effective and with few casualties. German defences in the sector crumbled but not before they had claimed one high profile success...

On the deck of an LCT during the voyage to Utah from England are soldiers from the 101st Airborne Division and the 4th Infantry Division.

The landings on Utah were intended as a follow-up to the airborne assault which had taken place during the early hours of D-Day. Combined, these two operations were meant to cut off the German forces located on the Cotentin peninsula and enable the capture of Cherbourg on its northern coast.

With this important port in hand, the Allies would be able to dramatically increase the flow of men and materials into Normandy from the south coast of England. As with Omaha, it was believed that the forces defending the coast at the base of the Cotentin peninsula were second rate 'static' units – including older soldiers and press-ganged captured Soviet troops.

In contrast to Omaha, Allied intelligence was right about Utah. The defenders, though numerous, suffered from low morale and were seriously under-equipped. Most of their tanks were obsolete French or Czech designs and their weaponry was a mixture of outdated captured stock and basic rather than advanced German materiel. What the Germans on the Cotentin did have plenty of, however, was powerful coastal gun batteries – nine of them on the same side of the peninsula as Utah.

The US Army's 4th Division was chosen for the amphibious D-Day attack. The lead unit would be the 8th Infantry Regiment with armoured support from the 70th Tank Battalion, which was highly experienced having already participated in the campaigns for both North Africa and Sicily.

They would go in on two landing zones, Uncle Red on the left and Tare Green on the right. Along the entire length of Utah were Widerstandsnester 1 to 14 but the invasion front was narrow to the point where only a handful of these would need to be overcome by frontal assault.

Two of the battalion's three medium tank companies were equipped with DD Shermans while the third was to land with regular Shermans. It had been planned to equip the third company's tanks with rocket launchers to help them breach concrete defences and blow apart beach obstacles but these were demonstrated to be ineffective so the idea was dropped.

Reconnaissance of the Utah sector revealed that the Germans had flooded

Infantry and vehicles head for the shore in this aerial view of the Utah landings.

The battleship *USS Nevada* fires on the German defences on Utah ahead of the invasion.

large areas immediately behind the landing zone and the only way inland was via a series of narrow causeways. Any men or vehicles attempting to cross these would be exposed and vulnerable to German forces defending the other end – which was why a large part of the plan for Utah relied on the airborne landings outlined in chapter 8.

The Germans felt these marshes made the beaches fronting them unattractive as a landing ground and this in turn led to the beach defences themselves being given a lower priority.

Utah had significantly fewer beach obstacles than neighbouring Omaha and the beach itself was flatter which would make it easier for the attackers to cross and harder for the defenders to shoot at anything beyond what was immediately in front of them.

Several of the Cotentin coast's numerous gun batteries were within range of Utah – particularly dangerous were those at St Martin-de-Varreville, which housed a quartet of 122mm guns captured from the Soviets; Azeville with four 105mm guns captured from the French; Morsalines with six French 155mms and Crisbecq which housed three monstrous 210mm guns made by Skoda in Czechoslovakia. They would have to be dealt with by bombing or by the airborne troops.

Force U's bombardment group consisted of the battleship *USS Nevada*, monitor *HMS Erebus*, heavy cruisers *USS Quincy*, *USS Tuscaloosa* and *HMS Hawkins*, cruiser *HMS Black Prince*, light cruiser *HMS Enterprise*, Dutch gunboat *Soemba* and eight destroyers – *USS Fitch*, *USS Forrest*, *USS Corry*, *USS Hobson*, *USS Herndon*, *USS Shubrick*, *USS Butler* and *USS Gherardi*.

There was less supporting naval firepower available at Utah – fewer truly big guns – but then resistance was expected to be less fierce than on other beaches.

LCT 475 drops B Battery of the 65th Armored Field Artillery Battalion on to Uncle Red mid-morning on D-Day.

US troops landing on Utah Beach. They were in the wrong place but the German defences were far weaker here than on Omaha.

OPENING SALVOS

The Crisbecq battery opened fire on the *USS Fitch* and *USS Corry* at 5.05am and the Morsalines battery started shooting at a minesweeper doing its job 10,000ft off the coast. *HMS Black Prince* responded while the *USS Nevada* also now came under fire. *USS Quincy* joined in at 5.37am and scored a direct hit on a machine gun emplacement at 6am. The other vessels began to pound their targets and the artillery duel continued for more than an hour.

Fire was directed at beach targets on Uncle Red and Tare Green from 5.50am onwards as per the original invasion plan, a mirror image of those being enacted up and down the Normandy coast as Overlord swung into action.

The Utah bombing unit's 269 USAAF B-26 Marauders began their bombing run on the beach defences at 6.05am but instead of remaining high above the clouds as their counterparts on Omaha did, the pilots decided to fly in below 3500ft so they could see exactly what they were targeting – even though this meant breaking the rules which said they were to remain at between 3500ft and 7000ft.

General Theodore Roosevelt III in Normandy.

They hit the Germans with 4300 250lb bombs and many found their targets. More aircraft flew in to lay a smokescreen in front of the navy vessels off Utah at 6.10am but the aircraft meant to screen the *USS Corry* was shot down by German anti-aircraft fire before it could accomplish its mission. A fire control man on board the *Corry*, Emil Vestuti, said: "There were two planes flying by laying smoke to protect the boats that were coming up and as this one plane was getting ready to cover us, it got shot down and that left us exposed. Then it seemed like everything on the beach just concentrated on *Corry*."

There was an almighty explosion and the whole ship shuddered violently. The engines coughed and died and at 6.41am the order was given to abandon ship. When *USS Butler* had collected as many survivors as possible, the final death toll stood at 24 with another 59 men wounded. At around the same time, beach control vessel PC-1261 took a direct hit, disintegrating immediately in a burst of fire and debris. A Landing Craft Tank, LCT-597, hit a mine and also went down, taking its four DD Shermans with it.

With the DD tank landings falling behind schedule and only 28 of the 70th Tank Battalion's 32 Shermans remaining, the naval officers in charge decided that they had to launch their cargo into the sea closer to shore. These swimming tanks therefore entered the water just 4500ft from the beach instead of the planned 15,000ft.

The first wave of infantry, four companies of the 8th Infantry Regiment, went in on board 20 LCVPs, landing at 6.30am. Companies E and F came ashore on Uncle Red while B and C landed on Tare Green. The tanks came in 10 minutes later.

It was clear that something had gone wrong. None of the landmarks matched up with what had been expected and it was quickly realised that the entire first wave had landed at La Grande Dune, 6000ft to the left of where it was supposed to be. Offshore currents and poor visibility caused by smoke from the bombing had left the 8th's carefully laid attack plans in tatters.

Luckily, the 8th had instead been put in an even better position than expected. Instead of coming ashore facing two strongpoints, they faced just one – WN5 – which had been partially demolished already by the USAAF's aerial attack.

When all 28 DD Shermans arrived, none of them having sunk, they rolled up on to the beach and began firing their main guns into WN5's surviving bunkers and the seawall.

Horrified by these tanks rising out of the sea, the commander of WN5, 23-year-old Eastern Front veteran Second Lieutenant Arthur Jahnke, said: "Here was a truly lunatic sight. I wondered if I was hallucinating as a result of the bombardment. Amphibious tanks – this must be the Allies' secret weapon."

Only a few minutes earlier, one of his elderly orderlies had run in shouting: "Everything's wrecked! Everything's wrecked! We've got to surrender!" but

A detachment of DUKWs heads for Utah beach carrying supplies.

A Dodge vehicle drives through the surf towards the beach north of WN5 in Uncle Red sector.

Jahnke was not going to give in without a fight. His position had one 88mm anti-tank gun, an old Renault tank turret mounted over a dug-in concrete position and a small selection of old machine guns and mortars.

He also had a number of the new Goliath remote controlled mines. These 4ft long tracked machines, packed with explosives, had been concealed in little shelters along the seafront ready to be driven out right under the tracks of attacking tanks and blown up. Unfortunately for Jahnke, the bombing had cut all the wires between his command bunker and these unusual devices, rendering them useless.

An explosion then tore into WN5 and Jahnke was rendered unconscious, his body half buried in sand and debris. When he came to at around noon there was an American pointing a rifle at him.

The first wave of US infantry had suffered very few casualties and now the second wave came ashore carrying demolition teams and engineers who immediately set about clearing the beach of obstacles.

ADVANCING INLAND

The eldest son of 26th American President Theodore Roosevelt, General Theodore Roosevelt III, was the first senior officer on the beach. At 56 he was also the oldest man to take part in the landings, having requested that he be put on the front line.

On being told that he and his men had landed in the wrong place, he walked up the beach with the aid of his cane – which he had been forced to use since suffering a heart attack – and noted that Exit 2 was visible behind the ruins of WN5. On returning, he approached the commanders of the 8th's first wave and told them it didn't matter that they'd gone off course: "We'll start the war from right here!"

The follow-up waves came in on the new landing zone rather than at the originally designated beaches. By 9am the 8th Infantry and the 70th Tank Battalion were streaming across the Exit 2 causeway.

The retreating German defenders had detonated an explosive charge resulting in a gap in the causeway but this was quickly

The scene on Utah on June 8. Temporary roadways have been constructed and vehicles continue to move ashore after landing on the beach.

covered with a makeshift bridge. Then the leading tank broke down, stalling the tank behind it which was then knocked out by a German anti-tank gun. The third tank wasted no time in destroying the gun, the wrecked tank was shoved off the causeway and the advance continued, only to be slowed by the causeway's narrowness.

Some units began wading through the flooded fields on either side with water up to their armpits. On the other side were minefields and as the soaked soldiers climbed up out of the water there were further delays while sappers cleared paths.

Once the 8th's 3rd Battalion was able to move directly inland from Exit 2 they encountered infantry from the German 1st Battalion of the 919th Grenadier Regiment, backed up by a platoon equipped with 75mm anti-tank guns. In the fierce and brutal firefight which followed 50 Germans were killed and the remainder, more than 100 men, surrendered. Once this obstacle was removed, the 8th sent forward a platoon of its own to make contact with troops of the 82nd Airborne Division near Chef-du-Pont.

The 2nd Battalion of the 8th moved down the sea wall rather than waiting for the congested causeway to become available, crushing small pockets of German resistance as it went. After smashing the poorly defended WN2a it reached Exit 1 near Pouppeville and linked up with the 501st airborne who had already mopped up German forces within the town.

While the 8th Infantry, which was still at close to full strength and barely blooded, was forging ahead, the rest of its parent division, the 4th, was landing on Utah along with another follow-up outfit, the 90th Division. The 12th and 22nd Infantry came ashore without difficulty and began moving north, as planned, although their progress was slowed by congestion. As D-Day itself ended, the American 4th Infantry Division had suffered just 43 men killed and 63 wounded out of 23,250 men landed.

Captain Frederick C Maisel, in the foreground crouched amid the marram grass, leads soldiers of I Company, 8th Infantry Regiment, 4th Infantry Division, off Uncle Red. The company has crossed the dunes and the two white cords indicate an area cleared of mines.

Soldiers of the 4th Infantry Division come ashore off Exit 1 from Utah beach supported by the DD Sherman of the 70th Tank Battalion.

Two columns of infantry from the 22nd Infantry Regiment, 4th Infantry Division, march through the flooded fields behind Utah en route to Saint Martin de Varreville.

CHAPTER 14

King Tigers and Moaning Minnies
German weapons of Normandy

Allied forces fighting their way inland from the beaches of Normandy came up against some of the deadliest weapons in the world. German tanks and infantry support weapons were highly advanced and, when they were available, the fighters and bombers of the Luftwaffe formed a first-rate fighting force.

The German soldiers charged with defending the Atlantic Wall went into action on June 6 wearing matt grey uniforms and short ankle boots, accompanied by canvas gaiters. Long gone were the shiny jackboots and glossy insignia of the early war 'Blitzkrieg' period.

The Waffen SS Panzer division infantry also wore a baggy pull-over camouflaged smock or 'tarnjacken' known as the M42. The German army had entered the war wearing the M1935 pattern helmet, the 'Stahlhelme', and by 1944 the standard helmet was the M1942. Both were similar to the design used during the First World War, but the M1942 in particular was of inferior quality. Its finish was rougher, paint was less well applied and the lining was sparser.

Webbing consisted of a leather belt with Y-straps that went over the shoulders and attached to this were pouches for ammunition, a bayonet, an entrenching tool, a bread bag, a gas-mask container, and a water bottle.

A wide range of weapons were used by front-line German soldiers, but the most common was the basic 7.92mm Mauser K98 bolt-action rifle. It had entered service in 1935, but was generally just an update of the M1898 rifle with which German infantrymen had fought the First World War. It had a five-round magazine and was reasonably accurate.

German soldiers engage in a spot of target practice. The two nearest the camera are wearing camouflaged smocks.

The German equivalent of the British Bren or American BAR light machine gun was the MG42, which fired the same ammunition as the K98 and was in the process of replacing the earlier MG34 by 1944. It was the heaviest of the three countries' light machine guns at 25.5lb, but had a much higher rate of fire at around 1200rpm.

Squad leaders, paratroopers and tank crews were sometimes equipped with 9mm MP40 sub-machine guns – the equivalent of the British Sten and American Thompson. It had a higher muzzle velocity than either, but was less accurate than the Sten at long range. Its rate of fire was on a par with the Sten, but both were beaten by the Thompson's incredible 600 to 1500rpm, depending on model.

The MP40 was often known as the 'Schmeisser' by the Allies, after Hugo Schmeisser, who had invented the first widely used submachine gun, the MP18, towards the end of the First World War. In fact, Schmeisser had no involvement in the MP40's design, it being the work of Berthold Geipel and Heinrich Vollmer, who were employed by Erma Werke.

Erma Werke even ended up suing Schmeisser for copyright infringement when he produced a version of the MP40 while working for Haenel, the MP41, which was essentially the same gun, but with a wooden stock. Erma won the case.

German soldiers carried a variety of pistols from the famous but antiquated 9mm P-08 Luger semi-automatic to the much more modern Walther P-38, introduced in 1940. The third main type was an American design – the Browning Hi-Power. John Browning had developed the design for the

German paratroopers armed with Panzerfaust and Panzerschrek shelter near an abandoned M4 Sherman in Normandy 1944.

This member of the Leibstandarte SS Adolf Hitler carries an MP40 sub-machine gun. It had a high muzzle velocity but a relatively low rate of fire.

The outdated MG34 light machine gun was still in use in Normandy in 1944.

French military, but died in 1926 before the gun was finalised.

The Hi-Power was finished off by Dieudonné Saive at Belgian firm Fabrique Nationale (known as FN) and it entered Belgian service in 1935. When the Germans occupied Belgium, FN was still making it so the Germans kept the production line going and began using it in large numbers.

Besides the K98, MG42 and MP40, German forces in Normandy also used a number of semi-automatic rifles – including the world's first true assault rifle. The first of these to have entered service was the Walther Gewehr 'rifle' 41 or G41, in 1941, but this proved to be unreliable and overly complex and was superseded by another Walther, the smaller, lighter and more reliable G43. It fired 7.92mm ammunition.

The German infantry's trump card, the Sturmgewehr, meaning literally 'assault rifle' entered limited service in October 1943. The StG44 was based on research which strongly indicated that most infantry gunfights took place at distances of less than 400m. It therefore sacrificed long-range accuracy for controllable fully automatic fire at short range and it had a long, curved detachable magazine holding 30 rounds. It was highly effective in combat, but very few examples were available in

Normandy until August 1944 onwards, due to political infighting and Hitler's meddling in the German armament industry – a fortunate situation for the Allies.

The German army still used the familiar Mod. 24 Steilhandgranate or 'stick grenade' in 1944, which was primed by pulling a cord which ran down the hollow handle. The Germans also had the smaller egg-shaped M39, which could be thrown further.

When it came to taking on tanks, the early Panzerbüchse 'tank rifle' had been replaced by the Faustpatrone Klein 30 'fist cartridge small' – the first in the highly successful Panzerfaust series, and its successor the Panzerfaust 30.

These one-shot disposable anti-tank weapons fired a pre-loaded high-explosive warhead capable of penetrating the armour of any Allied tank, though it only worked at relatively close range – about 100ft. Around

6% of all British tanks destroyed in Normandy had been hit by a Panzerfaust.

More effective still was the Panzerschrek 'tank terror' – effectively a copy of the American M1A1 Bazooka, but scaled up slightly to take larger ammunition. Its rocket-propelled-shaped charge warhead could punch through 200mm of armour – far more than any Allied design could boast – at 600ft.

Four main varieties of mortar were also employed by the Germans: the 5cm Granatwerfer 36, the 8cm Granatwerfer 34, the Granatwerfer 42, and the 8cm Granatwerfer 42.

ARMOURED SUPPORT
While the Allies relied heavily on armour to support their breakout from the Normandy beachhead, the Germans were even more reliant on it to stop them.

German Waffen-SS men pictured carrying a wide variety of equipment on the Eastern Front.

ZIMMERIT PASTE
German tanks and self-propelled guns manufactured between August 1943 and September 1944 were factory coated with a non-magnetic paste called Zimmerit, which gave their armour a ridged or patterned look up-close.

The paste, produced by Zimmer AG, was meant to prevent Allied troops from sticking magnetic mines to the vehicles' outer skin. The ridges were intended to increase the distance between the surface of the armour and any bomb that might be applied, since the magnetic fields were relatively weak.

The Allies did not use magnetic mines in Normandy – or in any other theatre of the war – but nevertheless the Germans persisted in applying the

paste for more than a year. It took around 200kg of the material to cover, for example, a Tiger tank to the required depth of 6mm.

Use of Zimmerit was discontinued in September 1944 because there were reports from frontline units that it could catch fire. The authorities tested armoured plates covered in the paste and refuted the suggestion but the Zimmerit ban remained in place.

In 2008, the SdKfz Military Vehicle Foundation, having restored a StuG, decided to scientifically replicate Zimmerit using the original recipe and test the claims that it was flammable. The tests found that Zimmerit prepared in cold weather – such as the winter of 1943/44 – would not 'cure' properly and since it contained benzene it became a significant fire risk.

With air cover frequently patchy or even nonexistent, the German army depended on its tanks and assault guns.

PANZER IV SD.KFZ.161

The most numerous German tank in Normandy was the Panzer IV Sd.Kfz.161. Designed as an infantry support tank as early as 1934, and entering production three years later, the Panzer IV was old. This, however, meant flaws had largely been ironed out and crews knew exactly how to extract the best performance from it.

Early versions were fitted with a stubby howitzer cannon mounted in the tank's turret, but by 1944, in Ausfuhrung or 'variant' H, this had been replaced by a long-barrelled 75mm cannon.

Also, by 1944 the Panzer IV was being used primarily as a medium tank rather than as a support vehicle. Its armour had been improved with the front becoming a single plate, 80mm thick, and side skirts were added to both its hull and turret to protect it from hollow-charge projectiles. Finally, Zimmerit paste was applied to all vertical surfaces to prevent infantry from sticking magnetic mines to it.

During fighting in bocage country in Normandy, it was not uncommon to see Panzer IVs with one or more plates missing from their side skirts. These were often torn off by obstacles such as trees or stone walls.

The Ausf H was the ultimate version of the Panzer IV, but a newer version could also be found in Normandy as the fighting progressed – the Ausf J. This was a cheaper, more easily produced, version of the tank which had had the electric motor that turned its turret replaced by an extra fuel tank. The J's unlucky crew could carry

A soldier eats his lunch beside his MG42 – the replacement for the MG34.

more precious juice, increasing range to 200 miles, but had to crank the turret around by manually turning a handle. The protective sideskirt armour plates were replaced with weight-saving wire mesh too.

PANZER V PANTHER SD.KFZ.171

When the Second World War began, the German army was equipped mainly with tanks designed several years earlier. The Panzer III was a 1935 design and even the most recent tank, the Panzer IV, dated from 1936. These proved to be more than a match for most of their Allied contemporaries, but in 1941 they came up against an enemy they could not overmatch

– the Russian T-34. This had highly effective sloped armour and a 76.2mm gun that could penetrate any German tank with ease.

The T-34's appearance among the ranks of a supposedly inferior enemy shocked the Germans and a rapid programme of development was begun to produce something to overcome or at least match it.

The result was the Panzer V Panther. It went from drawing board designs to full production in 18 months and featured sloping armour ,which was twice as thick as that of the T-34. Its main gun was a 75mm with exceptionally high muzzle velocity.

At the beginning of the Normandy campaign there were just 156 Panthers in France, but the number had risen to 436 by

GERMAN TANK SPECIFICATIONS

Panzer IV Sd.Kfz.161 Ausf H
Crew: Five (commander, gunner, loader, driver, radio operator/machine-gunner)
Weight: 25 tonnes
Engine: Maybach HL 120 TRM V12 petrol water-cooled, 11,870cc, 300hp
Maximum speed: 23mph road, 9mph cross-country
Range: 111 miles road, 75 miles cross-country
Armament: 75mm KwK 40 L/48 cannon, 2 x 7.92mm MG34 machine guns
Armour: 80mm maximum

Panzer V Panther Ausf G
Crew: Five (commander, gunner, loader, driver, radio operator/machine-gunner)
Weight: 45.5 tonnes
Engine: Maybach HL 230 P30 V12 petrol water-cooled, 23,880cc, 700hp
Maximum speed: 28mph road, 14mph cross-country
Range: 100 miles road, 62 miles cross-country
Armament: 75mm KwK 42 L/70 cannon, 2-3 x 7.92mm MG34 machine guns
Armour: 100mm maximum

Panzer VI Tiger Ausf E
Crew: Five (commander, gunner, loader, driver, radio operator/machine-gunner)
Weight: 55.5 tonnes
Engine: Maybach HL 230 P45 V12 petrol water-cooled, 21,353cc, 700hp
Maximum speed: 23mph road, 12mph cross-country
Range: 55 miles road, 37 miles cross-country
Armament: 88mm KwK 36 L/56 cannon, 2 x 7.92mm MG34 machine guns
Armour: 120mm maximum

It was a relatively old design in 1944 but the Panzer IV was still the most common German tank in Normandy. This one is pictured at the Tank Museum in Bovington, Dorset.

An early Panzer V Panther on the Eastern Front. The Panther was rushed into production to combat the Russian T-34.

July 30, 1944 – still pitifully few to combat the thousands of Shermans pouring ashore from the Allied beachhead. In addition, the Germans found its width and the length of its gun barrel made fighting in wooded areas or the narrow lanes and tall hedges of the Normandy countryside difficult.

Complaints also arose about its sensitive power train, a lack of spares and a perceived vulnerability to Allied fighter-bombers.

PANZER VI TIGER SD.KFZ.181

The most feared tank of the Second World War, the Tiger was produced in remarkably small numbers – just 1347 were built during a production run of two years from August 1942 to August 1944.

While the Panther was a direct result of German encounters with the T-34, the Tiger was the product of efforts to design a heavy tank that had been ongoing sporadically since 1937. While the Panther was being rushed into production, so too the process of making the Tiger a reality was stepped up.

While the T-34 compensated for relatively thin armour by sloping it, the Tiger simply had thick vertical armour plates that were stepped and welded together for added strength. So thick was the Tiger's armour in fact, that it was immune to frontal attacks from a Sherman's standard 75mm gun even at close range.

The Tiger's powerful 88mm gun, too, was an example of 'bigger is better' design theory. It gave armour penetration sufficient to knock out any Allied tank in existence at a range of more than 2000m and was also highly accurate.

Overall, the design was highly effective, though not entirely invulnerable. It was also difficult and expensive to build. As with the Panther, far too few Tigers were made to overcome the Allies' overwhelming numerical superiority.

An SS man carries an early StG44 assault rifle into combat.

PANZER TIGER II SD.KFZ.182

Taking the design theory behind the Tiger to the next level was the super heavy Tiger II, also known as the 'King Tiger' or even 'Royal Tiger'. While it shared its engine with the Tiger, and the Panther too for that matter, it was otherwise a new design.

Tiger Ausf B
Crew: Five (commander, gunner, loader, driver, radio operator/machine-gunner)
Weight: 69.7 tonnes
Engine: Maybach HL 230 P30 V12 petrol water-cooled, 23,889cc, 700hp
Maximum speed: 23mph road, 11mph cross-country
Range: 75 miles road, 50 miles cross-country
Armament: 88mm KwK 43 L/71 cannon, 2 x 7.92mm MG34 machine guns
Armour: 185mm maximum

Sturmgeschütz III Ausf G
Crew: Four (commander, gunner, loader/radio operator, driver)
Weight: 23.9 tonnes
Engine: Maybach HL 120 TRM V12 petrol water-cooled, 11,870cc, 300hp
Maximum speed: 25mph
Range: 75 miles road, 50 miles cross-country
Armament: 7.5cm StuK 40 L/48 cannon, 1 x 7.92mm MG34 machine gun
Armour: 80mm maximum

Hummel
Crew: Six (driver, five gun crew)
Weight: 24 tonnes
Engine: Maybach HL 120 TRM V12 petrol water-cooled, 11,870cc, 300hp
Maximum speed: 26mph
Range: 133 miles
Armament: 150mm sFH 18 L/30 howitzer, 1 x 7.92mm MG34 machine gun
Armour: 30mm maximum

Covered in extremely thick armour and equipped with an 88mm gun even more powerful than that of the Tiger it was a beast of a tank. Unfortunately, expecting the same engine used to haul around 45.5 tonne (Panther) and 55.5 tonne (Tiger) tanks to power a tank approaching 70 tonnes was asking for trouble.

Complexity and a critical shortage of materials meant only 492 Tiger IIs had been made by the end of the war. In addition, the tank was a notoriously unreliable gas guzzler. The figures given for its range belie the fact that this was only achieved by fitting massive fuel tanks capable of holding 860 litres, compared to the 568 litres of the Tiger I and 720 litres of the Panther.

In practice, although most Allied tanks had to be at point blank range to have any hope of puncturing a Tiger II's armour, they often didn't need to. The giant machines were often simply abandoned by their crews when they ran out of fuel or broke down.

Nicknamed 'Tiki', this Panzer VI Tiger belongs to the 2nd SS Panzer Division Das Reich.

STURMGESCHÜTZ III SD.KFZ.142

Originally conceived in the mid-1930s as a mobile artillery piece for supporting infantry assaults, the Sturmgeschütz or StuG III was essentially a fixed forward-firing gun mounted on the same chassis as the Panzer III, hence StuG III – there was never a I or II.

Operated by artillery crews rather than tank or infantry personnel, the StuG was designed to blast through improvised strongpoints, such as houses, and destroy soft-skinned vehicles such as trucks or jeeps.

Its role changed when German forces began to come up against concerted opposition on the Eastern Front. When tanks were unavailable, StuG IIIs were often called upon to fill in and proved to be quite capable of knocking out enemy armour.

Therefore, in early 1942, the StuG production line was altered to manufacture the Ausf. F version, which mounted a high-velocity 7.5cm StuK 40 L/43 gun and after only 120 had been made this was changed again to a longer 7.5cm StuK 40 L/48 –

essentially the same main gun as the Panzer IV Ausf. G and later the H and J too.

While the Panzer IV had a turret that could be rotated through 360° and the StuG's gun was fixed, the StuG was cheaper. A Panzer IV was a snip at 103,462 Reichsmarks (RM) compared to the Tiger's 250,800 RM but it was still expensive compared to the StuG's rock bottom 82,500 RM. It also had a crew of four, compared to the five required for most tanks.

These two factors made a big difference to a nation being brought to its knees by the costs of war and severe shortages of manpower. As a result, the StuG III became Germany's most-produced armoured vehicle of the Second World War, with around 10,000 being made. Numerous units operated it in Normandy.

HUMMEL SD.KFZ.165

Germany used a diverse range of mobile artillery machines, many converted from older German tanks or even captured tanks. These included the Panzer I-based Sturmpanzer I, the Panzer II-based Wespe, the Marder I, which was based on captured French-tracked vehicles, and the Grille, which was based on the Czech Panzer 38(t).

One of the most successful to see action in Normandy was the Hummel or 'Bumblebee'. Another product of the war in Russia, it mounted a huge 150mm sFH 18 L/30 howitzer on a tank body made from the best bits of the Panzer III – the steering mechanism – and the Panzer IV – the suspension and engine.

The crew compartment was open to the elements and it carried just 18 rounds. It was sometimes therefore accompanied by a Munitionsträger Hummel, essentially another Hummel, but with ammunition racks instead of a gun.

NEBELWERFER

While the German infantry had mortars for close artillery support and a range of field guns were available, particularly during the early part of the Normandy campaign, there was another weapon which could provide heavy indirect fire support. The Nebelwerfer 'smoke launcher' series of multiple rocket launchers had been in service since the outbreak of war in 1939 and by 1944 the most common types in front-line use were the Nebelwerfer 41 and 42.

The 15cm NbW 41 had six launch tubes clustered together on a gun carriage, originally designed for the 3.7cm PaK 36 anti-tank gun. Its high-explosive rockets were loaded from the rear and had a range of nearly 4.3 miles. An alternative version of the NbW 41, featuring an open-framed launcher, fired 32cm rockets or, with the aid of an adapter, 28cm rockets. The launch sequence saw all six rockets fired, although they left the launcher one at a time. The heavier ammunition meant its range was reduced to just 1.3 miles for the 32cm and 1.6 for the 28cm. From 1943, some, but not all, 28/32cm NbW 41 launchers were converted to fire 30cm Wurfkörper 42 rockets as the 30cm NbW 42.

In Normandy, nearly all of the available Nebelwerfers were employed against the British and Canadians, rather than the Americans. They called them 'Moaning Minnies' because of the sound they made when fired.

A Panther in garish camouflage at the Tank Museum in Bovington.

A Panzer VI Tiger on the Eastern Front, stalking between the remains of a T-34/76 on the left and a BT-7 on the right. It was the armoured fighting vehicle Allied tankmen feared the most.

German paratroopers hitch a ride on a mighty Tiger II.

Americans inspect a captured StuG III of the 10th SS Panzer Division Frundsberg.

The open-framed type Nebelwerfer.

The cluster-type Nebelwerfer rocket launcher is inspected by an Allied serviceman.

FIGHTER SUPPORT

By the time the Allies invaded France in June 1944 the clouds of fighters that had opposed the Dieppe Raid two years earlier had diminished to become a mere shadow of their former selves.

Efforts to create a successor to the reliable old Messerschmitt Bf 109, which had been continually upgraded in service since its introduction eight years earlier in 1937, had failed and the jet powered Me 262 was barely operational by the end of the Normandy campaign.

Many of the Bf 109's most experienced pilots had been killed on the Eastern Front but it was still being turned out in vast numbers – particularly the Bf 109 G-6.

The type continued to be plagued by deficiencies which had hardly seemed to matter 10 years earlier – its narrow track undercarriage made it difficult for the uninitiated to handle take offs and landings and its diminutive size limited the payload and weaponry it could carry.

Focke-Wulf's Fw 190 had been a shock to the Allies in late 1941, but now the design was reaching its limits, while the latest Spitfires, Thunderbolts and Mustangs surpassed it. Other types, such as the venerable Junkers Ju 88 and Dornier Do 17 light bombers, and Bf 110 and Ju 188 night fighters, were easy meat for the Allies.

OTHER TYPES

The Luftwaffe in France had been left with only the bare minimum of front line capable aircraft and a selection of obsolete machines, some of which found a new lease of life as night fighters.

The outmoded Bf 110 – which had been struggling even during the Battle of Britain – was used to attack bombers at night, as were its eventual replacement the Me 410 and the Ju 188.

The common types that had come to characterise the Luftwaffe during the early stages of the war – the Ju 87 Stuka dive bomber and the Heinkel He 111 bomber, for example – had been almost entirely phased out, with the former being replaced by Fw 190 types, adapted to carry bombs.

An upgrade of another common early type, the Dornier 217, a more powerful version of the Do 17, was used during the Normandy campaign for anti-shipping operations and also bombing raids on ground targets. ■

LUFTWAFFE FIGHTER SPECIFICATIONS

Messerschmitt Bf 109 G-6
Empty weight: 5893lb
Loaded weight: 6940lb
Engine: Daimler-Benz DB 605 A-1 liquid-cooled inverted V12 producing 1455hp
Maximum speed: 398mph at 21,000ft
Range: 528 miles or 621 miles with droptank
Maximum altitude: 39,370ft
Max rate of climb: 3345ft/min
Armament: 2 x 13mm MG 131 machine guns, 1 x 20mm MG 151 cannon – plus various optional kits to fit additional 20mm guns – rockets, a single 551lb bomb or four 110lb bombs.

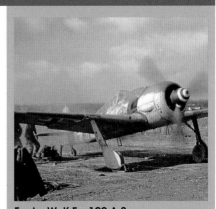

Focke-Wulf Fw 190 A-8
Empty weight: 7060lb
Loaded weight: 9735lb
Engine: BMW 801 D-2 radial engine producing 1676hp
Maximum speed: 408mph at 19,400ft
Range: 500 miles
Maximum altitude: 37,430ft
Max rate of climb: 2953ft/min
Armament: 2 x 13mm MG 131, 4 x 20mm MG 151 cannon.

CHAPTER 15

D-Day plus seven

Operation Perch and the Battle of Carentan, June 7-14

Having breached Hitler's Atlantic Wall in spectacular fashion on D-Day and made significant gains inland, the British all but ground to a halt the following day with the arrival of the fanatical SS Panzer Division Hitlerjugend. At the same time, the Americans went to work on cutting off the Cotentin Peninsula on the right of the invasion front.

An American para of the 505th rides a 'liberated' horse down the road in Sainte-Mère-Église on June 8.

The Germans had long known that the Allies' invasion of France was imminent but had been unable to work out exactly where it would come. Their plan, positioning units at strategic centres and moving them up as needed, was theoretically sound but the Allies' air supremacy made moving those units up to the front a major problem.

The bombing campaign ahead of the invasion had devastated French rolling stock, preventing the movement of troops and equipment by rail. Forced to use the road network, the tanks and vehicles rushing to the front were harassed all the way by Allied fighter-bombers. While the battered 21st Panzer Division fought on in front of the British assault at Caen, two Waffen SS tank divisions were racing to support it – the 12th SS Panzer Division *Hitlerjugend* and the Panzer Lehr Division.

Hitlerjugend had been formed the year before and was composed of 16,000 18-year-old members of the Hitler Youth. All of its regimental, battalion and company

Paratroopers of the 505th Parachute Infantry Regiment, 82nd Airborne, use horses to patrol Ravenoville, close to Utah beach, on June 7.

Ausf A and G Panther tanks of the Panzer Lehr Division at Juaye-Mondaye, south of Bayeaux, around June 10.

Canadian troops land east of the Seulles, Juno beach's Nan Green sector. While the forward units pushed inland after D-Day, the beaches were cleared and prepared for further reinforcements and supplies to come ashore.

commanders were drawn from seasoned SS or army units, primarily the 1st SS Panzer Division *Leibstandarte SS Adolf Hitler*. What its rank and file lacked in experience they made up for in sheer fanaticism. Morale was sky high and its lead units arrived between the British and Caen at 10am on June 7.

Panzer Lehr was created in January 1944 from Germany's elite training and demonstration tank formations, 'Lehr' meaning 'teach'. Like the *Hitlerjugend*, it was well equipped with Panzer IV and Panther tanks. It arrived beside the 21st and the *Hitlerjugend* on June 8.

Rommel's strategy, once the location of the invasion was revealed, was simple: hold the Allies in place until a strong enough force could be assembled to throw them back into the sea. The landscape of Normandy beyond the beaches, known as the 'bocage' or 'box country', favoured the German defenders. The countryside for up to 50 miles inland was a maze of small fields surrounded by high banks of earth and dense hedgerows, reducing visibility to a few dozen yards and causing disorientation.

In these conditions, battles often took place at close range and tanks were very vulnerable to infantry using anti-tank weapons. Fighting in the bocage resulted in heavy casualties on both sides.

On the morning of June 7, General Montgomery came ashore and established his headquarters while the Americans, having finally overcome the last resistance on Omaha, linked up with the British coming ashore on neighbouring Gold beach. Sword, Juno and Gold were also linked to form a single continuous front. The only beach not yet connected was Utah.

With the *Hitlerjugend* and Panzer Lehr arriving, Rommel set about gathering reinforcements to crush the invasion. Field Marshal von Rundstedt, who was in charge of the SS Panzer reserves, got Hitler's personal permission to release the *Leibstandarte SS Adolf Hitler* from Belgium to Caen and the 2nd SS Panzer Division *Das Reich* up from Toulouse in the south.

On the right side of the invasion front, survivors of the 716th Static Division, who had been manning the Atlantic Wall, and the 352nd Division, were reinforced by elements of the three German divisions stationed on the Cotentin peninsula – the 91st Airlanding Division, the 709th Static Division and the 243rd Static Division.

The base of the Peninsula, which the Americans needed to secure in order to cut the rest of it off from outside reinforcement and link Omaha with Utah, was anchored by the town of Carentan, which was held by the veteran German 6th Parachute Regiment.

Therefore, the American 101st Airborne from the direction of Utah and the 29th Division from the direction of Omaha began a march towards Carentan on June 7.

Rommel also recognised the importance of Carentan and sent four more divisions to the paratroopers' aid up from Brittany – the 3rd Parachute Division, the 77th Division, the 275th Division and the only elite SS unit in the region not pitted against the British and Canadians – the 17th SS Panzergrenadier Division *Götz von Berlichingen*.

Thanks to Allied air power and the destruction of France's railways by both bombers and the French Resistance, none of the divisions heading for the front line was able to arrive as quickly as planned.

On the British and Canadian front, *Das Reich* did not arrive until June 23 and it took the *Leibstandarte* until June 27-28. On the American front, the weaker static divisions located on the Contentin peninsula itself were already engaged in a large number of small fire fights and individual actions against the scattered US airborne forces.

Coordinating them into an organised and cohesive defensive line to protect Cherbourg or Carentan proved almost impossible.

The 3rd Parachute Division arrived by truck on the night of June 10, as did the panzergrenadiers of the *Berlichinge*n – although they ran out of fuel in the St Lô area and were delayed while further supplies were brought up. The 77th and 275th Divisions took longer to arrive due to train delays and other difficulties.

A barrage balloon flies over a field at Colleville-sur-mer filled with the bodies of American soldiers killed on D-Day and immediately thereafter. In the background a GMC truck is unloading more corpses.

OPERATION PERCH

The British renewed their assault on Caen on June 7. Operation Perch had originally been the name of the D-Day +1 plan to break out of Caen to the south east but since Caen was still in enemy hands it became the plan to encircle it instead.

I Corps, coming in from the Sword beach area, moved to the left while the Canadians from Juno and XXX Corps from Gold beach attempted to swing round the city to the right. Initial progress was made, Bayeux and Port-en-Bessin were captured, but counterattacks by the remaining German forces prevented further progress right across the front.

The Canadians in particular fared badly against the *Hitlerjugend*. The division's lead unit was the 25th SS Panzergrenadier Regiment, commanded by Kurt Meyer and supported by artillery plus 50 Panzer IV tanks from the 2nd Battalion of the 12th SS Panzer Regiment. Confident and utterly ruthless, Meyer told his men he had been ordered to "throw the fishes into the sea".

The SS units were already in position and preparing to attack when the Canadian North Nova Scotia Highlanders with their armoured support, the Sherbrooke Fusiliers tank regiment, came into view, advancing towards Carpiquet airfield west of Caen.

Meyer watched them from his command post on top of the tower of Ardenne Abbey, which was only a short distance away. The Canadians had not yet spotted his men and he had a ringside seat to what happened next.

Later, he wrote: "But what is this? Am I seeing clearly? An enemy tank is pushing through the orchards. My God, what an opportunity! The tanks are driving right across the 2nd Battalion's front! The unit is showing us its unprotected flank. I give orders to all battalions, the artillery and the available tanks: do not shoot! Open fire only on my orders.

"The commander of our tank regiment has positioned his command vehicle in the garden of the monastery. A radio link is quickly established with the tank. Wünsche,

Men of the Regina Rifles guarding a position in Cardonville, to the south of Bretteville-l'Orgueilleuse during the Hitlerjugend's attacks of June 8-9.

commander of the tank regiment, quietly transmits the enemy tank movements. Nobody dares raise his voice.

"An unbearable pressure now rests on me. It will happen soon now. The enemy spearhead pushes past Franqueville and starts across the road. I give the signal for the attack to Wünsche and I can just hear his order as he gives it: 'Achtung! Panzer marsch!'

"The tension is gone. There are cracks and flashes near Franqueville. The enemy tank at the head of the spearhead smokes

and I watch the crew bailing out. More tanks are torn apart with loud explosions."

The Canadians, caught by surprise, fell back but rallied at Buron and held the *Hitlerjugend* at bay, inflicting serious casualties in the process. The Sherbrooke Fusiliers reported 31 German tanks destroyed by the end of the day.

Far from pushing the Canadians back into the sea, Meyer had been checked and thrown back himself and the numerically superior Canadians began pushing through along the *Hitlerjugend's* right flank.

Spotting this ingress, Meyer attacked and in the process took around 150 Canadians prisoner.

On the evening of June 7, on Meyer's orders, five captive North Nova Scotia Highlanders and six Sherbrooke Fusiliers were lined up against a wall of the Ardenne Abbey and shot in the back of the head. Another seven Highlanders POWs were executed the following day – some shot, some beaten to death.

By June 9, Caen remained firmly in German hands. Montgomery met to discuss the situation with Lieutenant-Generals Miles Dempsey and Omar Bradley. They decided that a new pincer movement was the answer, with the 51st (Highland) Infantry Division and the 4th Armoured Brigade moving to the left of Caen while units from Gold beach's XXX Corps swung round to the right. The lead units of the Panzer Lehr were now beginning to arrive, positioning themselves in front of XXX Corps.

A Sherman Firefly tank from C Squadron 13th/18th Hussars in action near Bréville on June 11.

LEGENDARY BIG CAT

German heavy tanks fielded during the latter half of the Second World War rapidly acquired a fearsome and enduring reputation.

Even now, historians bemoan the dire state of Allied tanks, particularly the Cromwell and the Sherman, citing their poor armament and thin armour.

Praise is regularly heaped upon the Tiger and Panther to a point where it seems incredible that any British tank ever managed to knock one of them out. The reality, however, was somewhat different.

One encounter during Operation Perch illustrates a serious weakness in one of the German 'big cats'.

Approaching midday on June 9, a company of 12 Hitlerjugend Panther tanks and infantry advanced on a village recently captured by the Canadians – Norrey-en-Bessin west of Caen. They were ambushed by the Regina Rifles, equipped with PIAT projectors and several six-pounder anti-tank guns. Six Sherman tanks from the 1st Hussars provided armoured support.

When the trap was sprung, seven of the 12 Panthers were knocked out almost immediately. The infantry platoon who had been accompanying them suffered heavy casualties – 16 dead and 17 wounded.

It was later theorised that the Panthers had blown up easily because their fuel tanks, when half full, allowed for a fatal accumulation of fuel vapour. And this wasn't the only flaw.

Tests carried out on Panthers by the French after the war also found that the type's drivetrain was severely overstressed – it was a 45 ton tank running on a chassis designed for a 24 ton vehicle – meaning it could only manage about 100 miles before requiring a strip-down. The construction of the tank also meant that if a major failure occurred it could only be fixed by taking the turret off using heavy lifting equipment.

The teeth of its gears stripped easily if you weren't careful, particularly third, fuel consumption was appalling – as little as 0.2mpg cross country – and the slave labourers used in their construction often left internal bolts loose, stuffed wadded cloth or even cigarette butts into vital equipment.

At any one time, as many as 30-40% of all Panthers in Normandy were unavailable for front line combat duties due to mechanical unreliability issues. When it worked, when the fuel tank was full and it was directly facing its enemies, the Panther was superb but it fell short in many respects even to the supposedly inferior Shermans and Cromwells.

The fearsome looking Panzer V Panther suffered from serious design flaws.

XXX Corps' 50th (Northumbrian) Infantry Division, whose troops had been on the front line on D-Day, reached the town of Tilly-sur-Seulles late on June 9. Tilly was directly west of Caen, on the point of the right 'pincer', and it was here that they first encountered the tanks of the Panzer Lehr. Fierce fighting ensued with an attack by the Panzer Lehr being broken but only after a British company had been overrun.

The British pushed back the following day, now reinforced by the Sherman Fireflies and Cromwells of the 7th Armoured Division, and managed to take Tilly's central crossroads. That evening the Panzer Lehr and the *Hitlerjugend* took it back. The left side of the pincer on the eastern side of Caen, meanwhile, was delayed as I Corps struggled to get into position. The 6th Airborne units still holding the Orne bridgehead fought off several counterattacks on June 10 while waiting for I Corps forces to reach them.

The following morning, as the Panzer Lehr and XXX Corps licked their wounds on the opposite side of Caen and much further south, the 51st launched an assault on Bréville, north east of the city.

BATTLE FOR BRÉVILLE

The plan to capture Bréville, a crucial stepping stone on the way down the eastern flank of Caen, involved the 5th Battalion of the Black Watch attacking over 750ft of open ground supported by artillery and mortar fire. It proved to be too far. German machine gunners swept the space and turned it into a killing ground. Concentrated fire first halted and then repulsed the assault with the Black Watch suffering 200 casualties.

The survivors retreated to the nearby Château St Côme only to find that the

Germans were right behind them. This time it was the Germans' turn as the enraged British turned their machine guns on them, cutting through the enemy infantry.

Three tank troops from the 13th/18th Royal Hussars were ordered to go to the Black Watch's aid but as they approached the château they were fired on at close range by camouflaged German self-propelled guns. Three of the Hussars' tanks were knocked out and the rest pulled back.

Meanwhile further attacks were taking place in an attempt to force the right pincer forward. The Queen's Own Rifles of Canada and 'B' Squadron of the 1st Hussars tried to advance through the hamlet of Le Mesnil

Patry north west of Caen. With the tanks out in front carrying D Company of the Rifles, they were ambushed by the *Hitlerjugend*. The Germans had captured a radio set and signals codes from a wrecked Canadian tank on June 9 and knew precisely where and when the Rifles and Hussars would appear.

Using a combination of Panzerfausts and Panzerschrecks, the *Hitlerjugend* destroyed or disabled 51 Shermans – all but two of those involved in the advance. Men who had been riding on them were thrown to the ground as they caught fire and burned or exploded. The commander of the Rifles, Major Elliot Dalton was hit in the leg by

Burying the bodies of paratroopers from the US 101st Airborne killed during the battles immediately following D-Day.

An American temporary airfield under construction near Sainte-Mère-Église, inland of Utah beach. Work began on June 7 and was completed on June 17. The 371st Fighter Group, operating Republic P-47 Thunderbolts was based there from June 17-23.

Ten LSTs risk breaking their keels to urgently land the US 2nd Armored Division at Colleville sur Mer – Omaha beach – on June 9-10. Following the initial assault, it was critical to get as many men and as much materiel ashore as fast as possible.

A destroyed Hitlerjugend Panther tank. It was knocked out by soldier using a PIAT projector opposite the Regina Rifles' headquarters in Bretteville-l'Orgueilleuse on June 8.

mortar fire. The horrified leader of the Hussars, Lieutenant Colonel Ray Colwell, tried to order the retreat but it was too late.

A total of 61 Hussars and 55 Rifles soldiers were listed as killed or missing after the attack, a combined total of 35 were injured and 22 taken prisoner.

The following day, back at Bréville, a battalion of German infantry supported by six tanks and SPGs attacked the Black Watch holed up at the Château St Côme. The battle that followed saw most of the Black Watch's vehicles and anti-tank guns destroyed – leaving them powerless to fight the tanks. Under heavy fire, the survivors pulled back from the now ruined and burning château, joining elements of the 9th Parachute Battalion who were also being attacked by German panzers.

One German tank was hit by two PIAT mortar rounds but kept coming, destroying two British machine gun positions. Only after it was hit by a third PIAT round did it pull back, still mobile enough to retreat. The German infantry were still advancing however and it took a Canadian counterattack to prevent the British being

completely overrun. Bréville was finally taken later that day by the 12th Battalion of the Parachute Regiment – who suffered 141 casualties out of 160 men in the process. After these punishing encounters, the left pincer movement of Operation Perch was shut down on June 13.

The left pincer may have stalled but the right was still moving. As the British coming in from Gold beach linked up with the Americans from Omaha it became apparent that a gap in the German line was opening up and the battle that ensued is described in chapter 16.

CAUSEWAY ASSAULT

Away to the west, the Americans were getting to grips with Carentan. It was a port surrounded on three sides by waterways – the River Douve to the west and north, a basin to the northeast and the Vire-Taute Canal to the east.

There were four bridges carrying a single highway, running south from Saint Côme-du-Mont, into the north of the town. For its last mile, this highway was raised above a flooded area on a 6-9ft high

causeway on four bridges. On June 9, two battalions of the German 6th Parachute Regiment and survivors of other units prepared to defend Carentan.

At the same time, the American 101st Airborne, the 'Screaming Eagles', had been gathering its scattered forces together, including the 501st, 502nd and 506th Parachute Infantry Regiments (PIRs) and the 327th Glider Infantry Regiment. It was also now supported by the 2nd Armored Division which had rolled its Shermans in off Omaha beach.

The Americans' plan was to attack over the bridges from the north and sweep round to attack from the east too. The bridges seriously held up the attack because No. 2 had been blown and No. 4 was blocked with a Belgian gate. After some scouting, the full scale assault began at noon on June 10. An improvised footbridge was erected beside Bridge No. 2, allowing the infantry to pass it during the early afternoon. The men then crawled towards Bridge No. 4 to avoid an 88mm gun covering it.

By 3pm, most of the men were past No. 2. Then Germans hidden in a large farmhouse to the right front of Bridge No. 4 opened fire with machine guns. Another machine gun positioned behind a hedge just 100 yards away then joined in and the Americans were forced to pull back, having suffered several casualties. Now men all along the causeway were being hit.

As his men were being killed and the attack stalled, the 29-year-old leader of the 502nd Lieutenant-Colonel Robert G Cole went back to bridge No. 2. As he walked along in view of the enemy snipers, bullets zinging off the ground, he shouted to his men: "God damn it, start firing and keep firing. God damn you, listen. Spread out. How many times must I tell you?"

The 3/502nd was ordered to continue the attack at 4am and Companies G and H managed to get most of their men through the gap on Bridge No. 4. Ahead lay the enemy-held farmhouse and hedgerows. When the men leading the attack got close to the farmhouse they were suddenly subjected to rifle, machine gun and mortar fire. An artillery strike called down on the

Four paratroopers of the US 101st Airborne ride a German Kübelwagen through Carentan while other American soldiers rest. The photo was taken some time between June 12 and June 14.

farmhouse seemed to have little effect so Cole decided there was no option but to fix bayonets. He gave the order and shouted across the road for Stopka, to pass it on. He failed to do so. Smoke shells were used to lay a screen in front of the farmhouse and at 6.15am Cole blew his whistle and led the charge. Just 20 of his 250 men followed him.

When Stopka realised that he had failed to pass on Cole's order, he tried to rally the men nearby saying: "Come on! Let's go! Follow the colonel!" and about 40 men got up. Halfway across a field, Cole looked back and saw no one was following him. Then he saw that several men were trying to do so but were being deterred by the bullets and shrapnel whizzing around.

He turned around and strode back towards them, shooting his pistol, shouting: "God damn, I don't know what I'm shooting at but I gotta keep on! These goose-stepping Heinies think they know how to fight a war. We're about to learn 'em a lesson!" Some of the men actually laughed and they along with the rest got up and kept going.

Reaching the farmhouse, the Americans found it had been abandoned. The Germans had withdrawn to rifle pits and machine gun positions to the rear and right of the building along a hedgerow. By now the charge had gathered momentum, with more men – seeing that the first wave had not been cut down – running to catch up.

Passing the farmhouse, the attack fell upon the hedgerow and the Germans were wiped out using a combination of grenades and close quarter combat.

Cole wanted to push on into the Germans' positions on the outskirts of Carentan itself but the 3/502nd was broken and exhausted. On the morning of June 11, the Germans launched a counterattack on the farmhouse but Cole's men repulsed it with machine gun fire both from the

Jeeps roll into Carentan past closed shop fronts on June 14.

outlying position and the house itself. After a lull in the fighting, the Germans launched another assault which stretched the 502nd close to breaking point.

Germans soldiers advanced to within one hedgerow of the farmhouse and there were too few survivors left to stop them. Just then Captain Julian Rosamund, the forward artillery officer, finally managed to reach the batteries he'd been out of contact with all day and called down fire on the Germans, who were only 300ft away.

The shells whizzed past very low overhead and exploded. In just five minutes most of the Germans were dead or dying and the remainder retreated. At 8pm, the 2/502nd moved forward to take over from the remnants of the 3/502nd and 1/502nd. The 506th was then sent in to finish the job.

TAKING CARENTAN

While the 502nd was fighting along the causeway, the 327th Glider Infantry was sweeping around Carentan to the left. After fighting off a large German force en route, it was ordered to secure a rail bridge, a road bridge and a footbridge over the canal to block the town's eastern exits.

By midnight on June 10, the American battalions had reached the canal and taken the road bridge intact – the other two bridges having been demolished by the retreating Germans. By June 11, the Americans had crossed the canal and were advancing towards the town.

At 2am on June 12, 1/506th and 2/506th reached the farmhouse which Cole and his men had held. The 2/506th then swept down the right-hand side of Carentan and reached the main road that led into it from the south west. It then turned and advanced into the town, meeting up with the 1/401st, which had entered from the north east.

The 327th and 501st piled into the town too but it rapidly became clear that most of the German defenders had escaped to the south west overnight – just before the 2/506th could block their last exit. Carentan was now in American hands.

Pushing south the following morning, on June 13, the 501st and 506th encountered a strong German counterattack supported by heavy armour. The 17th SS Panzergrenadier Division *Götz von Berlichingen* had finally arrived and joined up with the survivors of the 6th Parachute Regiment.

This assault pushed the Americans back to within 1500ft of the town but at 10.30am dozens of Sherman tanks arrived, having been thrown into the fight by General Bradley himself, who had heard a garbled communication that made it seem as though Carentan was being entered by 150 German tanks. The Germans were repulsed with 500 casualties and Carentan was fully secured by June 14.

Aerial view of Carentan in American hands.

CHAPTER 16

Tigers unleashed

The Battle of Villers-Bocage

As British forces poured through a gap in the German defensive line, they came up against a small force operating the formidable Tiger tank. The battle that ensued has become one of the most infamous encounters between armoured fighting vehicles in history...

With the disintegration and withdrawal of the German 352nd, who had been holding the centre, a ragged hole was exposed in the front line facing the British and they moved swiftly to drive as much armour through it as possible.

The 7th Armoured Division was earmarked for the attack. Its Cromwells and Sherman Fireflies would punch through and seize the strategically important town of Villers-Bocage before wheeling around, advancing on a ridge 1.6 miles east of it known as Point 213 and heading for the rear of the hard-pushed Panzer Lehr.

It was hoped that this would force the Panzer Lehr to pull back, enabling the 50th (Northumbrian) Infantry Division, who'd been keeping the Waffen-SS men busy in the meantime, to envelope Caen to the west.

At noon on June 12, the 7th Armoured began disengaging from combat and by 4pm was motoring through the hole, dubbed the Caumont Gap, with its armoured reconnaissance regiment, the 8th King's Royal Irish Hussars, scouting ahead.

The division advanced for 12 miles almost unopposed then halted for the night to carry out maintenance. The 8th Hussars probed the Panzer Lehr's flank just under two miles away to the left while the division's armoured car regiment, the 11th (Prince Albert's Own) Hussars, linked up

A column of Cromwells and Shermans on the move. These were the primary fighting vehicles of the 7th Armoured Division as it rolled through the Caumont Gap on June 12.

with the US 1st Infantry Division to the right, near Caumont itself. Naval artillery fire was used to 'soften up' Villers-Bocage ahead of the next day's advance.

The Germans were deeply concerned about the Caumont Gap without being completely aware of the large force already driving through it. The 1st SS Panzer Korps commander Sepp Dietrich had ordered his reserve, the 101st SS Heavy Panzer Battalion, to move up and stopper the gap while other units were rushed to the front. The 101st had arrived in Normandy on June

12 after a five day, 160 mile drive west from Beauvais, north of Paris, with just 17 battle-ready Tiger I tanks. It normally fielded 45 but it had been continually harried by fighter-bombers on the journey and the Tigers, which were not designed for prolonged treks, kept breaking down.

The 1st Company of the 101st based itself 5.6 miles northeast of Villers-Bocage, close to the Panzer Lehr, while the 2nd Company, commanded by 30-year-old Eastern Front tank ace Captain Michael Wittmann, was just south of Point 213. Wittmann could usually count on 12 Tigers but by the following day, June 13, just six were available: Tigers 212, 213, 214, 224, 231 and 232.

Brigadier William 'Loony' Hinde, commander of the 7th Armoured, drew up his plan on the night of June 12. The 4th County of London Yeomanry (Sharpshooters) and a single battalion of the Rifle Brigade would drive straight through Villers-Bocage and occupy Point 213.

The 1/7th Queen's Royal Regiment (West Surrey) would occupy Villers-Bocage while the 5th Royal Tank Regiment and another company of the Rifle Brigade would move on to another ridge to the southwest near another town – Maisoncelles-Pelvey.

This would leave a gap between the 4th Yeomanry and the 5th Royal Tank, which would be plugged by the 260th Anti-Tank Battery of the Norfolk Yeomanry, equipped with M10 Achilles tank destroyers. The 5th Regiment, Royal Horse Artillery, with its

Panzer VI Tiger of the 101st SS Heavy Panzer Battalion before the Normandy invasion.

Tank ace SS-Untersturmführer (Second Lieutenant equivalent) Michael Wittmann, left, and his crew on the Eastern Front with their Tiger before the Normandy campaign.

Tiger tanks of the 101st SS Heavy Panzer Battalion en route to plug the gap in the German front line around the Allied beachhead.

Sexton self-propelled artillery pieces, would follow on while the 1st Royal Tank and the 1/5th and 1/6th battalions of the Queen's Royal Regiment (West Surrey) would be held in reserve in the Livry area.

At 5.30am on June 13, Hinde's plan was put into effect. The 7th Armoured moved en masse towards Livry and was greeted by cheering French civilians. Beyond Livry, as the column closed in on Villers-Bocage, the British spotted a German eight-wheeled Sd.Kfz.231 armoured car, its commander watching them carefully.

Before the car could be fired on by the nearest British tank, it turned around and sped off. Entering Villers-Bocage, another German vehicle, this time a Volkswagen Kübelwagen, was seen driving rapidly away.

The 8th Hussars, still on scouting duties, encountered more German eight-wheeled armoured cars and reported seeing German tanks approaching the village. Undaunted, the British pressed on. The Sharpshooters' A Squadron drove through and quickly covered the 1.6 miles to Point 213, knocking out a solitary Kübelwagen along the way.

The following Rifle Brigade was ordered to move its personnel carriers to the side of the road to allow further tank reinforcements through and it did just that, parking them nose to tail.

Not far from Point 213, Wittmann and his men looked on with alarm. The British had arrived sooner than expected. Wittman later said: "I had no time to assemble my company; instead I had to act quickly, as I had to assume that the enemy had already spotted me and would destroy me where I stood. I set off with one tank and passed the order to the others not to retreat a single step but to hold their ground."

A sergeant of the Rifle Brigade noticed Wittmann's Tiger approaching at 9am and broke radio silence to report it. Moments later, the Tiger reached the main road and put a shell into the rearmost Cromwell tank of A Squadron at Point 213, knocking it out. The next tank, a Sherman Firefly, its engine revving, pulled forward and tried to sight

Wittmann's tank. Seeing it, Wittmann's gunner fired again, setting the Firefly ablaze and wrecking its engine. Powerless, it coasted to a halt, blocking the road to and from the ridge.

The remainder of A Squadron was now trapped and the rest of Wittmann's command approached, their Tigers' powerful 88mm guns firing round after round into the thin-skinned Cromwells and Shermans, destroying three more.

Wittmann himself turned around and sped back towards Villers-Bocage.

STREET FIGHTING

Seeing the Tiger coming at them head on, the tanks of the Sharpshooters in the village tried to escape – but it was too late. One fired two shots at the Tiger, neither causing any damage, before it was destroyed. An M5 Stuart light tank was also blown up. Two Cromwells drove into the gardens of houses to get away, only one successfully 'hiding'.

The Tiger then rammed the smouldering Stuart out of the way and approached the

village centre, putting a hole through and disabling another Cromwell en route. In the main street, Wittmann destroyed a pair of observation post tanks belonging to the 5th Regiment, Royal Horse Artillery, a Cromwell and a Sherman. An officer's scout car and a medical half-track were next.

Approaching the section of road where the Rifle Brigade's carriers were lined up, the Tiger hit one after the next until they were all burning. At the eastern end of Villers-Bocage, a trio of M5s blocked Wittmann's path – he hit one and it exploded violently, then he knocked out the other two.

Now the Cromwell that had 'hidden' in the garden earlier on, and which had been surreptitiously shadowing the Tiger since then, hoping for a shot at its weaker rear armour, finally took the shot – and it bounced off. Wittmann's crew traversed their turret round and killed the Cromwell with a shell that punched right through it.

Continuing on, Wittmann's Tiger came to the outskirts of Villers-Bocage, where it

With the French rail network largely out of action, this was the only way the Tigers of the 101st could get into position. They are pictured here in Northern France heading for the front on June 7. Bundesarchiv, Bild 101I-299-1804-07 / Scheck / CC-BY-SA

encountered a 6-pounder anti-tank gun crew aiming their weapon squarely at it. Wittmann's rampage was finally brought to an end by a shot to his Tiger's tracks, which disabled it. Neither Wittmann nor his crew were injured and they managed to scramble out of the tank and retreat on foot, walking the 3.7 miles back to the 101st's HQ.

Following the 101st's attack on Point 213, the Sharpshooters' A Squadron comprised nine serviceable tanks including a pair of Sherman Fireflies and a Cromwell observation point tank. The unit was ordered to hold its ground supported by a section of riflemen.

At 10am, just an hour after Wittmann's attack began, the 101st's 5th Company turned up on the battlefield and started rounding up British tank men and riflemen who had remained in the area between the ridge and Villers-Bocage. The 1/7th Battalion of the Queen's Royal Regiment now held the village itself and captured three men from the 2nd Panzer Division – an advance party for the division, which was now beginning to arrive in the combat area.

With the Germans now holding the area between the village and the ridge, A Squadron of the Sharpshooters was cut off. A breakout was planned and a single Cromwell attempted to escape via a roundabout route but it was quickly disabled by a German tank.

The Germans then began to fire into the trees around Point 213, causing a cloud of splinters to descend on the beleaguered tankmen. After five minutes, A Squadron decided to surrender and 30 Sharpshooters were taken prisoner, although a handful managed to escape back to British lines.

In the village, the Queen's Royal Regiment readied itself. A Company took up positions around the railway station while B and C Companies were posted to the eastern side of the village. Before long, German forces began to infiltrate the eastern side and skirmishes broke out.

A pair of German tanks rolled down the approaches but were damaged with anti-

The 101st approaches Villers-Bocage. Bundesarchiv, Bild 101I-738-0267-18 / Grimm, Arthur / CC-BY-SA

tank guns and withdrew. Realising that the last had not been seen of the 101st and its Tigers, the British prepared an ambush in the village square.

Lieutenant Bill Cotton of the Sharpshooters' B Squadron positioned a Firefly, commanded by Sergeant Bobby Bramall, a handful of Cromwells, a 6-pounder gun and members of the 1/7th armed with PIATs at carefully selected points and settled down to wait.

At Château d'Orbois, the Panzer Lehr's headquarters, Wittmann briefed Lieutenant-Colonel Kurt Kauffmann on the situation and was given a Volkswagen Type 166 Schwimmwagen which he drove back to Point 213, still in the hands of the 101st.

Kauffmann ordered Captain Helmut Ritgen to block the northern exits from Villers-Bocage. Ritgen took a small force of Panzer IVs and advanced but ran into British anti-tank gunners who blew a hole in one tank, setting it on fire. Four of Ritgen's Panzers managed to enter the village from the south but the two in front were

destroyed by anti-tank gun fire and the rest pulled back.

A second attempt to enter from the south was made at 1pm by another four Panzer IVs and although two of these were also knocked out, this time they did not withdraw. Tigers from the 101st were sent in to support them and succeeded in taking out the British anti-tank gun position.

Four Tigers led by a Panzer IV then moved down the main road towards the village square. When they got there, they found Cotton and his men still waiting. Bramall's Firefly shot at the Panzer IV but missed, seconds later however the 6-pounder crew did the job and destroyed it. Three of the Tigers then dispersed into the back streets. One was killed by a British anti-tank gun and the others were tackled at close range by PIAT crews hidden in buildings. One was blown up and the other was rendered immobile.

The fourth Tiger had stopped in the middle of the road short of the ambush site, seemingly waiting for the British to break cover. Bramall spotted it through the windows of a corner house.

He got off two shots, one of which damaged the Tiger's gun mantlet, before it reversed away and shot down a side street. A Cromwell in another side street on the opposite side of the main road gunned its engine, crossed the main road and knocked the Tiger out from behind.

Next, a Panzer IV was knocked out by Bramall. There then followed a lull in the fighting when Cotton and Bramall used blankets and petrol to set fire to the knocked out German tanks lying around to prevent their later recovery and repair.

The armoured attack having failed, the Germans next moved in with a strong force of infantry – drawn from the 2nd Panzer Division. B Squadron fought them off, inflicting heavy casualties. Another Panzer IV was knocked out then both sides called down artillery fire which rocked the village.

Knocked out Cromwell in Villers-Bocage. Bundesarchiv, Bild 101I-494-3376-19A / Zwirner / CC-BY-SA

Yet more out-of-action Cromwells. Bundesarchiv, Bild 101I-738-0269-07 / Grimm, Arthur / CC-BY-SA

Cromwell knocked out by Wittmann's Tiger in Villers-Bocage. Bundesarchiv, Bild 101I-738-0276-25A / Grimm, Arthur / CC-BY-SA

Bren gun carriers of the Rifle Brigade were destroyed one by one. Bundesarchiv, Bild 101I-738-0275-11A / Grimm, Arthur / CC-BY-SA

His forces under increasing pressure from the 2nd Panzer Division's fresh units, Hinde decided to withdraw at 6pm. During the Battle of Villers-Bocage on June 13, the British had lost 25 tanks, 14 armoured cars and 14 Bren gun carriers. The Germans lost between eight and 15 tanks, including six Tigers. This last was particularly costly because there had only been 36 Tigers in Normandy at the start of the day.

BOMBED OUT

When the British had finally abandoned Villers-Bocage, the Germans moved in and reoccupied it, killing or capturing any surviving British soldiers they found. The following day, the Panzer Lehr pushed hard on the British who had already come through the Caumont gap and succeeded in driving them back.

The moment of opportunity had slipped away and the front line was straightened on both sides once again – as it had been

before the Caumont Gap opened up. On the night of June 14, to cover the withdrawal, a force of 337 RAF bombers, 223 Avro Lancasters, 100 Handley Page Halifaxes and 14 de Havilland Mosquitos dropped 1700 tons of high explosive bombs on targets around Villers-Bocage, destroying another of the 101st's Tigers – leaving 29 in Normandy – and damaging three others.

Just over two weeks later, on June 30, another bomber force, this time comprising 151 Lancasters, 105 Halifaxes and 10 Mosquitos, dropped 1100 tons of bombs on Villers-Bocage. There were no Germans in the village at the time, although they had been using it as a transit point, and only French civilians were killed.

Although the Battle of Villers-Bocage, particularly Wittmann's jaw-dropping assault on June 13, has come to be regarded as a textbook example of the superiority of German tanks over their British counterparts; the passage of time has seen a

rather different picture emerge.

The Tiger was superior to the Cromwell or Sherman given the right circumstances, but at Villers-Bocage they were knocked out by British PIAT anti-tank guns, an unglamorous 6-pounder anti-tank gun and even by the much-derided Cromwells.

While Wittmann's initial assault has gathered plaudits for the sheer guts it took, in reality it put the British on the defensive and therefore directly contributed to the losses the Germans took later in the day.

A combination of the tenacity of the Panzer Lehr and the 101st, and the British inability to capitalize on their initial gains at Villers-Bocage, led to the failure of the attack through the Caumont Gap. Precisely why Villers-Bocage was abandoned on June 13 when all German attempts to take it had failed remains something of a mystery, but it seems impossible to shake the idea that the fear generated by the Tiger tank was at least partly responsible. ∎

After Wittmann's rampage through Villers-Bocage, the British laid a trap for the Germans and this was the result – a burned out Panzer IV and a Tiger sit side by side. Bundesarchiv, Bild 101I-494-3376-08A / Zwirner / CC-BY-SA

Further down the road from the first pair – another wrecked Tiger in Villers-Bocage. Bundesarchiv, Bild 101I-494-3376-12A / Zwirner / CC-BY-SA

Another Tiger knocked out during the vicious fighting for Villers-Bocage. Bundesarchiv, Bild 101I-494-3376-05A / Zwirner / CC-BY-SA

More knocked out Cromwells just outside Villers-Bocage. Bundesarchiv, Bild 101I-494-3376-26A / Zwirner / CC-BY-SA

German soldiers examine an abandoned British Sherman beside two more Cromwells. Bundesarchiv, Bild 101I-738-0275-02 / Grimm / CC-BY-SA

CHAPTER 17

Monty's big push

Cherbourg and Operation Epsom, June 15-July 1

German heavy armour was piling in to defend Caen against the British, but despite the odds facing him Montgomery still believed he could break through. The Americans meanwhile deliberately stalled their advance south to concentrate on securing the essential deep-water port facilities of Cherbourg...

A Churchill tank of 7th Royal Tank Regiment moves up to the front line on June 25 in readiness for Operation Epsom.

The commander of the German Cherbourg garrison, Lieutenant General Karl-Wilhelm von Schlieben (helmeted and obscured by US soldier in the centre) and Rear Admiral Walter Hennecke, to the right of him in hat and coat, are taken prisoner by US forces outside the entrance to their underground command post – a converted quarry.

With Carentan secure at the base of the Cotentin Peninsula, the US forces already ashore, and those continuing to land every day at the Mulberry harbour off Omaha beach, Mulberry 'A', focused their energies on taking more permanent and secure port facilities – those of Cherbourg on the northernmost tip of the peninsula.

Specifically, this was to be the task of VII Corps commanded by Major General Joseph Lawton 'Lightning Joe' Collins. The corps consisted of the 4th, 9th, 79th and 90th Infantry Divisions, the 82nd and 101st Airborne Divisions, the 6th Armoured Group and several other formations.

The German forces facing VII Corps south of the port were a ragged mixture of units from several divisions, most of which had already suffered crippling losses during the first fortnight of fighting after D-Day. They had few tanks or other vehicles and knew they were unlikely to be reinforced or even resupplied in the near future.

Major-General 'Lightning Joe' Collins and Eisenhower climb out of the vast V-2 rocket complex captured while still under construction at Sottevast near Brix, south of Cherbourg.

Valognes, in the centre of the Cotentin peninsula, was on the line of advance to Cherbourg for US troops, but they were hampered by damage done to the town during earlier aerial bombardments. This image, taken on June 24, shows a jeep called 'Always Ruth' of the 298th Engineer Combat Battalion. In the background, rubble is shoved aside to aid the passage of convoys to Cherbourg.

Rommel believed the best course of action for this ad hoc fighting force was for it to pull back to Cherbourg and settle in for a long siege. The city was ringed by concrete fortifications embedded in three ridges that covered every possible line of approach. Just south of the city was a fortress known as Fort du Roule and within the city was the fortified Arsenal. Beside the harbour were a number of navy forts too.

Hitler, however, had other ideas. On June 16, he demanded that the depleted divisions and demoralised battlegroups south of Cherbourg remain in position and hold a defensive line against the Americans outside the city. The following day, he conceded that they could withdraw but only as far as an arbitrary defensive line, still outside Cherbourg, which spanned the full width of the peninsula.

Most of VII Corps had been collected on the eastern side of the peninsula, having landed there on Utah or Omaha, but by June 18 the 9th Infantry Division had reached the western side. A day later, the 4th, 9th and 79th Infantry Divisions were advancing up the peninsula on a broad front. What German forces they encountered were swiftly overcome or hastily withdrew ahead of them.

During the march they found numerous V-1 flying bombs and even an unfinished V-2 rocket launching bunker site at Sottevast, near Brix. It took just two more days to reach Hitler's 'defensive line' and pass it.

The city's German garrison, commanded by Lieutenant General Karl-Wilhelm von Schlieben, consisted of 21,000 men. These were the remains of four divisions, various naval gunners and labourers who had been working to improve Cherbourg's defences when the invasion came. They had little ammunition or even food. Having ignored Collins' call to simply surrender on June 21, von Schlieben set about trying to demolish as much of the port as he could before the Americans could get their hands on it.

At noon on June 22, four squadrons of RAF Typhoons and six squadrons of RAF Mustangs began attacking targets in the city. Next came all 12 fighter-bomber groups of the American 9th Air Force and 11 groups from the 9th Bomber Command which, between them, dropped 1100 tons of explosives on von Schlieben's forces.

Collins then launched the ground assault, which saw fierce fighting on all three of the defensive ridges. It soon came down to a laborious process of knocking out one pillbox or bunker after another. A method was developed where fighter-bombers and artillery would initially make the Germans take cover, then a lighter artillery barrage would keep their heads down while the Americans advanced to within 1200ft. The infantry would take over, shooting their own heavy weapons into the firing slit while engineers moved around to the rear, blew the door off and threw in grenades.

This process kept American casualties low and proved to be highly effective. After less than two days, on the afternoon of June 23, the defensive ring had been breached in several places and the Americans were advancing towards the city proper.

On June 24, the 4th Infantry Division reached the northern coast of the peninsula, east of the city, and the next day the 4th and 9th divisions, supported by heavy naval gunfire, moved along the coast and into the outskirts of Cherbourg. The 79th attacked the Fort du Roule and when this was taken on June 26, von Schlieben was captured.

The German commander refused to order the Arsenal and navy forts to surrender, but the man in charge of the 400-strong Arsenal garrison, Major-General Robert Sattler was a

A US soldier followed by a column of German prisoners walks down the street in Valognes.

Major-General Joseph Lawton Collins, commander of VII Corps, receives the formal surrender of Cherbourg from Lieutenant-General Karl-Wilhelm von Schlieben, centre, in the Chateau de Servigny.

The damaged wharf at Cherbourg port. In the background is the ferry terminal. The entire dockyard was reduced to rubble and wreckage by the Germans before the city was surrendered.

realist. Knowing exactly what equipment the Americans had at their disposal, he told them he would not surrender unless tanks were deployed against him. The tanks were duly deployed, a few shots were fired, and Sattler's force came marching out with their bags already packed.

The harbour forts held out longer, the last surrendering on June 29, but by then it was all over. The last German resistance on the Cotentin peninsula, at the Cap de la Hague, on its furthest northwestern tip, surrendered on June 30. The entire peninsula was now in American hands.

Cherbourg proved to be a disappointment however. The Germans had devoted a lot of time and effort to making it unusable. One American engineer, surveying the damage done, described it as "a masterful job, beyond a doubt the most complete, intensive, and best planned demolition in history".

Quay walls had been shattered, sunken ships and hundreds of mines blocked the harbour, the breakwater was broken and, naturally, anything resembling a crane had been reduced to a pile of twisted scrap.

American engineers removed the debris and repaired the physical damage while teams of British engineers deactivated the mines, but it wasn't until July 16 that the first large cargo ship was able to enter the harbour. In the meantime, the British Mulberry at Arromanches, Mulberry 'B', and the smaller ports taken by the Allies picked up the slack. Mulberry 'A' had been wrecked by a storm which ravaged the Normandy coast from June 19-22.

ROLLING THUNDER

After the heavy fighting at Villers-Bocage and the withdrawal from the Caumont Gap, plans were laid for another major British offensive, Operation Dreadnought, but it never materialised because of the storm. The endless columns of supply ships that had been trawling back and forth from the south coast of England to the Mulberry harbours since D-Day came to a halt.

Some were able to retreat back to safe harbour, but more than 140,000 tonnes of counted-on supplies were lost to the enormous waves and about 800 craft were stranded on the beaches of Normandy when the surging sea retreated.

Allied aircraft, which had ruled the skies since the offensive began, were grounded. This gave the Germans an opportunity to move up yet more reinforcements unmolested, reorganise their defences, add new minefields and position nearly 70 88mm anti-tank guns to cover the approaches to Caen.

The last opportunity for a quick tactical victory had vanished at Villers-Bocage. In addition, the German 2nd SS Panzer Corps now began to arrive – the extra troops Rommel needed for an offensive of his own, which on June 20 Hitler had given him a direct order to carry out.

But Montgomery knew the vital importance of maintaining British momentum, so much of which had now been lost, and therefore the next offensive, Operation Epsom, was prepared. It would involve the whole of Lieutenant-General Richard O'Connor's VIII Corps – including the 11th Armoured, 15th (Scottish) and 43rd (Wessex) Divisions. All together, some 60,000 men and 600 tanks would advance down the right-hand side of Caen.

The attack began at 7.30am on June 26 under covering fire from a barrage of 500 artillery pieces, some of them firing from the warships still anchored off the coast. A soldier of the King's Own Scottish Borderers later recalled: "Concealed guns opened fire from fields, hedges and farms in every direction around us, almost as if arranged in tiers. During short pauses between salvoes more guns could be heard, and right away, further guns, filling and

Captain W H Hooper and some of his men lead a column of German prisoners up the Avenue de Paris in Cherbourg, following the garrison's surrender.

A piper leads 2nd Argyll and Sutherland Highlanders forward to the battalion's forming up area on the afternoon of June 25, ahead of Operation Epsom.

reverberating the very atmosphere with a sustained, muffled hammering. It was like rolls of thunder, only it never slackened. Then the guns nearby battered out again with loud, vicious, strangely mournful repercussions."

The three-hour barrage caused some damage, but the German defensive line was now several miles deep and well dug in. After the big guns had ceased fire, the fanatical *Hitlerjugend* emerged from their shelters and fought as tenaciously as ever. After three miles the advance was halted.

Rain poured down, turning roads into mud and obscuring any potential safe routes

through minefields. By the end of the first day, both sides had suffered heavy casualties in the dense bocage country where every narrow sunken lane became a shooting gallery and every field with its thick earth boundaries and tall hedges became a small fortress to be stormed.

VIII Corps had failed to reach its initial objectives, including the northern banks of the River Odon, which ran all the way south-west from Caen to Villers-Bocage. The British were disappointed but the Germans, despite their sterling defence, were dismayed. Epsom had come far too close to the Odon for comfort and the front-line

units were being seriously stretched as they tried to contain VIII Corps.

Rommel was forced to cancel the offensive Hitler had ordered and use the 2nd SS Panzer Corps to shore up the line north of the Odon instead. The Germans counterattacked with 70 tanks on June 27, but British anti-tank guns forced them to retreat. At 7.30am the 2nd Battalion of the Argyll and Sutherland Highlanders attacked the Odon crossing at Tourmauville with the 227th (Highland) Infantry Brigade.

While the Germans engaged the 227th, the Highlanders and their armoured support, the 23rd Hussars got as far as

British 5.5in gun firing in support of 15th Division's attack on June 26.

Sherman tanks of 23rd Hussars moving up to the front line just after dawn on June 26 at the start of Epsom.

Colleville. The garrison there knocked out several of the Hussars' tanks with 88mms and held up the advance until the afternoon. Then the Highlanders pushed through, captured the bridge at Tourmauville and established a bridgehead on the south bank of the Odon. By 7pm, two battered squadrons of 23rd Hussars and a company from the 8th Rifle Brigade had crossed.

The rest of the Epsom battlefront was a series of small engagements as the 15th (Scottish) and 43rd (Wessex) fought back and forth over small areas against the grenadiers of the *Hitlerjugend*, supported by Panther tanks from the 2nd Panzer Division.

That night, a 2500 strong battlegroup from the 2nd SS Panzer Division *Das Reich* arrived and was placed under the command of the *Panzer Lehr*. Early the next morning, another battlegroup, this time from the 1st SS Panzer Division *Leibstandarte SS Adolf Hitler* turned up and was placed under the command of the *Hitlerjugend*.

Later that day, both Rommel and von Rundstedt were summoned to a conference with Hitler. The general commanding the German Seventh Army, Friedrich Dollmann, then died suddenly throwing the German high command into disarray on June 28.

At 3pm, Hitler received word of what had happened and appointed the II SS Panzer Corps' Senior Group Leader Paul Hausser as head of the Seventh Army, making him the supreme commander of all forces in the invasion area. Two hours later, the forces facing the British around Caen, Panzer Group West, were taken off him and given to General Leo Geyr von Schweppenburg.

While all this was going on, the battle raged. The 15th (Scottish) tightened their grip on the northern bank of the Odon by taking another nearby village, Grainville-sur-Odon, and German attempts to counterattack were blocked and a larger German attempt to pinch off the top of the British thrust and encircle the forces at the Odon bridgehead was defeated.

The Argyll and Sutherland Highlanders south of the Odon advanced along the riverbank at 9am to try and capture another bridge, this time at Gavrus, which was closer still to Caen. Heavy fighting ensued, but the Scots were once again victorious. Even closer to Caen, the village of Baron-sur-Odon was taken by the 11th Armoured

Men of the 6th Royal Scots Fusiliers advance through the mist and smoke that masked their attack at 7.30am on June 26.

A lorry carrying ammunition explodes on the Epsom battlefield.

Division and the 23rd Hussars. The target of this thrust was nearby Hill 112 – a feature dominating the landscape.

The Hussars dislodged the Germans from the northern slope and summit, but were unable to occupy them because of strongly held *Hitlerjugend* positions on the reverse slope. The Hussars were relieved by the 3rd Royal Tank Regiment at 3pm, but they were unable to break the stalemate. By the end of the day, the 11th Armoured Division had lost 40 tanks on Hill 112.

THE END OF EPSOM

The rain finally began to let up on June 29 and the Allies' fighter-bombers resumed their attacks. The RAF claimed a total of more than 200 vehicles destroyed during the day. Reconnaissance overflights of the area revealed a disturbing picture however.

German reinforcements were still arriving from all over France and threatening to overwhelm VIII Corps, which was now out on a limb on the western side of Caen. O'Connor halted any further

A pause in the attack while a mortar barrage is fired on a village on the morning of June 26.

Men of 9th Cameronians in a sunken lane in Le Haut du Bosq. The British infantry had to advance cautiously as they entered villages for fear of snipers, booby traps, machine guns and tanks. June 26.

D Company of the 7th Seaforth Highlanders, advancing to make contact with the enemy.

The 7th Seaforths attacking through a cornfield during Operation Epsom.

A column of British Sherman tanks pass knocked out Panther 204.

Men of the 6th Royal Scots Fusiliers entering St-Manvieu-Norrey on the morning of June 26.

attempts to press on and ordered his men to take up defensive positions along the Odon. Desperate to eject the British from their positions south of the river, Hausser ordered the 9th SS Panzer Division *Hohenstaufen* to hit the British positions to the north, isolating those on the south side.

The *Hohenstaufen's* assault began at 2pm and two SS infantry regiments, supported by Panzer IVs, Panthers and StuGs overran a company of British infantry before ploughing into VIII Corps' flank.

The fighting was fiercest at Grainville-sur-Odon, with the small village changing hands several times during the day. When evening fell, however, it was held by the British. The *Hohenstaufen* had been stopped in its tracks by 9pm, with yet more heavy casualties suffered on both sides.

Hausser gathered his reserves west of Caen but intensive attacks by Typhoons and bomb-dropping Spitfires broke up his formations. The *Frundsberg* division was also delayed by aerial attacks and didn't manage to begin its part of the offensive until 2.30pm. Nevertheless, when this large

formation's weight was thrown at the Scottish infantry defending Gavrus, they struggled to hold on. Before long, they were forced back to the bridge north of the village where they prepared for a last-ditch defence. This proved unnecessary since the Germans fell back after an artillery barrage.

O'Connor received reinforcements in the form of the newly arrived 53rd (Welsh) Infantry Division and further strengthened his defences, expecting another day of attacks on June 30.

The *Hohenstaufen* renewed its attacks that night in the dark, but made little progress facing the tanks of 11th Armoured Division. The *Frundsberg* and *Hitlerjugend* began an attack on Hill 112, without realising that the British had already abandoned it. Hausser suspended his counterattacks and told

Rommel that this was a result of "tenacious enemy resistance". The British called off Operation Epsom and settled down for more defensive fighting to come.

The German attacks continued on July 1 with the *Frundsberg* finally ejecting the 11th Armoured Division from Baron-sur-Odon, before it was retaken by the 31st Tank Brigade a few hours later. The British hit Hill 112 with a heavy artillery bombardment which went on for several hours. Patrols later found between 300 and 400 dead *Hitlerjugend* panzergrenadiers still in their positions on the northern slope.

There was fighting throughout the day, but by the end the front lines were more or less where they had been to start with. It was a stalemate again and the end of the third British attempt to take Caen. ■

CHAPTER 18

Ruined cities and hedgerow heroes

Operation Windsor to the Battle of Saint-Lô, July 2-18

The final assault on Caen was long and bloody. Thousands were killed on both sides as the Germans threw their reserves into the action and the British, losing face with their Allies, desperately tried to break the deadly status quo.

A flail tank seen in the foreground, Red Cross vehicle and Sherman tanks ready to move off to Caen.

Sherman tanks make their way across open countryside in preparation for the attack on Caen - Operation Charnwood.

While VIII Corps had forced a corridor right down the western side of Caen, there were still German forces holding out to the north and west of the city.

A key objective now became Carpiquet – a village to the west of Caen with a nearby airfield. By now engineers from five construction wings had built or were in the process of building 20 forward airfields inside the British landing zone – enabling whole squadrons of fighters and fighter-bombers to operate on the Continent.

Still, more were needed and if Carpiquet could be taken it could become not only an additional air base but also a staging post for assaults into Caen itself. On D-Day, Carpiquet had been an unreached objective of the 3rd Canadian Infantry Division, so

now the 3rd was called upon again. Operation Windsor was intended to take the village and the airfield with support from RAF Typhoons and the nine 16in guns of the battleship *HMS Rodney* – firing at an extreme range of 15 miles.

The Germans also realised the importance of Carpiquet and had fortified it heavily. It was garrisoned by a battalion of the 26th SS Panzergrenadier Regiment – part of the *Hitlerjugend* – supported by 15 tanks, and ringed with emplacements housing anti-tank and machine guns.

Windsor began at 5am on July 4. The Canadian infantry advanced under a creeping artillery barrage while the tanks of the Sherbrooke Fusiliers attacked from the north. An hour and a half later outskirts of both village and airfield had been reached. While the Canadians at Carpiquet began the

Sherman tanks from C Squadron of the 33rd Armoured Brigade move forward passing other tanks and crews in a prelude to Operation Charnwood.

A Sherbrooke Fusiliers Sherman passes through Buron, the scene of heavy fighting, on July 8 during Operation Windsor.

difficult process of winkling out the *Hitlerjugend* in bitter house-to-house fighting, the attack on the airfield stalled and could only proceed with fire support from Shermans of the Fort Garry Horse.

The last defenders of the village were cleared out with flamethrowers and AVRE tanks and the airfield attack continued with airstrikes by two squadrons of Typhoons.

Eventually, the airfield's hangars were reached but the Canadians were still unable to evict the stubborn *Hitlerjugend* defenders. As the day drew to a close, the airfield attack was called off.

The battalions in Carpiquet, now ruined, dug themselves in. They were just one mile outside Caen – the closest Allied units to the city anywhere on the battlefront.

In the early hours of July 5, a large force from the *Leibstandarte SS Adolf Hitler*, comprising tanks, infantry and Nebelwerfer rockets, began a counterstrike against the Canadians. The Fort Garry Horse, despite having suffered the loss of 13 tanks the day before, managed to hold off the panzer division's armour with the help of Typhoon air strikes.

It took until July 9 to finally capture the airfield and eliminate or capture the last surviving *Hitlerjugend* defenders. During Operation Windsor, the Canadians lost 127 men and another 250 were wounded. The Fort Garry Horse lost 17 tanks. The Germans lost 155 men and 20 tanks.

OPERATION CHARNWOOD

Four days earlier, with the Carpiquet airfield still untaken, Montgomery decided that the only option to finally take Caen was a full frontal assault and Operation Charnwood was drawn up.

The objective would be to enter the city from the north on as broad a front as possible and drive the Germans out of it all the way down to the Orne River, which bisected the city from the north east to the south west. While this was going on, further British forces would sweep round and capture strategic bridgeheads in the south eastern half of the city.

At 10pm on July 7, ahead of the attack, 467 RAF Lancaster and Halifax bombers dropped 2000 tons of high explosive bombs across the northern half of the city. This achieved very little – other than to turn Caen into a wasteland of ruins.

Six squadrons of de Havilland Mosquitos bombed specific targets at 10.50pm and at 11pm 636 artillery pieces and the 16in guns of the battleship HMS *Rodney* opened fire on the villages north of Caen.

The artillery barrage began to creep forwards into Caen at 4.30am and the British 59th Infantry Division, plus the Canadian 3rd advanced. There was a further bombing raid by 192 B-26 Marauders at 7am which managed to hit the *Hitlerjugend's* headquarters.

The British on the left, attacking the villages directly north of Caen, managed to cut through the German defenders there with minimal difficulty. Attempts were made to reinforce the positions with the battle hardened veterans of the 21st Panzer but these failed when air attacks prevented them from reaching the front.

The *Hitlerjugend* put up much stiffer resistance. At Buron, northwest of Caen, 200 SS men inflicted 60% casualties on the companies attacking them but the village had still fallen by noon. A counterattack south of the village dissolved when 13 of the *Hitlerjugend's* Panzer IV and Panther tanks were smashed by the M10 Achilles SPGs and 17-pounder anti-tank guns of the 62nd Anti-tank Regiment.

Carpiquet airfield in 1944, looking south-east, with the northern hangars on the right.

By the early evening the German defensive positions had been rolled over and British forces were striking south into the heart of Caen. At 7.15pm, the Germans gave up most of their positions north of the Orne and retreated over the river, giving the British and Canadians possession of the northern half of Caen.

A number of bridges across the Orne remained in one piece despite the German withdrawal but all were either choked with rubble or else held by the Germans in readiness for future attacks. The south of the city was still in German hands but by now only around 800 members of the fanatical *Hitlerjugend* remained alive.

The Allies had lost more than 100 tanks during Operation Charnwood while the Germans had lost fewer than 30 – but these were losses that the Germans could ill afford. The next day, July 10, another punishing offensive began against the Germans, this time the forces positioned south of Caen. The 10th SS Panzer Division *Frundsberg* still held Hill 112 southwest of Caen, following the bitter fighting of Operation Epsom and now this force was to be on the receiving end of Operation Jupiter.

Naval big guns and Typhoons had already spent two days hammering the *Frundsberg* ahead of Jupiter so when it came, spearheaded by the 43rd (Wessex) Infantry Division and a pair of armoured brigades, the Germans were quickly pushed back. By 8am the 43rd Wessex were fighting on the slopes of Hill 112 but the Germans clung on to it tenaciously.

The Tiger tanks of the 102nd SS Heavy Panzer Battalion and the Panthers, Panzer IVs and StuG IIIs of the *Leibstandarte SS Adolf Hitler* were committed to the battle and even though the British gained the summit of Hill 112 at one point, they were still driven back by the evening.

On July 11, the hill changed hands several times as the armies fought back and forth over it and by the evening a stalemate position had been reached. Operation Jupiter lasted for just two days but resulted

A Sherman tank of the Fort Garry Horse by the wrecked hangars of Carpiquet airfield following the successful conclusion of Operation Windsor.

in more than 2000 casualties being inflicted on the 43rd (Wessex) Infantry Division and its armoured support units.

There was a lull in the fighting after Charnwood and Jupiter and the Allies used the opportunity to clear up the northern half of Caen – which now flew the Tricolore.

Rommel, as ever, used the time he had to further reinforce his defensive positions south of Caen – now manned by an assortment of survivors from the *Leibstandarte SS Adolf Hitler, Hohenstaufen* and *Hitlerjugend* SS panzer divisions. He had already removed what was left of the Panzer Lehr and *Das Reich* divisions and sent them to face the Americans on the western side of the battlefront.

PANIC AND FRIENDLY FIRE

Since the beginning of Charnwood, the Americans had been struggling to overcome German forces south of their invasion beaches, centred on Saint-Lô,

about 15 miles south of Carentan. The main force pressing south was XIX Corps.

Launching its primary thrust on July 7, the lead division, the 30th Infantry, found its way blocked by two waterways – the Vire River and the Vire-Taute Canal.

The 30th, nicknamed 'Roosevelt's SS' by the Germans, was highly regarded and comprised the 117th, 119th and 120th Infantry Regiments. Crossing the Vire first and almost unopposed was the 117th. The whole regiment was over by noon and the 119th started across it too.

Having overcome this obstacle, the 117th moved west and towards another village, St-Jean-de-Daye. Resistance was stronger here so the village was bypassed as the advance through increasingly dense bocage country continued only to be slowed by sniper fire.

The 30th Division had trained hard ahead of its arrival in Normandy in mid-June but it encountered the same problems as the British around Caen in bocage fighting. It was difficult to locate enemy positions and doubly difficult to bring a significant amount of firepower to bear on them. Artillery co-ordination and communication were hampered by the geography and it was easy to become lost in the maze of hedges.

By the afternoon of July 7, the 30th had made acceptable progress and had not encountered any sizeable enemy opposition – it looked as though the Germans had failed to shore up the sector with any major force. General Bradley therefore decided to have the 3rd Armoured Division make a "power drive" through the bridgehead opened up by the 30th down to the southwest of Saint-Lô.

In the early hours of July 8, the 113th Cavalry Group – a reconnaissance outfit of tanks and infantry – crossed the Vire-Taute Canal but made little progress. When the 3rd Armoured Division tried to make Bradley's "power drive" it found itself stuck in a tangle of different units as the 30th's

The Fort Garry Horse saw heavy fighting during the battle for Carpiquet airfield.

North of Saint-Lô on July 15, soldiers of the 175th Infantry Regiment of the 29th US Infantry Division dig in behind a hedge, shortly before the great offensive to take the town.

Battling in the bocage – a Sherman fitted with a bulldozer blade pushes its way through a hedgerow, barrel pointed down, ready to shoot.

A Priest self-propelled gun passes a Humber scout car from the 30th Armoured Brigade whose mine clearing Sherman flail tanks assisted during the advance on July 8.

regiments and the 113th all tried to advance at the same time. Traffic jams ensued.

Finally, at 6.42am, the 3rd's Combat Command B managed to start its drive southwest through the hedgerows, pausing only briefly to smash a small counterattack by four Panzer IVs of the *Das Reich*. Progress was still painfully slow however, with the 30th continuing to get in the way. Right across the front, the Americans only managed to cover about a mile in one day despite only weak opposition.

The following day, July 9, VII Corps' 9th Division, which had had a prominent role in clearing the Cotentin peninsula, arrived to

support XIX Corps' attack – which did little to help the traffic situation. While the Americans continued to struggle at a snail's pace along slippery tracks, across muddy fields and through holes bulldozed in the sides of hedges, units harassing one another with their own crossfire, they began to receive reports of large German tank movements around Saint-Lô.

At 11.40am, the 117th reported hearing enemy tanks moving up from the south; at 12.30pm, its 2nd Battalion was reportedly fighting off a counterattack involving German infantry. At 2.25pm, XIX Corps' command heard that the 3rd Battalion of the

117th had been driven back, but when contacted the 117th denied that there had been any counterattack. The 3rd Battalion itself reported an attack by SPGs at 3pm and at the same time the headquarters of the 120th regiment received a message from the 743rd Tank Battalion asking whether the 2nd Battalion of the 120th had pulled out.

Furthermore, the 743rd reported that it had lost three fifths of its tanks. The 2nd Battalion reported at 3.10pm that it was being pressed by German tanks and infantry. In reality, a relatively small force from the *Das Reich's* Engineer Battalion had succeeded in causing mass hysteria along

At last – a patrol moves through the streets of Caen on July 10.

Infantry of 130 Infantry Brigade, under mortar fire, take cover by the roadside as they advance to take Verson.

Two GIs check out the body of a sniper they have just killed during the drive on Saint-Lô.

Three GIs advance carefully along the side of a hedgerow.

the American front line as the numerous strung out units heard snippets of information, overheard the sound of gunfire but couldn't trace its source amid the hedges and panicked.

There were several instances of friendly fire and at least two American Shermans were knocked out by M10 tank destroyers failing to properly identify their targets.

Another day had passed with little ground covered for a loss of 267 casualties – most of them from artillery fire. The night passed without enemy attack.

PANZER LEHR'S FAILURE

As July 10 began, the American 30th was now flanked on one side by the veteran 9th Division and on the other by yet another new force, the 35th Division, which had landed in Normandy on July 5-7. The tank attack of the 3rd Armoured Division

continued with Combat Command B now approaching the village of Hauts-Vents – still less than halfway to Saint-Lô from the bridge at Saint-Fromond. The traffic problems persisted.

Meanwhile, the Germans were experiencing problems of their own. The Panzer Lehr, being brought up to stiffen the front against the Americans, had suffered continual air attacks on the way. Even when it set off it had been severely under strength as a result of a month spent fighting against the British – 5000 of its 15,000 men having become casualties.

Now the Panzer Lehr launched a two-pronged counter offensive. While one force met the leading American units – the 119th and 120th Infantry Divisions and 3rd Armoured Division's Combat Command B – head on, the other hammered into its western flank, smashing into two formations

that had thought they were well back from the front – the 39th and 47th Infantry Divisions. The Panzer Lehr's tanks piled into a gap between the 39th and the 47th and overran the command post of the 3/47th. All communication between the 39th and 47th was lost as they struggled to recover from the lightning fast assault.

It was a great opportunity but the sheer weight of American numbers was decisive and numerous Panzer Lehr Panthers were destroyed, mainly by M10 SPGs.

THE BATTLE FOR SAINT-LÔ

The advance towards Saint-Lô was painfully slow and different units developed their own tactics as the fighting progressed.

The 2nd Battalion of the 116th, part of the 29th Division, used small mixed teams operating as a single unit. One infantry squad, one tank and a handful of engineers would take each field one at a time.

The infantry would seize the hedgerow at the beginning of the line of attack, the tank, with iron prongs welded on its final drive housing at the front, rolled forward and made holes in the hedgerow, firing its machine guns into the field and hedgerow ahead. Next, two engineers ran forward and filled the prong holes with explosives.

These would be blown and the tank would then roll through the gap and fire its main gun at the corners of the field – where the Germans would typically have set up their machine guns – while raking the area with fire before the infantry then advanced.

By July 13, the area immediately north of Saint-Lô was reached but the Americans were again bogged down fighting well-prepared German defensive positions. A breakthrough was achieved on July 14 but the gap was swiftly filled by the Germans who brought up the last of their reserves.

Approaching Saint-Lô from the north-west, the 30th Infantry Division was fought to a standstill by the tenacious Panzer Lehr. The final phase of the offensive to take Saint-Lô began on July 15 with XIX Corps taking the lead. Its divisions set off at 5.15am and by noon they were only making

An American Sherman nicknamed Hun Chaser in a street littered with rubble in Saint-Lô. The vehicle is from the 747th Tank Battalion Company Task Force Cota of the 29th US Infantry Division.

slow progress in vicious field by field actions against German paratroops. At least half a dozen US tanks were destroyed accompanying the 30th Infantry Division alone. Its commander, Major-General Leland S Hobbs, told his superiors that the day's fighting had turned into a "slug fest".

The 30th was advancing to the right of Saint-Lô, on the western side of the river Vire – with the town being on the opposite bank. Taking the town itself was left to XIX Corps' other two divisions – the 29th and 35th. Out in front for the 29th was the 116th regiment, heading for Martinville, a hamlet of fewer than a dozen farmhouses on a ridge two miles east of Saint-Lô.

When the 3/116th approached the hamlet, it was hit by a furious German artillery barrage and suffered heavy losses. A company from the 747th Tank Battalion lost seven Shermans during the same indirect attack and American aircraft were unable to spot the well camouflaged German artillery pieces doing the damage.

With the 3/116th halted, the 2/175th tried a flanking manoeuvre to the southwest but it too was stopped in its tracks by heavy fire from well prepared positions. The 35th Infantry Division meanwhile did better as it took a prominent feature between Martinville and Saint-Lô – Hill 122.

A counterattack followed with a German tank advancing down the Martinville road, firing its main gun into a hedgerow where American forces were holed up. It raked the hedge from end to end, blowing huge holes in it and causing casualties with every shot. A bazooka team tried to knock it out but was killed. The bazooka was picked up by two more soldiers but they were forced to retreat when the tank found their range.

An entire company of US soldiers was demolished and forced to pull back, dragging their wounded with them.

The survivors, led by Sergeants Harold E Peterson and Thomas E Fried, and a man the official US history refers to as "a full-blooded Indian known simply as Chief", staged a flanking attack. Peterson, carrying a grenade launcher, worked his way around until he could see the tank through a hedge and opened fire, scoring six direct hits. The tank, still mobile, withdrew.

The 116th received 269 new personnel ready for another push on July 17. By the following day, the 29th Division commanded the inner slopes of hills that led directly into Saint-Lô. On the right, the 35th Division also made significant gains and found that the German defenders between it and the town were now retreating, abandoning large amounts of equipment behind them.

Task Force C of the 29th Division, a column of M8 Greyhound armoured cars from the 29th Reconnaissance Troop, M10 tank destroyers and Shermans rolled into the east end of the town at 6pm and an hour later the town was taken.

It was 95% destroyed and once in American hands it was mercilessly shelled by the Germans.

THE BOMBING OF SAINT-LÔ

Saint-Lô was devastated by American bombs long before the ground war ever got near it.

Since the German occupation of the town in 1940, the war had been uneventful for its inhabitants but at noon on June 6, 1944, two American bombs knocked out their power.

As evening fell, huge formations of B-17 Flying Fortresses and other bombers were seen passing overhead. Later, one man recalled seeing two small planes leave a group, each trailing a narrow plume of white smoke. They were marking the corridor for the first bombardment of Saint-Lô.

Three squadrons of Martin B-26 Marauders flew over and, at two second intervals between each squadron, dropped their bomb loads directly onto the town – 60,000lb of ordnance in six seconds. It devastated a huge area.

Some of the town's residents decided to stay on after the attack, believing it was a mistake, but many opted to evacuate to the surrounding countryside.

Those that stayed hunted through the rubble, hoping to find survivors. One man, Mr Leclerc, was called to help by a young boy whose brother and sister were buried under their house. He said: "We dig through stones, bricks, earth, clothes, things. We throw mementos at the feet of the mother, who collects them in a neat little pile. It goes on for hours and night falls. Some men leave, to go across the street, there are six victims under the ruins, a whole family.

"We find the remains of a bed, the boy's bed, empty. We keep looking. What for? There can only be squashed bodies in there, under such a mass of burnt beams, collapsed walls and plaster dust. Then, suddenly, a hand touches something soft. It is tiny and warm. We dig deeper, faster, half an hour more, and now, a muted yell.

"We find the foot, the leg, blood. At last, we retrieve the little mass of living flesh, covered with dust. Now, the only light comes from the fires. The little boy is still in there. We go back to work. A new miracle, a cry: 'Mummy!' He wants to cry, he does not understand. 'What happened?' A priest, his black habit covered with white dust passes by on his way to the hospital, we give him the little girl, he takes her in his arms. She is dead."

A second attack came shortly after midnight. More bombs fell. Another resident, Mr Bernard, said: "With a deafening noise, bombs keep falling, and I cannot distinguish individual explosions. It becomes a continuous hellish rumbling, laced with the frightening screech of engines and the deadly whistling of falling bombs.

"From the sea of fire boiling in front of me erupt blinding lighting strikes and geysers of sparks. In minutes, the whole west side of the town was an immense inferno, its reddish yellow glow reverberating in the sky between huge columns of smoke.

"From time to time, their underbelly catching the light of a thousand fires, three or four planes would wind around the swirling columns of smoke, like fish in an aquarium full of aquatic plants – horsemen of the Apocalypse, riding across the red sky, to the sound of an infernal orchestra, made up of colossal gongs, titanic cymbals and gigantic drums, sowing in their wake terror, misery, destruction and death."

Later on, an American soldier, whose name was not recorded for posterity, took one look at the ruin of Saint-Lô and remarked: "We sure liberated the hell out of this place."

Saint-Lô in ruins in August 1944. The houses are in ruins but the streets have been cleared.

CHAPTER 19

The death ride

Operations Goodwood and Atlantic – July 18-21

After six weeks of intense fighting, British infantry reserves were dwindling, but tanks were in plentiful supply. Therefore, a plan was conceived to launch a massive armoured assault around the eastern side of Caen. Success could smash German resistance around the city. Failure could mean dozens of tank crews riding to their deaths...

The British had taken northern Caen up to the Orne and Odon rivers during Operation Charnwood on July 9, but the Germans still held the southern half of the city. A meeting was held on July 10 where Generals Montgomery, Dempsey and Bradley discussed their next moves. Bradley outlined a plan for his forces to break the deadlock around Saint-Lô and sweep down behind the front line.

This was the outline for what would become Operation Cobra. Montgomery agreed with Bradley's idea and decided that Dempsey's forces around Caen should launch an attack that would tie down as much German armour as possible and force Rommel to throw whatever reserves he might have left into the fray.

Manpower shortages were already beginning to bite for the British, who had suffered horrendous casualties over the preceding weeks in the battle for Caen so it was decided that Dempsey's attack should be an armoured assault with minimal infantry support – the British Army had 2250 medium tanks and 400 light tanks in Normandy with another 500 held in reserve.

Dempsey discussed the plan with his five corps commanders at 10am on July 13 and later that day the first order for Operation Goodwood was issued. VIII Corps' 7th Armoured Division, 11th Armoured Division and Guards Armoured Division would drive through the bridgehead over the Orne to the north-east of Caen and loop right around to the south of the city.

The target of the 11th was Bras, Hubert-Folie, Verrières and Fontenay-le-Marmion. Wherever strong entrenched resistance was encountered the tanks would just bypass it, leaving it to be mopped up by follow-up forces. The division's 159th Infantry Brigade would capture Cuverville and Démouville. Following the 11th, the Guards would go for Cagny and Vimont and the 7th, setting off last, would aim for the Garcelles-Secqueville. The 3rd Infantry and 51st (Highland) Infantry Divisions would secure VIII Corps' eastern flank. Meanwhile, the II Canadian Corps would capture the southern portion of Caen itself. This last part of the plan was codenamed Operation Atlantic.

A target start date of July 18 was set. It was decided that the element of surprise would be critical and the plans included provision for diversionary attacks by XII and XXX Corps on the opposite (western) side of Caen. In addition, a rolling barrage would

Shermans near Verrières during Operation Atlantic on July 20.

Soldiers of the 3rd Infantry Division accompanied by Sherman tanks of the 27th Armoured Brigade advance on July 18.

WHO NOBBLED ROMMEL?

Thirty miles away from Caen, to the south-east, on July 17, Field Marshal Erwin Rommel was being driven back to his headquarters in his black open-topped Horch 830BL staff car, registration number WH948205.

He had been visiting the headquarters of SS Senior Group Leader Josef 'Sepp' Dietrich and was close to Saint-Foy-de-Montgommery when RAF aircraft appeared overhead and strafed the road. Rommel's driver stepped on the accelerator and tried to get off the main road, but was hit in the arm with a 20mm round.

Leaving the road, the car crashed into a tree stump. Rommel's skull was fractured in three places. In addition, glass shards from the 20mm round passing through the windscreen had embedded themselves in his face.

He was hospitalised and unable to lead the German forces in the vicinity of Caen when Goodwood was launched.

Precisely which RAF aircraft 'got Rommel' has been the subject of fierce debate. There are two main contenders out of a total of more than seven. Ontario-born Charley Fox of 412 (Canadian) Squadron was flying a reconnaissance mission in his Spitfire Mk.IX, VZ-F, at about the right time, 1.15pm, in the right place and destroyed a staff car during a strafing attack. He made his claim more than 60 years after the fact, but his logbook entry for the day confirmed his story. He died in 2008.

South African pilot Johannes Jacobus 'Chris' le Roux of 602 (City of Glasgow) Squadron also attacked a staff car near Saint Foy while flying a Spitfire Mk.IX, but said that it overturned into a ditch. He was, and still is, credited with the attack by the RAF but died during an aircraft accident just over two months later on September 19, 1944.

creep ahead of 11th Armoured Division and an aerial barrage would soften up the German positions.

Close air support would be provided by the RAF's 83 Group and from July 13-16 six new road bridges across the Orne were constructed to increase the rate at which the British tanks could get across. Gaps through minefields were cleared and marked.

It was clear to the Germans by July 17 that an attack was imminent. Aerial reconnaissance, a rare commodity for the Germans, had shown a flow of traffic over the Orne into the bridgehead and an RAF Supermarine Spitfire was shot down while taking photos of the defences, south of Caen. Its camera and film were captured despite British attempts to destroy them.

Panzer Group West had already established a defensive belt 10 miles deep behind Caen, arranged into four lines, with every village in the area being fortified with strongpoints and anti-tank guns.

The front line to the north-east of the city was held by the German LXXXVI Corps'

346th Infantry Division, while the east was held by what was left of the 16th Luftwaffe Infantry Division. Behind them was a battle group of the 21st Panzer Division's 125th Panzergrenadier Regiment with 30 StuGs led by Colonel Hans von Luck.

Further armoured elements of the 21st and 10 Tiger IIs of the 503rd Heavy Panzer Battalion were based at Cagny, slightly further south, and the rest of the 21st was spread out on the plains south-east of Caen, near the Bourguébus Ridge.

LXXXVI Corps had 78 anti-tank field guns, including many 88mm weapons; a

further four 88mms were positioned at Cagny and 44 of them were positioned in the villages along the ridge.

South of Caen, I SS Panzer Corps' 272nd Infantry Division defended Vaucelles and elements of the *Leibstandarte SS Adolf Hitler* were held in reserve at the village of Ifs.

GOODWOOD GETS UNDER WAY

The diversionary attack mounted by XII Corps, codenamed Operation Greenline, started on July 15 and made good progress, capturing a strategic point known as Hill 113. The 9th SS Panzer Division *Hohenstaufen* ultimately repulsed it on July 16, but the British kept the hill. The operation, having done what it set out to do, was wound down the following day and Hill 113 was abandoned.

While the battles of Greenline were going on, XXX Corps' diversion, Operation Pomegranate, was launched. Again, it started well on the first day, July 16, but the *Hohenstaufen* steadily drove it back around Noyers-Bocage, a little way down the road towards Caen from Villers-Bocage. Combined, Greenline and Pomegranate resulted in 3500 British casualties, but succeeded in keeping the 2nd Panzer Division and 10th SS Panzer Division *Frundsberg* on the front line. The Germans suffered 2000 casualties.

The main attack opened at 5.45am on July 18 with a huge aerial bombardment. Fifty-five minutes later the opening artillery barrage began and the 11th Armoured Division got going at 7.45am.

The leading tank regiments of the 11th Armoured Division's 29th Armoured Brigade, the 2nd Fife and Forfar Yeomanry and the 3rd Royal Tank Regiment, had passed through the German minefields by

Cromwell tanks of the 2nd Northants Yeomanry approach their start line on July 18.

8.05am and reached the railway line which ran east from Caen to Troarn.

The already weakened 16th Luftwaffe Division had collapsed under the preliminary barrage and most of its front line units simply surrendered. Crossing the railway line itself was difficult however, and when the barrage resumed at 8.50am the tanks struggled to keep up with it.

By 9.35am, the leading armoured units had reached the next railway line three miles further south – this one from Caen to Vimont. The 23rd Hussars, trailing behind the Yeomanry and 3rd Royals were delayed when they were forced to engage a unit of StuGs from the 200th Assault Gun Battalion which they wrongly believed to be Tiger tanks. As the two forward regiments began to pass the 21st Panzer positions at Cagny they came under fire from the battery of 88mm guns dug-in there. It took just a few minutes for these deadly weapons to disable 12 British tanks. Undaunted, the Yeomanry bypassed the village and continued south.

The 3rd Royals came under fire from another village, Grentheville, but similarly bypassed it and continued south towards Bras and Hubert-Folie. The two regiments were now way out in front of any other British forces including their own reserves and facing heavy anti-tank fire from prepared positions as they pressed their attack on the Bourguébus Ridge.

The Guards caught up with the 11th at 10am. By 11.15am the British were spread out and being attacked from behind by the positions they had so rapidly bypassed earlier in the day. General Heinrich Eberbach, now in charge of Panzer Group West, saw an opportunity. He ordered the *Leibstandarte SS Adolf Hitler* to mount a full-frontal assault, while the 21st Panzer Division attacked from Cagny – catching the British in a steel trap. This began at noon, and although the 11th Armoured units called in Hawker Typhoon air strikes to break up the enemy attack, they still lost 16 tanks to a loss of six German Panthers.

Not long after the German counterattack began, the 2nd Armoured Grenadier Guards, part of the Guards division, was

THE PLOT TO KILL HITLER

As the British and Americans were consolidating their gains at Caen and Saint-Lô, respectively, between 12.40pm and 12.50pm on July 20, a bomb went off at Hitler's Wolfsschanze (Wolf's Lair) headquarters in East Prussia, Germany.

The explosion was the culmination of a plot to assassinate the Führer that was conceived and executed by a group of high-ranking German military personnel. A bomb had been carried into a meeting of Hitler and his inner circle by Colonel Claus von Stauffenberg – an officer and aristocrat who had lost his left eye, right hand and two fingers on his left hand during the German campaign in Tunisia two years earlier.

While four men died as a result of wounds sustained in the blast, Hitler survived with only minor injuries because a table leg had been between him and the bomb. He wasted little time in rounding up von Stauffenberg and his fellow conspirators and having them executed.

He also used the failed attempt on his life as an excuse to rid himself of anyone else who had voiced dissent over his regime. Around 7000 people were arrested and after a series of show trials in August, 4980 of them were put to death.

Rommel, who had been commanding the defence in Normandy up until he was injured on July 17, was also implicated in the plot. A number of conspirators reportedly said his name while undergoing extreme torture.

Hitler did not want to execute the popular field marshal so he offered him a choice of show trial or death by suicide. Rommel chose the latter, taking a cyanide capsule on October 14, 1944. He was buried with full military honours.

Colonel Claus von Stauffenberg tried, unsuccessfully, to assassinate Adolf Hitler while British forces were fighting east of Caen during Operation Goodwood.

attacked by 19 tanks from the 21st Panzer and 503rd Heavy Panzer. The fighting was so intense that two German King Tigers were knocked out by their own side.

One King Tiger, separated from the rest, was trying to turn around when a similarly separated Irish Guards Sherman stumbled across it. Facing the German tank's weaker rear armour, the Sherman crew fired into it and then rammed their

tank into it. Other British units then caught the King Tiger with anti-tank fire and knocked it out. It took the rest of the day to finally capture Cagny with the total loss of 15 tanks and damage to a further 45. The 7th Armoured Division, having started last, played little part in the battle except for mopping up bypassed German positions.

That night the 11th Armoured Division pulled back to the line of the Caen-Vimont railway and received replacement tanks. Forty had been destroyed during the day and a further 86 were damaged. The Germans attempted a number of minor counterattacks, one led by a captured Sherman tank, but these were thrown back.

The three armoured divisions suffered a total of 521 casualties. The fighting continued close to the ridge for two more days, before Dempsey called a halt on July 21. Seven miles of territory east of Caen had been taken and the Germans had barely been able to contain the assault.

Around 2000 German soldiers were taken prisoner and around 100 German tanks destroyed. The British suffered around 1000 casualties in total and 314 tanks were immobilised, 130 of them completely destroyed. Historian Alexander McKee, writing in his 1964 book Caen: Anvil

Cromwell tanks of the 2nd (Armoured Reconnaisance) Welsh Guards await the order to advance during Operation Goodwood.

Cromwell tanks and other Guards Division vehicles wait in their assembly area during Operation Goodwood.

of Victory described Operation Goodwood as the "death ride of the British armoured divisions" because so many tanks were destroyed – although subsequent historians discovered that many of the 'destroyed' tanks were actually recovered and repaired. Many of their crews also survived.

OPERATION ATLANTIC

While the three British armoured divisions engaged German tank formations in combat to the east and south-east of Caen, the Canadians initiated Operation Atlantic – the taking of Caen, south of the Orne.

When the northern half of the city was captured, the southern half remained in German hands – including the Colombelles steel works. This had six huge chimneys that made it an ideal observation position for the Germans.

Lieutenant-General Guy Simonds of II Canadian Corps, charged with planning the assault, came up with a two-pronged attack which required the 2nd and 3rd Canadian Infantry Divisions to take Colombelles and the southern banks of the Orne.

The 3rd would lead the way on July 18, crossing the Orne near Colombelles before heading south, clearing the city of its remaining German defenders. The 2nd would attack to the south-east and capture Vaucelles, before heading still further south to attack the Germans on the high ground

Infantry pose for the camera on a Sherman tank near Ranville on the morning of July 18. A Sherman Firefly and a Crab flail tank are to the rear.

near Verrières Ridge, three miles south of the city. Everything went according to plan and the Canadians swept through Caen. The whole city was now, finally, in Allied hands. By early morning on July 20, leading elements of the 2nd took Colombelles and the surrounding industrial suburbs. They were now in a position to reach their final objective – the German forces on the slopes of the ridge.

While other German forces had been engaged in fighting the British around Caen, elements of I SS Panzer Corps had been busy fortifying the 90ft-high ridge with concreted-in anti-tank guns, dug-in Tiger tanks, Nebelwerfers and machine guns.

Therefore, when the Canadians attacked it on July 20 they were quickly forced to withdraw. The situation wasn't helped by torrential rain that made it difficult for tanks to reach the ridge and for infantry to gain purchase on the muddy ground. Lacking

armoured support, the leading Canadian infantry, the South Saskatchewan Regiment, took 282 casualties during its failed attack.

The German defenders, made up of *Hitlerjugend* and *Leibstandarte SS Adolf Hitler* units, then counterattacked with tanks, shoving the reeling Canadians back past their original starting positions. As the battle continued, the South Sasks' supporting battalion, the Essex Scottish Regiment, also suffered heavy casualties.

Simonds threw more men into the fight to try and stabilise the front line until eventually, on July 21, the German advance was halted. The Canadians suffered around 1500 casualties and failed to take the ridge – but their other goals had been achieved.

In the wake of this failure, Simonds began to draw up plans for a second offensive that, if successful, would break the German defences and carry the Canadians past the Verrières Ridge – Operation Spring.

A Sherman Firefly waiting for the attack east of Caen.

Soldiers of the 1st/7th Queen's Regiment, 7th Armoured Division, comb through the ruined village of Demouville directly east of Caen on July 19.

CHAPTER 20

Breakthrough

Operation Cobra – July 22-August 7

With Saint-Lô to the west and Caen to the east now secure and the Germans' heaviest armour concentrated around Caen, an opportunity presented itself for a breakthrough south of Saint-Lô. The Americans rose to the occasion and readied an immense hammer blow for the already wavering panzer armies...

The original D-Day plan had called for the British to swiftly take Caen and hold off the Germans until the Americans had taken Cherbourg 15 days later. In practice, while the Americans under Lieutenant-General Omar Bradley pursued their mission, the British and Canadians ended up fighting nearly all of the German reinforcements sent to meet the invasion.

As the battle around Caen coagulated into a bloody war of attrition, the Americans took Cherbourg and held up their end of the southern invasion front. With the port secure, the American VII Corps led by Major-General 'Lightning Joe' Collins began pushing south again at the beginning of July.

On July 10, Bradley had revealed plans for a strong thrust southwards to begin on July 18. He called it Operation Cobra.

Monty approved the plan and ordered Operation Goodwood as a distraction. Bradley gave his officers their Cobra briefing on July 12. Rather than being a broad sweeping movement, it would involve units from VII Corps making a hole less than two miles wide in the German front line and then steamrollering through it with overwhelming air support from both heavy bombers and fighter-bombers plus artillery support from more than 1000 heavy guns.

In total, Bradley's forces included 1269 Shermans, 694 Stuarts and 288 M10s, vastly overmatching the German armour ranged against them. As the start date for Cobra approached, the British offensive around Caen petered out and Eisenhower himself became concerned that the 'distraction' had evaporated. Therefore II Canadian Corps' commander Lieutenant-General Guy Simonds was ordered to get moving with his second offensive on the Verrières Ridge – Operation Spring.

This began at 3.30am on July 25 with Operation Cobra being launched some six hours later. The first Canadians into action were the North Nova Scotia Highlanders, who attacked Tilly-la-Campagne to the left of Verrières the village and after an hour of fierce fighting managed to take it.

Verrières the ridge was captured by the RHLI, the Royal Hamilton Light Infantry (Wentworth Regiment), an hour later. Further to the right, the Calgary Highlanders tried to take May-sur-Orne and

An M8 armoured car, nicknamed Colbert, from C Squadron of the 82nd Armored Reconnaissance Battalion enters Canisy south west of Saint-Lô during the Operation Cobra breakout on July 26. The house has been set on fire by an American artillery barrage.

Bourguébus Ridge but despite taking the former they struggled to hold on to it as the Germans launched a series of punishing attacks causing heavy casualties.

The Black Watch were tasked with taking St-Martin-de-Fontenay on the eastern banks of the Orne but found themselves being fired on not only from within the village itself but also from the ridge to the left and the opposite bank of the river to the right. This blistering crossfire gave the Canadians nowhere to hide and slaughtered them. All but 15 were killed or wounded.

The Germans believed that the Canadian assault was the Allies' attempt at a decisive breakthrough and threw everything they had into defeating it. The 9th SS Panzer Division *Hohenstaufen* and 12th SS Panzer Division *Hitlerjugend* launched vicious attacks on May-sur-Orne and Tilly-la-Campagne over the next few days, forcing

the Canadians there to retreat. They gave Verrières the same treatment but the RHLI managed to weather the onslaught and keep a firm grip on the village.

By the end of July 27, Operation Spring had come to an end but it had achieved its objective – when Operation Cobra began, there were still seven panzer divisions in the Caen area with 750 tanks including every Tiger tank and Nebelwerfer brigade in Normandy. Standing in the way of Bradley's breakout offensive were just two panzer divisions capable of fielding, at best, 190 tanks.

THE COBRA STRIKES

Ahead of Operation Cobra, the Americans launched a massive bombardment. Beginning on the night of July 24, US bombers pounded targets within the unusually narrow corridor of attack around the road from Saint-Lô to Periers. During

Americans demonstrate an attack on a Panzer V Panther in Periers during Operation Cobra. The tank was already immobilized and abandoned or the infantry would have been taking a foolhardy risk approaching it so directly. There is a good chance that the crew would have survived the initial blast and manned their machine guns at the first sign of American soldiers.

General Bernard Montgomery and General Dwight D Eisenhower on July 26. They are awaiting news of the successful American breakthrough. Monty's dog Rommel is in the background. Field Marshal Rommel himself was still in hospital and had only woken up two days earlier having been knocked unconscious when his staff car was strafed by a British fighter-bomber on July 17.

A peasant leans on her rabbit hutch as a column of soldiers from the 4th US Infantry Division passes her in La Hommet d'Arthenay, north west of Saint-Lô, on July 23 during the first phase of Operation Cobra.

this raid, a number of bombs fell short and landed on the 30th Infantry Division, killing 25 men and injuring 131.

The next day, 2730 bombers and fighter-bombers dropped 3300 tons of bombs and napalm canisters into the corridor, which was four miles long and 1.4 miles wide. A total of 140,000 artillery shells were fired into it too. In spite of the 'friendly fire' incident of the day before, the same mistake was made again and the loads of 35 heavy bombers and 42 medium bombers landed on the 30th Infantry. This time 111 men were killed and 490 wounded.

Among the dead was Lieutenant-General Lesley J McNair who had been in his foxhole when a bomb landed on it. Bradley later said: "The ground belched, shook and spewed dirt to the sky. Scores of our troops were hit, their bodies flung from slit trenches. Doughboys were dazed and frightened. A bomb landed squarely on McNair in a slit trench and threw his body 60ft and mangled it beyond recognition except for the three stars on his collar."

The Germans stationed within the corridor, suffered far worse. At the beginning of the attack, Field Marshal Günther 'Hans' von Kluge ordered Lieutenant-General Fritz Bayerlein, commander of the Panzer Lehr, to hold the line. After the bombardment, Bayerlein told von Kluge's messenger that he wanted to send a reply: "Out in the front everyone is holding out. Everyone. Not a single man is leaving his post. Not one. They're lying in their foxholes mute and silent for they are dead. Dead. Do you understand? You may report to the field marshal that the Panzer Lehr Division is annihilated."

In fact, Bayerlein still had around 2200 men and 45 armoured vehicles at his disposal and these were readied to meet the American advance. 'Lightning Joe' Collins' VII Corps led the way. The first day of Cobra was disappointing and just 1.25 miles were gained. Still, the small pockets of resistance encountered did not form a continuous line – the Germans were too few in number – and could be bypassed. The next day VIII Corps joined the battle but again, gains were small.

As the third day of Cobra dawned it became clear that the remaining German forces facing the two huge American formations had withdrawn. VII Corps' 9th Infantry Division was the first unit to capitalise on the gap and drive through it. The entire German front line facing the Americans folded on July 28. Scattered counterattacks were launched but these were desperate and uncoordinated as the Germans realised the terrible scale of the breakthrough and fled.

Among these were elements of the 2nd SS Panzer Division *Das Reich*, Panzer Lehr survivors, the 17th SS Panzergrenadier Division and the 353rd Infantry Division. Reinforcements sent by von Kluge moved in from the west but these were intercepted by the American XIX Corps.

The plan was working and VII and VIII were penetrating far beyond what was left of the German defences. To help maintain the American momentum, the British launched Operation Bluecoat on July 30 from Caumont-l'Éventé to the west of Villers-Bocage, pushing south parallel to the American line of advance towards Vire. Units from the British VIII Corps and XXX Corps managed to gain five miles in a day.

The next day, the ceaseless American advance saw leading units finally breaking free of the restrictive bocage landscape into open countryside.

From August 1-4, seven American divisions swept down coastal routes to Avranches and into Brittany. Still more had advanced as far south as Mortain nearly 15 miles further on from Vire. Failing to grasp the enormity of the breakthrough, Hitler ordered von Kluge to counterattack Avranches and Mortain but most of his forces were either in the process of disintegrating or were desperately fighting defensive actions elsewhere on the front line.

Even so, an order from Hitler could not be ignored and on August 7 Operation Lüttich was launched against Mortain by the 2nd Panzer, *Leibstandarte SS Adolf*

Soldiers of the Royal Winnipeg Rifles advance near the French village of Ifs on July 25 during Operation Spring – the mission to distract the Germans while the Americans broke through their lines to the west.

Canadian troops move forward from Vaucelles south of Caen on July 25 during Operation Spring.

Hitler and *Das Reich* divisions. Between them they scraped together 75 Panzer IVs, 70 Panthers and 32 StuGs but the Americans were barely put off their stride. By August 8, Le Mans had fallen – a city around 80 miles south of Caen.

This sudden rapid movement by huge forces that were still fresh and combat ready left the Germans reeling and the battered remains of numerous divisions had become encircled.

Bradley said: "This is an opportunity that comes to a commander not more than once in a century. We're about to destroy an entire hostile army and go all the way from here to the German border."

All attention was about to focus on a hitherto unnoticed French town – Falaise. ■

A pair of Jagdpanthers – the tank destroyer version of the Panzer V Panther – belonging to the 2nd Company of schwere Heeres-Panzerjäger-Abteilung 654 in Bourgtheroulde-Infreville following the Allied breakout.

The remains of a locomotive torn apart by a massive explosion at Canisy station during Operation Cobra.

CHAPTER 21

Hell's cauldron

Crushing the Falaise Pocket – August 8-22

The astonishingly rapid advance of American forces after the Operation Cobra breakthrough took everyone by surprise after almost two months of near-stalemate. Germany's battered divisions, turning to flee, found themselves trapped in a deadly 'cauldron' from which it seemed there was no escape…

A Canadian soldier receives medical attention next to burning German StuG III amid heavy rubble near Falaise. The panzer has been shoved off the road by advancing Canadian tanks.

The Western Front was unravelling by August 8. To the east, a massive Russian offensive – Operation Bagration – was nearing its conclusion with the almost total collapse of several large German military formations. No reinforcements would be coming from the east to help the beleaguered divisions facing the Allies in Normandy.

The American drive south and then west had led to the near encirclement of the German forces that had been maintaining the front line due south of the original June 6 beachheads. The Allies rushed to capitalise on this with a new plan – Operation Totalize.

The intent was to have Canadian forces break through the weakened German defences south of Caen and drive hard for high ground north of Falaise nearly 20 miles further south. If these forces could meet up with the Americans sweeping across from the West, the Germans would be boxed in – and utterly destroyed.

Standing in the way was Verrières Ridge, where the Germans still had upwards of 100 anti-tank guns dug-in with a tattered remnant of the once mighty 12th SS Panzer Division *Hitlerjugend*, with about 50 tanks, in reserve.

Canadian commander Lieutenant-General Guy Simonds came up with an innovative idea to break through by enabling his infantry to keep up with his tanks using armoured infantry transports.

He had 102 M7 Priest SPGs converted into Kangaroo armoured personnel carriers (APCs). The Priest was based on a Sherman tank chassis and turning it into an APC meant it could go anywhere Allied tanks

Sherman tanks of the Polish 1st Armoured Division on August 8 awaiting the launch of Operation Tractable.

The remains of a motorised column in the Falaise pocket. Fleeing German units were mercilessly hunted down by rocket firing Allied fighter-bombers.

could go and was nearly as well armoured.

Simonds' armoured columns rolled out at 11.30pm on August 7 and by noon the next day, the attack force had taken the whole of the previously unassailable Verrières Ridge.

Just after midday, two *Hitlerjugend* battlegroups launched a counterattack from Cintheaux supported by Tiger tanks. The Canadians repulsed them but the German battlegroups were now severely hampering the Allied advance. Worse still, a bombardment intended to smash the *Hitlerjugend* before the Canadians reached them missed – because the SS division's established foxholes at Cintheaux had all been vacated.

As darkness fell on August 8, after a promising start, Totalize had ground to a halt. Simonds tried to jump start the operation in the early hours of August 9 by ordering a column of Kangaroo mounted infantry and 52 tanks to attack and capture a point known as Hill 195 halfway between Cintheaux and Falaise. The assault team got lost however and ended up being broken up by repeated German attacks. Another column was then sent to take Hill 195, which it successfully did on August 10.

Totalize was ended on August 11 having failed to reach Falaise. The Canadians again took heavy casualties but at the same time managed to inflict a similar level of punishment on the weary Germans.

OPERATION TRACTABLE

After Totalize, Simonds busied himself preparing for the next major assault of the encirclement – Tractable. Meanwhile, Lieutenant-General George S Patton's US Third Army had passed through Bradley's Operation Cobra breakout forces and was now moving up from the south to close the trap on the Germans.

On August 12 he captured Alençon and just 24 hours later his leading forces had advanced 35 miles up the road and taken the area surrounding Argentan, which was strongly held by the Germans. Patton had been ordered to advance north to Falaise but Bradley was worried that his units might run straight into those of the British or Canadians, causing friendly fire casualties. Therefore, he told Patton to remain where he was, leaving a gap in the encirclement.

Now it was the Canadians' turn again and Operation Tractable was activated to try and close up the gap from the north instead. Simonds and his Canadian First Army were this time supplemented by the 10,000 strong Polish 1st Armoured Division which had arrived in Normandy in early August.

The target was again Falaise and the opposition was, again, the *Hitlerjugend*. The SS division was now down to about 500 men, 15 tanks and 12 88mm anti-tank guns.

At noon on August 14, after a force of RAF bombers had pounded the Germans, the attack began. The *Hitlerjugend* launched continual counterattacks but the combined force pressed forward. The Poles took Potigny late on in the afternoon and as night

A Canadian Ram artillery observation tank advances towards Cintheaux on the afternoon of August 8. In the background an ammunition truck burns fiercely.

fell the Canadians reached Point 159 on the northern outskirts of Falaise.

With growing concern that the town was still in enemy hands, Simonds ordered the Canadian 2nd Infantry Division forward to continue the attack. More heavy fighting followed as the Germans battled to keep the gap open and allow more forces to escape the trap. Some 350,000 Germans were now encircled.

The 2nd broke into Falaise on August 16 and began mopping up the remains of the German defenders. Now the final targets were Trun, to the east of Falaise and Chambois on the same road.

The Polish and Canadian forces set off for Trun on August 16 and by August 17 the Polish 1st Armoured had successfully flanked the surviving *Hitlerjugend* and the town was liberated on August 18. By the evening of the same day, three Polish battlegroups were positioned immediately north of Chambois. Simonds' plan for August 19 was to have the Canadian 4th

Armoured Division attack Chambois with two battle groups from the Polish 1st. Two more Polish battlegroups would now strike east to take Hill 262. Everything went as planned and Hill 262 was captured by the early afternoon, the Polish forces having destroyed a company of German infantry who had been defending it.

A couple of hours later, the Canadians and Poles linked up with the American 80th and 90th Divisions – sealing the pocket and completing the encirclement of the remaining German forces in Normandy. Desperate to escape, the remnants of the 2nd and 9th SS Panzer Divisions, the *Das Reich* and *Hohenstaufen*, attacked the Polish forces dug-in on Hill 262 on the morning of August 20. The *Hitlerjugend* and German 2nd Parachute Division also attacked and by mid-morning more than 2000 Germans had managed to slip through the gap created.

A wider hole was opening up when 32-year-old Major David Currie arrived with a small force of tanks, SPGs and infantry from

This Tiger, turret number 214, was knocked out by a Cromwell of the Polish 1st Armoured Division. The Cromwell's shell penetrated the turret rear escape hatch.

The Canadian crew of a Sherman tank of C Squadron, 29th Reconnaissance Regiment (The South Alberta Regiment) south of Caen. The unit was commanded by Major David Currie.

the Canadian South Alberta Regiment. He attacked and took the strategic village of St Lambert-sur-Dives – through which the Germans needed to pass.

During a day and a half of fighting, Currie's force knocked out seven German tanks, 12 88mm guns and 40 other vehicles. Some 300 German soldiers were killed, another 500 were wounded and 2100 were taken prisoner. The escape route remained closed and Currie was awarded the Victoria Cross. As Currie's men fought on August 20, the Polish 1st continued to hold out on Hill 262. A *Das Reich* attack forced a path through their line however and by mid-afternoon around 10,000 Germans had managed to escape through it. The Poles were so critically low on ordnance that they were forced to watch as still more Germans escaped the trap.

Canadians examine an abandoned Tiger tank of the 101st Heavy SS Panzer Battalion. The unit lost nearly all its remaining Tigers during the heavy fighting in the Falaise pocket and the subsequent German retreat.

SURRENDER

Sporadic fighting continued as night fell and German attacks resumed in earnest on the morning of August 21. The remaining Polish tanks used the last of their ammunition and had to be abandoned. At noon, the last remaining SS units launched their final assault and the Polish defeated them at close range with the very last of their bullets. Most of those Germans who had not managed to escape surrendered.

During the course of Operation Tractable, Polish forces had suffered horrendous casualties – 325 men killed, 1002 wounded and 114 missing. Most of the dead were killed during the defence of Hill 262.

But the Panzer Lehr had been destroyed and the *Hitlerjugend* had lost 94% of its tanks. More than 100,000 Germans were taken prisoner too. Two days later, the German 7th Army dug-in along the Seine River to prepare for the defence of Paris. ■

Some of the 480 tanks deployed at the start of Tractable near Bretteville-le-Rabet on August 14. This mixed group, probably from the 2nd Canadian Armoured Brigade, fields an M10 tank destroyer and a Churchill Crocodile as well as a Sherman and Churchill tanks.

A Sherman of the Sherbrooke Fusiliers, 2nd Canadian Armoured Brigade, covers Mount Royal Fusiliers in Rue des Ursulines in Falaise on August 17.

CHAPTER 22

The end of the beginning

The liberation of Paris – August 23-25

With German forces reeling from the Allied breakthrough, Eisenhower was keen to drive them back all the way to Berlin and particularly to get there ahead of the Soviets. Paris was not a priority until, that is, General Charles de Gaulle stepped in...

The momentum of the Allied assault was building as the battered and broken German divisions withdrew from Normandy minus most of their materiel.

Already, the vast Soviet tank armies were rampaging through Ukraine and Poland, driving ahead of them the shattered remains of German armies far larger than those faced by the Allies in the west.

The end game was coming and the winning team-mates – America, Britain, the USSR and their Allies – were already looking well ahead to a time when Hitler was out of the picture.

Churchill and Roosevelt, and through them Eisenhower, were acutely aware of the consequences for Europe if Stalin succeeded in taking Berlin ahead of them. It would put Stalin in a powerful position to dictate what would happen next – and based on the rocket and jet powered weapons already used against the Allies, who knew what technological wonders might be found as Germany itself was subdued?

There were strong suspicions, largely unfounded as it later transpired but very real at the time, that Hitler's formidable scientific community was working on a German A-bomb and other 'wonder weapons' including magnetic railguns and

sub-orbital bombers.

Above all other considerations however, the Americans were keen to see the Western war won so they could concentrate maximum effort on the Pacific campaign against the Japanese.

All of this amounted to the fact that, in August 1944, the Americans and British had little interest in liberating the French capital, Paris. There was the added consideration that no one really wanted to see the beautiful city turned into a warzone during a protracted siege with all the associated suffering and problems of supply.

For the French themselves, however, Paris was vital. They cared far less for the

Crowds of Parisians line the Champs Élysées to cheer the tanks and half tracks of General Leclerc's Free French 2nd Armoured Division as they pass through the Arc de Triomphe following the liberation of Paris on August 26, 1944.

overall fate of Europe than they cared for their own liberation after four long years of defeat, occupation and humiliation. Paris was also the national centre of administration and politics and the heart of the extensive French railway and road network.

With the future governance of France hanging in the balance, there were numerous factions that dreamed of leading the nation out of Nazi rule. Chief among these was the Free French Army commanded by General Charles de Gaulle. De Gaulle was determined that he should lead the country's new government as he already did the Free French government in exile in London.

As De Gaulle made his plans, unrest grew in Paris. The Allies had swept through and then encircled the forces opposing them in the west but still the Germans maintained their grip on the city.

Police officers, post office workers and employees of the Paris Metro went on strike on August 16 and were soon joined by other workers across Paris to create a general strike. On the same day, 35 members of the Resistance were executed by machine gun fire in the Bois de Boulogne – a park on the city's western edge.

By August 18, German-controlled newspapers in the capital had ceased publication, police had largely disappeared from the streets and several anti-German demonstrations were staged.

Members of the Resistance, of whom there were around 20,000 in Paris, began to show themselves openly and took possession of public buildings such as police stations, newspaper offices and government ministries.

They also destroyed road signs, disabled German vehicles, cut telephone lines, blew up fuel depots and carried out attacks on German personnel wherever possible.

Resistance leaders, via an intermediary, negotiated a truce with the commander of the German garrison General Dietrich von Choltitz that evening. Perhaps fearing for his own life, he agreed to hand over some parts of the city directly to the Resistance.

The following day, a large proportion of the Germans garrisoning the city hastily formed a convoy of tanks, half-tracks and trucks on the Champs Élysées and drove away. Then a series of skirmishes began between armed Resistance fighters and the small German force that had remained behind.

Barricades were erected on the streets on August 20 and members of the Resistance broke into the Fort de Romainville concentration camp for women on the north eastern side of the city and freed the inmates. Numerous civilian vehicles were commandeered and used to ferry supplies across the city to different groups of French fighters.

With most of the streets now in free French hands, the remainder of the German garrison stayed indoors. The sporadic fighting reached a peak at 9am on August 23 when several German units attempted to break out of their strongpoints. Tanks opened fire on barricades and Hitler ordered von Choltitz' men to destroy as much of Paris as they could before the leading Allied military units arrived. It "must not fall into the enemy's hand except lying in complete debris".

The Resistance fought back and it has been estimated that between 800 and 1000 French fighters were killed or wounded during running street battles.

The next day, Free French General Philippe Leclerc disobeyed his American commander Major-General Leonard T Gerow and sent a vanguard into Paris to tell the Resistance that the rest of his force, the 2nd Armoured Division, would arrive the following day.

The vanguard was the 9th Armoured Company led by Captain Raymond Dronne. It was made up mainly of Spanish Civil War veterans, driving Sherman tanks, M2 half-tracks and American General Motors Company trucks, and was welcomed by huge crowds.

By the time the rest of the division had arrived, most of the German garrison had left. Allied airmen and other servicemen who had been long hidden by the Resistance were now brought out of hiding just in time to witness Free French leader General Charles de Gaulle's arrival.

THE IMMENSE LESSON

Von Choltitz formally surrendered the city on August 25 at the Hotel Meurice – now the headquarters of General Philippe Leclerc – and was held prisoner by the French until 1947. In 1950 he released a memoir Is Paris Burning? in which he described himself as the saviour of Paris for failing to carry out Hitler's destruction order.

Later on August 25, Charles de Gaulle moved into the War Ministry building on the Rue Saint-Dominique before making a speech to the crowd from the Hôtel de Ville which emphasised the achievements of the French themselves and, despite everything, deliberately said very little about the role played by the British and Americans in liberating France.

He said: "Why do you wish us to hide the emotion which seizes us all, men and

American soldiers pause to admire the Eiffel Tower shortly after the liberation.

women, who are here, at home, in Paris that stood up to liberate itself and that succeeded in doing this with its own hands?

"No. We will not hide this deep and sacred emotion. These are minutes which go beyond each of our poor lives. Paris! Paris outraged! Paris broken! Paris martyred! But Paris liberated! Liberated by itself, liberated by its people with the help of the French armies, with the support and the help of all France, of the France that fights, of the only France, of the real France, of the eternal France!

"Well! Since the enemy which held Paris has capitulated into our hands, France returns to Paris, to her home. She returns bloody, but quite resolute. She returns there enlightened by the immense lesson, but more certain than ever of her duties and her rights.

"I speak of her duties first, and I will sum them all up by saying that for now, it is a matter of the duties of war. The enemy is staggering, but he is not beaten yet. He remains on our soil. It will not even be enough that we have, with the help of our dear and admirable Allies, chased him from our home for us to consider ourselves satisfied after what has happened. We want to enter his territory as is fitting as victors.

"That is why the French vanguard has entered Paris with guns blazing. This is why the great French army from Italy has landed in the south and is advancing rapidly up the Rhône valley. This is why our brave and dear forces of the interior will arm themselves with modern weapons. It is for this revenge, this vengeance and justice, that we will keep fighting until the final day, until the day of total and complete victory.

"This duty of war, all men who are here and all those who hear us in France know that it demands national unity. We, who have lived the greatest hours of our history, we have nothing else to wish than to show ourselves, up to the end, worthy of France. Long live France!"

A victory parade down the Champs-Élysées was held the following day even though a handful of German snipers were still active in the city. A combined French and American parade was held three days later on August 29.

German officers captured by Free French forces during the liberation of Paris await their fate at the Hôtel Majestic, which had been their headquarters during the occupation of the city.

Afterwards, the French quickly set about establishing a new governmental structure, something De Gaulle had been quietly doing ever since he had landed in Normandy on June 14. This was primarily to prevent the Americans and British from establishing a military government to rule over France as they later ended up doing in both Germany and Japan.

An AMGOT (Allied Military Government for Occupied Territories) had been planned for France all along but De Gaulle was determined to generate enough prestige for himself and his government to avoid it. In the end, his slightly overblown and jingoistic approach, which downplayed the achievements and sacrifice of the Americans and British, succeeded because he was able to unite the various French political factions under his new 'national unanimity' government on September 9, 1944.

The Americans and British officially recognised the Provisional Government of the French Republic on October 23, 1944, but the complete liberation of France had largely been achieved by the end of September.

After liberating Paris, the Allied armies paused to regroup before pushing onwards to the Rhine and ultimately the defeat of Hitler's Germany in May 1945. ∎

NOTHING LESS THAN FULL VICTORY

Long before the liberation of Paris, during the fear and anticipation that gripped every British and American serviceman on the eve of D-Day, Eisenhower gave his famous 'full victory' speech, but nestled in his pocket was another speech.

It was shorter, hastily scribbled in pencil on a small piece of card, and dated July 5, 1944 – Eisenhower nervously writing 'July' when he meant 'June'.

It read: "Our landings in the Cherbourg-Havre area have failed to gain a satisfactory foothold and I have withdrawn the troops. My decision to attack at this time and place was based on the best information available. The troops, the air, and the navy did all that bravery and devotion to duty could do. If any blame or fault attaches to the attempt it is mine alone."

He never had to give it and he only rediscovered it weeks later, when victory was no longer in doubt, still in his uniform pocket.

Just in case (above): Eisenhower's scribbled note accepting responsibility for a defeat that never came.

Three days after Free French forces paraded down the Champs Élysées, the Americans did the same.